SECOND EDITION

RUNNING

MS DOS®

SECOND EDITION

RUNNING

MS DOS®

By VAN WOLVERTON

The Microsoft® Guide
to Getting the Most
Out of the Standard
Operating System
for the IBM® PC
and 50 Other
Personal Computers

Drawings by Rick van Genderen

PUBLISHED BY
Microsoft Press
A Division of Microsoft Corporation
10700 Northup Way, Box 97200
Bellevue, Washington 98009

Library of Congress Cataloging in Publication Data
Wolverton, Van, 1939–
Running MS-DOS.
Includes index.
1. MS-DOS (Computer operating system).
2. IBM Personal Computer—Programming.
3. Microcomputers—Programming.
I. Title.
QA76.76.063W65   1985   005.4'469   85-18951
ISBN 0-914845-68-3

Printed and bound in the United States of America.

1 2 3 4 5 6 7 8 9 FGFG 8 9 0 9 8 7 6 5 4

Distributed to the book trade in the
United States by Harper and Row.

Distributed to the book trade in
Canada by General Publishing Company, Ltd.

Distributed to the book trade outside the
United States and Canada by Penguin Books Ltd.

Penguin Books Ltd., Harmondsworth, Middlesex, England
Penguin Books Australia Ltd., Ringwood, Victoria, Australia
Penguin Books N. Z. Ltd., 182-190 Wairau Road, Auckland 10,
*   New Zealand*

British Cataloging in Publication Data available

For Jeanne,
who makes it all worthwhile

CONTENTS

ACKNOWLEDGMENTS

Writing is sometimes called a lonely job, implying that a book is one person's solitary effort. That's not so in this case; this book is the result of the vision and effort of many people, some of whom will never receive the recognition they deserve. I'll single out a few, but stop short of an Academy Awards acceptance speech.

First the Microsoft Press staff: Nahum Stiskin, of course, for asking me to write the book; Salley Oberlin, for doing so well all the things a Managing Editor must do; Karen-Lynne de Robinson, for really caring about form and function; Larry Levitsky for providing the readers; and Barry Preppernau and Mark Zbikowski for technical direction. But special (and inadequate) thanks to JoAnne Woodcock, who exists only as a voice on a telephone and nudging comments on thousands of those little yellow stick-on notes. *Editor* is so inadequate a label to pin on someone with such wide-ranging responsibilities. Her patience, insight, determination, and sense of humor helped turn this from an outline to a manuscript to a book. Thanks, JoAnne.

Thanks, too, to Dan McCracken, who taught me to write the examples first.

Most of all, though, I thank my family. It wasn't their idea for me to write this book, but they had to make it part of their lives, too. Thanks to Bill, Kay, and Andy for knowing that their father's single-mindedness was temporary, for realizing that the work only *seemed* to be more important than anything else. Thanks to Jeanne, who has truly been my managing editor for 23 years; were it not for her understanding, fortitude, and wisdom, the book wouldn't have been written.

Scotts Valley, CA
March 1984

TO THE SECOND EDITION

I know I said I would stop short of an Academy Awards acceptance speech, and no, I haven't forgotten the Oscar winner of a few years back who should also get the Best Satire award for "I'd like to thank everyone I ever met." But I really should thank some others who contribute so much with so little recognition.

Karen Meredith shamelessly promotes the book as if it were her own; nice job, Karen.

Editorial and Production, the shock troops of a publishing house, have a host of heroes. Lia Matteson, another person I have come to know without ever meeting, answered questions and solved problems via telephone and express delivery packages. Proofreaders Marianne Moon and Lee Thomas read the book again and again, ever vigilant to prevent those embarrassing errors that everyone else overlooks ("But I read that sentence 20 times!"). Chris Banks tended the sometimes temperamental typesetter; Nick Gregoric and Greg Hickman gave us the artwork that breaks up those dreaded seas of gray prose. And Lesley Link-Moore, one of the world's unsung heroes, tried to keep track of it all, to wrest order from chaos and steer a course around the murderous Shoals of Entropy.

And everyone I thanked before.

Van Wolverton
Scotts Valley, CA
September 1985

INTRODUCTION

It may be tempting to skip these opening words and "get to the meat of it," but please read this introduction anyway. The information here is both useful and brief.

You may want to know whether this book applies to you. It does, if your computer uses MS-DOS. The book itself was written with an IBM Personal Computer but, with the exception of a few commands, the contents of the book apply equally to any machine that uses MS-DOS.

You bought this book—or at least took the time to pick it up and glance through it—despite the hefty manual you got with your copy of DOS. Why? What else can a book like this offer? It can offer simplicity. The DOS manual is thorough and complete. It is your official, comprehensive reference guide to DOS, but it also includes a good deal of technical information you don't really need in order to *use* DOS.

This book does not show you how to set up your computer, nor does it describe in detail the pieces of the system, such as the keyboard or display. These matters should be covered thoroughly in the manuals that came with your computer.

The book assumes neither that you are, nor that you aspire to become, a programmer. It doesn't try to explain how DOS works, and it leaves to the DOS manual the task of explaining some of the less frequently used commands and features. The book does assume that you have access to an IBM Personal Computer, or one of the many other machines that run MS-DOS, and that you want to put the machine to work. It includes dozens of examples, and is organized by what you want the computer to do, not by how DOS itself is structured. The examples reflect real–life situations.

You don't have to be a mechanical engineer to drive a car well, but you do need experience. You don't have to be a computer scientist to use DOS well, either, and this book starts you on your way.

WHAT'S IN THE BOOK, AND WHERE

Part 1, Chapters 1 through 4, describes the pieces of the computer system, defines some terms and concepts, and provides hands-on examples that show you the major capabilities of DOS.

Part 2, the bulk of the book, includes Chapters 5 through 18. These chapters show you how to operate your computer system and manage all its parts with the DOS commands.

Chapters 5, 6, and 7 show you how to manage your files, diskettes, and computer devices. Chapter 8 shows you how to control the way DOS displays the date and how to type special characters in other languages. Chapter 9 describes the DOS multi-level filing system that allows you to set up a personalized computer file system that matches the way you work. Chapter 10 shows you how to back up and restore files.

Chapters 11 and 12 make up an extended example that shows you how to create and modify files of text with Edlin, the DOS text editor. Chapter 13 shows you how to create your own commands to automate tasks you perform frequently.

Chapter 14 shows you how to use a special set of commands called filter commands to control where the other DOS commands get their input and where they send their output. Chapters 15 and 16 show you how to create more advanced commands of your own. Chapter 17 shows you how to tailor your system to suit your needs. It includes several useful techniques that can make DOS immediately useful in its own right. And Chapter 18 introduces you to the capabilities and commands of Microsoft Networks, which works with Version 3.1 of DOS.

Part 3 is a reference section. Chapter 19 provides a brief description of each DOS command covered in the book and includes page referencing to the detailed discussions and examples in the preceding chapters. Finally, Appendix A shows you how to prepare the fixed disk on an IBM Personal Computer XT or AT. Appendix B briefly describes some advanced DOS commands that you won't need for routine system operation. Appendix C, the Glossary, defines the terms used in this book, plus a few others you may have heard or seen.

If you plan to use your computer for word processing, spreadsheets, database management, or perhaps a household accounting package and some games, this book is probably all you'll need. Not only does it show you how to use DOS so you can run your programs, it shows you how DOS can make your computer a more valuable tool without additional software.

HOW YOU CAN USE THE BOOK

This book covers all versions of DOS, through 3.10, used with machines that have one diskette drive, two diskette drives, or both a fixed disk drive and a diskette drive. How you use the book depends on which computer you have and which version of DOS you're using.

If You Are Using Diskettes

You can use any version of DOS with the IBM Personal Computer, unless you have installed an expansion unit and a fixed disk, in which case your system is effectively a Personal Computer XT. If you're using an IBM-compatible machine, check the documentation to see which versions of DOS you can use.

If You Are Using a Fixed Disk

You must use Version 2.00 (or a later version) with the IBM Personal Computer XT, or Version 3.00 (or a later version) with the IBM Personal Computer AT. This requirement is also true of most compatible machines that use a fixed disk; check your documentation to be sure.

If you have an IBM Personal Computer XT and have not yet prepared your fixed disk, follow the instructions in Appendix A, "Preparing Your Fixed Disk," before you start trying the examples in the book.

If You Are Using an IBM PCjr

You must use Version 2.10 with the IBM PCjr. Because you have one diskette drive, some of the disk operations—such as copying an entire diskette—require you to exchange diskettes during the operation. DOS displays a message that explains what to do each time you must exchange diskettes.

ABOUT THE EXAMPLES

The best way to learn how to put DOS to work is to use it. This book, therefore, is devoted primarily to examples. Terms and concepts are defined as you need them to follow the examples. Because the book covers several versions of DOS and several types of machines, there are variations of some examples; these alternatives are identified. Unless an example specifically states it is for an earlier version, the DOS displays shown in this book are the IBM Version 3.10 responses. If you are using a different version, the responses you see may vary somewhat. Do not be concerned.

What to Type and When

There's an awkward mismatch between a computer and a book that shows you how to use it. The computer is dynamic: It displays messages, moves data back and forth between disks and memory, prints words and pictures, chirps now and then to announce completion of another task. When you use the computer, you enter into a dialogue: You type something, the computer responds, you type something else, and so on, back and forth, until your work is done.

A book, however, is static. It can only show snapshots of your dialogue with the system, yet it must describe that dialogue well enough so that you can take part in it. In this book, we have to show what you type and how the computer responds. We have to distinguish parts of this dialogue, such as the names of files and messages displayed on the screen, from the surrounding prose. Here are the conventions we've adopted to cover those situations:

- Hands-on examples are shown in different type, on separate lines, just as you would see them on your display. The characters you type are printed in lowercase, colored type (DOS doesn't care whether you type in uppercase or lowercase, but lowercase seems to be easier). Here is an example showing these conventions:

```
A> format b:
Insert new diskette for drive b:
and strike any key when ready
```

- Occasionally, similar information occurs in text. In these instances, the interaction between you and DOS is printed in italics to distinguish it from the surrounding text. For example, you may see: "Type *n* when DOS displays *Format another (Y/N)?*"

- Many DOS commands include options, or parameters, that allow you to specify a particular disk drive, file, or piece of equipment, or to use a particular form of the command. Options are shown in angle brackets < > when they represent a variable entry, such as the name of a file. When they must be entered exactly, they are shown in the form you must use. For example, here are the options of the Format command used in the preceding examples (don't worry about understanding the command at this point):

format <drive> /V /1 /4 /8

Now it's time to meet DOS. This book was written to be used at the system, so put it beside your keyboard, turn to Chapter 1, and get ready to put DOS to work.

PART

1

GETTING
TO KNOW DOS

Part 1 describes the terms and the basic operating principles of DOS. The chapters show you how to start DOS and control the system with DOS commands. The information is primarily tutorial, and many examples are included. Later parts of the book contain all the detailed reference information that describes the DOS commands and their capabilities.

Part 1 introduces you to the concept of an operating system: What it is, what it does, and why you need it. These chapters give you the foundation for using DOS effectively in your daily work with the computer.

CHAPTER

1

WHAT IS DOS?

Y ou've got your computer and you've probably got one or two programs, such as a word processor or a spreadsheet, to use with it. But what is this thing called DOS? Why do you hear so much about it, and why have hundreds of pages of instructions been written for it?

DOS IS A PROGRAM

DOS is a program, but it's not just any program. Chances are none of your other programs would work without it, because DOS controls every part of the computer system. DOS not only makes it possible for your other programs to work, it also gives you complete control over what your computer does and how it does it. DOS is the link between you and your computer.

To appreciate the role DOS plays, take a quick look at the pieces of your computer system and what they do.

HARDWARE MAKES IT POSSIBLE

Your computer equipment, called *hardware,* probably includes a keyboard, display, printer, and one or more disk drives. The purposes of the first three are straightforward: You type instructions at the keyboard, and the system responds by displaying or printing messages and results.

The purpose of a disk drive isn't quite so obvious, but it quickly becomes apparent as you use the system: A disk drive records and plays back information, much as a tape deck records and plays back music. The computer's information is recorded in files on disks; you'll find that disk files are as central to your computer work as paper files are to more traditional office work.

SOFTWARE MAKES IT HAPPEN

No matter how powerful the hardware, a computer can't do anything without *programs,* called *software.* There are two major types of software: *system programs,* which control the operation of the computer system, and *application programs,* which perform more obviously useful tasks, such as word processing.

Each program uses the hardware. It must be able to receive instructions from the keyboard, display and print results, read and write files to and from a disk, send and receive data through the computer's communications connection, change the colors on a color display, and so on through all the capabilities of the hardware.

So that each program doesn't have to perform all these functions for itself, a system program called the *operating system* manages the hardware. The operating system allows an application program to concentrate on what it does best, whether it's moving paragraphs about, tracking accounts receivable, or calculating stress in a bridge beam. DOS is an operating system.

DOS IS A DISK OPERATING SYSTEM

The operating system for many computers, including the IBM personal computers, is the Disk Operating System from Microsoft. It is called a disk operating system because much of its work involves managing disks and disk files.

What Does an Operating System Do?

An operating system plays a role something like a symphony conductor. When the score calls for the violins to play, the conductor cues the violins; when the score says the cellos should play more softly, the tympani should stop, or the entire orchestra should pick up the tempo, the conductor so instructs the musicians.

The players in the orchestra and their instruments represent the hardware. The experience and skill of the conductor represent the operating system. The score represents an application program.

When one score is replaced by another—Vivaldi's Mandolin Concerto is put aside and replaced by Haydn's Surprise Symphony, for example—the same musicians use the same instruments, and the same conductor uses the same experience and skills. A different sound, a different mood, perhaps, but the elements are the same.

When one application program is replaced by another—an accounting program is put aside and replaced with a word processor, for example—the same hardware carries out the instructions of the same operating system. A different program, a different purpose, perhaps, but the elements are the same.

DOS coordinates the computer system, just as the conductor coordinates the orchestra. Your application programs run in concert with DOS, trusting it to keep the system humming.

Much of what DOS does is invisible to you, such as how it stores a file on a disk or prints on the printer. But DOS lets you control the things you care about, such as which program to run, what report to print, or what files to erase. These functions share an important characteristic: They need disks and disk drives.

Disk Drives

Personal computers use two types of disk: a flexible disk in a protective plastic jacket, called a diskette, which you can remove from the drive, and a permanently mounted platter called a fixed disk. A fixed disk can hold 30 to 60 times as much information as a standard diskette and is much faster. Most personal computers have one of the following three combinations of disk drives:

- Two diskette drives.

- One fixed disk and one diskette drive.

- One diskette drive.

To distinguish between the two types of disk, this book uses diskette to mean only a flexible disk and fixed disk to mean only a fixed disk. The word disk alone is used to refer to either type.

Disk Files

Just as you organize and store your written records in paper files, you organize and store computer information in disk files.

A disk file—usually just called a file—is a collection of related information stored on a disk. It could be a letter, an income tax return, or a list of customers. It could also be a program, because most of the programs you use are stored in files.

Virtually all your computer work will revolve around files. Because one of the major functions of DOS is to take care of files, much of this book is devoted to showing you how to create, print, copy, and otherwise manage files. As you go through the practice sessions, you'll notice references to some versions of DOS that have more file-handling abilities than other versions.

Different Versions of DOS

DOS has been revised several times; the first version was numbered 1.00. Each time you start up your system, DOS displays the version number that you are using. DOS is revised to add more capability, to take advantage of more sophisticated hardware, and to correct errors.

A change in the number following the decimal point—3.00 to 3.10, for example—marks a minor change that leaves DOS substantially the same as the previous version. A change in the number preceding the decimal point marks a major change. Version 2.00, for example, has almost three times as many commands as Version 1.10.

This book covers all versions of DOS. Even though newer versions have much more capability than earlier ones, all the versions are compatible. If you start with Version 1.00, you can still use all your knowledge and experience, plus all your files and diskettes, when you move to a newer version.

For simplicity, this book refers to all 1.xx versions of DOS as Version 1, all 2.xx versions of DOS as Version 2, and all 3.xx versions as Version 3.

What Is Compatibility?

You may have seen the terms DOS-compatible or PC-compatible used in an article or advertisement. What does compatible mean? Although some technical issues are involved, the most meaningful measure of compatibility is the extent to which you can use the diskettes from one system in another:

- If two systems are totally compatible, you can freely exchange diskettes. This situation is rare.

- If two systems are incompatible, you cannot exchange diskettes, because neither system can read files stored by the
  other. That's why you can't use a diskette from an Apple
  computer in an IBM Personal Computer. This situation is
  common.

- If two systems are partially compatible, you can interchange
  some diskettes, particularly those that contain files of information rather than programs.

This last level of partial compatibility is what is usually meant
by MS-DOS-compatible, and is one of the advantages of using an
operating system that runs on so many different machines.

Even among DOS-compatible machines, there may be a few
differences in how DOS works on them. For example, to maintain
consistency, this book describes how DOS works on the IBM PC, IBM
PC XT, IBM PC AT, and IBM PCjr. If you are using DOS on a different
machine, some commands described in this book may not be available on your system, and some may work a bit differently. These
differences are pointed out where they occur in the book.

WHAT CAN YOU DO WITH DOS?

DOS coordinates the operation of the computer for your application programs. That's valuable—essential, really—but DOS has
much more to offer. You can use DOS, controlling it with instructions called commands, to manage your files, control the work
flow, and perform useful tasks that might otherwise require additional software.

For example, DOS includes a program called Edlin that lets you
create and revise files of text. Although it's not a word processor,
Edlin is fine for writing short memos and lists. Using Edlin, you
can write and print short documents in less time than it might take
to find the diskette that contains your word-processing program
and start the program running.

You can tailor DOS to your specific needs by creating powerful
commands made up of other DOS commands, and you can even
create your own small applications. For example, this book shows
you how to create a simple file manager—a program that lets you
search through a file for specific information—using nothing but
DOS commands.

Your use of DOS can range from just enough to use a single application program to the full range of capabilities in the later versions. But no matter how far you go, you needn't learn to write a program. It's all DOS, and it's all in this book.

CHAPTER SUMMARY

This quick tour of DOS may have introduced several new terms and concepts. Here are the key points to remember:

- A computer system needs both hardware (equipment) and software (programs).

- DOS (Disk Operating System) coordinates the operation of all parts of the computer system.

- A file is a collection of related information stored on a disk. Most of your computer work will involve files.

- Besides running your application programs, DOS is a valuable tool in its own right.

The next chapter starts you off at the keyboard.

CHAPTER
2
STARTING DOS

N ow that you have been introduced to some of the things DOS does for you, it's time to start your system and do something.

Whenever you start your computer, whether it is to use a word processor, accounting program, or DOS itself, you begin by *loading* DOS into the computer's workplace, its memory. Loading the DOS program and starting it running is sometimes called "booting the system" or "booting the disk." This term is borrowed from the phrase "pulling yourself up by your bootstraps," because DOS essentially pulls itself up by its own bootstraps, loading itself from disk into memory, where it then waits for a command from you.

The examples in this chapter assume you have set up your system and are familiar with its control switches. If you're using a fixed disk, the examples also assume you have prepared the fixed disk so DOS can use it. If you haven't yet prepared the fixed disk and you need some assistance, turn to Appendix A. Follow the instructions there—including those for copying the DOS programs onto the fixed disk—before continuing with the examples in this chapter.

ENTERING DOS COMMANDS

The instructions you give DOS are called *commands*. For the first few commands you enter in this session, you need only the standard typewriter keys on the keyboard. Two of those keys, Enter and Backspace, are shown in Figure 2-1 and are worth separate mention.

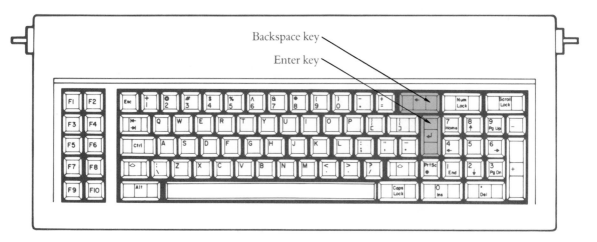

Figure 2-1. The Backspace and Enter keys on the IBM keyboard

The Enter Key

The Enter key is labeled with a bent left arrow (↵). Like the return key on a typewriter, it is used to mark the end of a line. In general, DOS doesn't know what you have typed until you press Enter, so remember: You end a command by pressing Enter.

The Backspace Key

The Backspace key is labeled with a long left arrow (←). It erases the last character you typed; use it to correct typing errors.

STARTING THE SYSTEM

If you're not using a fixed disk, open the latch of drive A (the left-hand drive) and put in the DOS system diskette. The diskette goes in with the label up and away from the machine, as shown in Figure 2-2. When the diskette is all the way in, close the latch.

Figure 2-2. Inserting the DOS system diskette

Turn on the power switch, located at the rear of the right side of the system unit. The computer seems to do nothing for several seconds, but this is normal. Each time you turn the power switch on, the computer checks its memory and all attached devices to be sure everything is working properly. The system beeps after it has made sure that all is well.

If you're not using a fixed disk, DOS is copied into the system's memory from the diskette in drive A. If you are using a fixed disk with DOS on it, the DOS program is copied into the system's memory from the fixed disk (known to DOS as drive C). As soon as the program is loaded, DOS is running and ready to go to work.

Date

The first thing you see after the computer beeps at you is the following message:

```
Current date is Tue  1-01-1980
Enter new date (mm-dd-yy): _
```

The blinking underline that follows the colon is the *cursor.* It shows where DOS will display whatever you type next. It also tells you that DOS is waiting for you to type something—in this case, a date in response to its *Enter new date* request. Such a request is called a *prompt;* DOS frequently prompts you to enter information, so you don't have to memorize operating procedures.

To enter the date, you type the numbers that represent the month, day, and year, separated by hyphens, and then you press the Enter key. You do not type the day of the week; as you will see later in this chapter, DOS figures out the day for you and displays both the day and date whenever you ask for them.

For this example, set the date to October 16, 1985 by typing the following (be sure to press Enter after the last number):

```
Current date is Tue  1-01-1980
Enter new date (mm-dd-yy): 10-16-85
```

Note: You can also use a slash, /, or a period to separate the numbers. Whichever you use, if you don't do it exactly right (in other words, in a way that DOS recognizes), DOS displays Invalid date *and waits for you to try*

again. If you make a mistake or enter the wrong date, don't be alarmed. As you'll see in the next example, it's easy to fix such errors.

After it accepts the date, DOS displays a message asking you to enter the time and again waits for you to respond. The screen looks something like this:

```
Current date is Tue  1-01-1980
Enter new date (mm-dd-yy): 10-16-85
Current time is  0:01:30.00
Enter new time: _
```

Before you enter the correct time, try the following exercise to see how easily you can fix typing errors.

Backspacing to correct typing errors

Try out the Backspace key. Type some characters, such as the following, at random, but don't press Enter:

```
Current date is Tue  1-01-1980
Enter new date (mm-dd-yy): 10-16-85
Current time is  0:01:30.00
Enter new time: w710273_
```

This isn't a valid time; if you were to press Enter now, DOS would display the message *Invalid time* and wait for your next attempt. Correct your typing "error" by pressing the Backspace key until all the characters are erased and the cursor is back to its original position, just to the right of the colon. The screen looks like it did before:

```
Current date is Tue  1-01-1980
Enter new date (mm-dd-yy): 10-16-85
Current time is  0:01:30.00
Enter new time: _
```

Time

You enter the time by typing the numbers that represent the current hour and minute, separated by a colon or a period. DOS keeps track of seconds and hundredths of seconds for you, so don't worry about them. For this example, set the time to 8:15 a.m. by typing the following (don't forget to press Enter):

```
Current date is Tue  1-01-1980
Enter new date (mm-dd-yy): 10-16-85
Current time is  0:01:30.00
Enter new time: 8:15
```

Note: DOS works on the basis of a 24-hour clock, so remember that 1:15 p.m. is typed as 13:15, 10:00 p.m. is typed as 22:00, and so on.

If you just press Enter in response to the date and time prompts when you start the system, DOS does not change its baseline date and time of midnight on January 1, 1980. This way to start up is quick, but DOS marks all the disk files you use with the time and date; such information is useful, so it's a good idea to set the correct time and date each time you start the system.

Start-up

After you have entered the date and time, DOS displays a start-up message to identify itself and the version you are using, and waits for further instructions. The exact wording of the lines that give the name of the operating system and the version number depend on which computer and version of DOS you're using. The following message (truncated here), which shows the date and time you just entered, appears on an IBM Personal Computer running Version 3.10 of DOS:

```
Current date is Tue  1-01-1980
Enter new date (mm-dd-yy): 10-16-85
Current time is  0:01:30.00
Enter new time: 8:15

The IBM Personal Computer DOS
Version 3.10 (C)Copyright Internat... B... M... 1985
              (C)Copyright Microsoft...

A>_
```

If you're using a fixed disk, the last line is C>, instead of A>, because C is the letter DOS uses to identify the fixed disk.

The System Prompt

The A> (or C> if you're using a fixed disk) is called the *system prompt,* because the system program (DOS) is prompting you to type a command. At this point, DOS is at what is often called the *command level,* because it is ready and waiting for a command.

The system prompt also identifies the *current drive,* the drive where DOS looks for a file. DOS identifies your drives by letter. On a system with two diskette drives, the left-hand drive is drive A, the right-hand drive is drive B; on a system with one diskette drive and one fixed disk, the left-hand (diskette) drive is identified as both A and B, the right-hand (fixed disk) drive is drive C.

If you're not using a fixed disk, your system is set up so that DOS is loaded from drive A. DOS thus assumes that drive A is the current drive, so the initial system prompt is A>. If you are using a fixed disk with the DOS programs on it, DOS is loaded from the fixed disk (drive C), so DOS usually assumes drive C is the current drive, and the initial system prompt is C>.

This book contains many examples for you to try. Throughout, the system prompt is shown as A>, unless stated otherwise. If you are using a fixed disk, you are told specifically when and how to prepare for an example. If there are no instructions, simply proceed through the example, but bear in mind that where you see A> in the book, you will see C> on your screen.

COPYING THE DOS DISKETTES

You've probably heard or read about the importance of copying valuable diskettes to protect yourself from loss in case of damage. If you have not made copies of your DOS diskettes, follow the step-by-step procedure given here, under the heading that describes your system. Don't worry if you don't yet understand everything that is happening. It's important that you do this copying as soon as possible, so that you don't chance damaging the originals.

If you have already made copies of your DOS diskettes, go on to the heading "Changing the Current Drive." If you are not using IBM's version of MS-DOS, prepare a new diskette according to the instructions in your documentation before you proceed.

If You Have Two Diskette Drives

These instructions assume that your DOS system diskette is in drive A, that you have performed the start-up steps of entering the date and time, and that you have the DOS system prompt, A>, on the screen.

1. Put a blank new diskette in drive B.

2. Type the following (but not the A>):

   ```
   A>diskcopy a: b:
   ```

   This command tells DOS to copy everything on the diskette in drive A to the diskette in drive B. DOS responds:

   ```
   Insert SOURCE diskette in drive A:

   Insert TARGET diskette in drive B:

   Press any key when ready...
   _
   ```

3. Your source (DOS) and target (blank) diskettes are in the appropriate drives, so press the space bar, or any other key. The system responds with a message like this one:

   ```
   Copying 40 tracks
   9 Sectors/Track, 2 Side(s)
   ```

   A short while later, DOS displays:

   ```
   Formatting while copying
   ```

   (The wording and timing of the messages may vary, depending on the version of DOS you are using.) It takes about a minute to copy the diskette. When the diskette is copied, DOS responds:

   ```
   Copy another diskette (Y/N)?_
   ```

4. Remove the diskette from drive B and label it DOS SYSTEM DISKETTE. Use a felt-tip, not a ballpoint pen, to avoid damaging the surface of the diskette.

5. Remove the DOS system diskette from drive A and put it in its plastic sleeve in the manual binder (or some other safe place).

6. You have another diskette to copy, so type *y*. DOS replies with the messages to put the source and target diskettes in drives A and B as in step 2.

7. Put the DOS Supplemental Programs diskette in drive A.

8. Put a blank new diskette in drive B.

9. Press the space bar, or any other key. DOS responds as in step 3.

10. When the copy is complete and DOS asks if you want to make another copy, remove the DOS Supplemental Programs diskette from drive A and put it in its plastic sleeve in the manual binder.

11. Remove the copy from drive B, label it DOS SUPPLEMENTAL PROGRAMS, and put it with your other working diskettes.

12. Put your new copy of the system diskette in drive A and close the drive latch.

13. Type *n* to answer the *Copy another diskette* question. DOS responds with the system prompt. Go on ahead now to the heading "Changing the Current Drive."

If You Have a Fixed Disk or One Diskette Drive

DOS prompts you to exchange the source and target diskettes in the drive several times. Follow the prompts, and remember that the DOS diskette is the source and the blank diskette is the target.

1. Type the following (don't forget to press Enter):

```
A>diskcopy
```

DOS responds:

```
Insert SOURCE diskette in drive A:

Press any key when ready...

_
```

2. The DOS diskette is already in drive A, so press the space bar or any other key. DOS responds:

```
Copying 40 tracks
9 Sectors/Track, 2 Side(s)
```

This message may vary, depending on the version of DOS you're using. DOS reads as much of the system diskette as it can, then asks you to exchange diskettes:

```
Insert TARGET diskette in drive A:

Press any key when ready...
-
```

3. Remove the DOS diskette, put in a blank new diskette, and press the space bar or any other key. DOS responds:

```
Formatting while copying
```

DOS writes the data it read from the system diskette onto the blank diskette, then requests that you put the system diskette back in the drive:

```
Insert SOURCE diskette in drive A:

Press any key when ready...
-
```

4. Continue exchanging diskettes as DOS prompts you. After the last exchange, DOS tells you it has finished:

```
Copy another diskette (Y/N)?_
```

5. Put the DOS SYSTEM DISKETTE in its plastic sleeve in the manual binder (or some other safe place).

6. Remove the diskette to which you copied DOS from drive A and label it DOS SYSTEM DISKETTE. Use a felt-tip, not a ballpoint pen, to avoid damaging the surface of the diskette.

7. You have another diskette to copy, so type *y* in answer to the *Copy another diskette* question. DOS replies with the message to put the source diskette in drive A as in step 1.

8. Put the DOS Supplemental Programs diskette in drive A.

9. Press the space bar or any other key. DOS responds as in step 2. When DOS prompts you to exchange diskettes, remove the DOS Supplemental Programs diskette, put in a blank new diskette, and press the space bar or any other key.

10. Continue to exchange the diskettes as you did before. When the copy is complete and DOS asks if you want to make another copy, remove the DOS Supplemental Programs diskette from drive A and put it in its plastic sleeve in the manual binder.

11. Remove the diskette to which you copied the supplemental programs, label it DOS SUPPLEMENTAL PROGRAMS, and put it with your other working diskettes.

12. Put your new copy of the system diskette in drive A and close the drive latch.

13. Type *n* to answer the *Copy another diskette* question. DOS responds with the system prompt.

CHANGING THE CURRENT DRIVE

If you don't want DOS to assume that your files are on the diskette in drive A, you can change the current drive by typing the letter of the new drive, followed by a colon. To change the current drive to drive B, for example, type:

```
A> b:

B> _
```

Now the system prompt is B>, confirming that DOS will look in drive B unless told otherwise. (If you are using a fixed disk, you have a message on your screen telling you to insert a diskette in drive B. That's DOS telling you that your diskette drive is empty; don't worry about it, you'll return to drive C in a moment.)

If you're not using a fixed disk, change the current drive back to drive A by typing the following:

```
B> a:

A> _
```

The system prompt returns to A>.

If you are using a fixed disk, change the current drive back to drive C by typing the following:

```
B>c:

C>_
```

The system prompt returns to C>.

CHANGING THE DATE

The computer has an electronic clock that keeps time to the hundredth of a second. DOS uses this clock to keep track of both the time of day and the date. If you're using the system when midnight arrives, the date advances to the next day (and, if necessary, the next month and year).

The clock doesn't run when the system is shut off, so each time you start the system DOS sets the date to January 1, 1980 (1-01-1980) and sets the time to midnight (0:00:00.00). That's why DOS prompts you for the correct date and time whenever you start the system.

You can change the date whenever you want with the Date command. To tell DOS you want to change the date, type:

```
A>date
```

Just as when you start the system, DOS displays the current date (which is the date you set earlier) and prompts for the new date:

```
Current date is Wed 10-16-1985
Enter new date (mm-dd-yy): _
```

Press the Enter key. DOS leaves the date unchanged and displays the system prompt. If you had typed a new date, DOS would have set its calendar to the new date.

You can check and change the time the same way, with the Time command.

PRINTING WHAT IS ON THE SCREEN

The screen display shows you a record of your commands and the responses from DOS. The screen can show a maximum of 25 lines. When all the lines are filled, each additional line causes the entire screen to shift up, or *scroll,* to make room for the new line at the bottom; the top line disappears from view.

Because a copy of what is on the display is often useful, most microcomputers make it easy to print what's on the screen. If you are using an IBM personal computer, locate the key labeled PrtSc, just to the right of the right Shift key. Make sure your printer is turned on, hold down the left Shift key, and press PrtSc (this combination is referred to in this text as Shift-PrtSc).

Each line of the screen is printed. Another way to print what is on the screen is described in the next chapter.

Note: If you are using another computer and do not have these keys, check your documentation for the procedure to follow with your system.

CLEARING THE SCREEN

Sometimes, when the screen is filled with commands and responses, you might want to clear it before continuing with your work. You can erase everything on the screen with the Clear Screen (cls) command. Try it by typing:

```
A>cls
```

The screen is cleared, except for the system prompt in the upper left corner.

TURNING THE SYSTEM OFF

If you're using DOS, all you have to do to shut the system down is turn off the power switch. You can do it anytime, except when the red light on a disk drive is on; turning the power off while a drive is in use can cause you to lose the data on the disk.

Some devices attached to your system may have special requirements for shutting down, such as a specific sequence in which they should be turned off. Be sure you know any special instructions for the devices attached to your system.

When you shut the system down, be sure to remove any diskettes you are using and store them where they will be safe. Remove your diskettes before you turn off the power, as long as the disk drive is not in use.

CHAPTER SUMMARY

You have completed your first session with DOS. It wasn't very long, but you started the system, entered a few commands, and printed what was on the screen. These are the key points:

- You control DOS by typing commands. End each command by pressing the Enter key.

- DOS doesn't know what you have typed until you press the Enter key.

- The system prompt tells you that DOS is at the command level, ready to accept a command.

- The letter in the system prompt identifies the current drive; you can change the current drive by typing the new drive letter, followed by a colon.

- The computer keeps track of the time and date. You set the date and time when you start up DOS, and you can also set them with the Date and Time commands.

- The Backspace key erases the last character you typed.

- Pressing Shift-PrtSc prints the contents of the screen.

- Typing *cls* clears the screen.

CHAPTER

3

TAKING A
TEST DRIVE

Whuhen you test drive a car, you already know how to start it. The test drive is to help you become familiar with the controls, the steering, the brakes, the overall "feel" of the car. Now it's time to take a test drive with DOS. You learned how to start DOS in the last chapter. Now it's time to begin learning to control DOS, how to "steer" it in the direction of one task or another, and how to call a halt when you want or need to.

That's what this chapter is all about. It introduces you to the directory of files that DOS keeps on each disk, and shows you how to use the special keys on your keyboard. You use these keys to tell DOS to cancel lines or commands, to freeze the display, and to restart DOS itself.

To try the examples given here, start up your computer, as you did in the last chapter. Enter the appropriate date and time, so that DOS responds with the system prompt, A> (C>, if you are using a fixed disk). Don't worry about leaving your computer on while you read the text between examples; DOS is patient.

Note: Part of this chapter deals with keys that have special meaning for DOS. If you are not using an IBM personal computer, you may want to check your documentation for equivalent keys on your system.

THE DIRECTORY

Recall from Chapter 1 that information stored on a disk is stored as a file. DOS automatically keeps and updates a list of every file you save on every disk you use. This list is called the *directory*. If you create and save a new file, DOS adds it to the list. If you revise an old file, DOS keeps track of that, too. The directory eliminates the need to keep a separate record of everything you save on each disk. You can tell DOS you want to see the directory whenever DOS is displaying the system prompt.

The example in the next section serves the double purpose of showing you a directory and showing you around the DOS system disk itself. As you use the system more, you will come to recognize many of the DOS files as DOS commands. Before you look at a directory, though, you should know a little about how DOS saves your files.

Whenever you create a file, you give it a descriptive name, called the *file name,* of up to eight characters. If you wish, you can add a suffix, called the *extension,* of up to three more letters. (Chapters 4 and 5 present more on files.)

Whenever you ask DOS to show you the directory of a disk, it lists your files by file name (and extension, if there is one). It also shows you the size of your file, in units called bytes, and gives you the date and the time the file was either created or last changed (that's why DOS prompts you for the date and time).

Note: A byte is the amount of storage required to hold one character in computer memory or on disk. Here are a few familiar items and their sizes, in bytes: the letters abcd, *4 bytes (1 byte per letter); the words* United States, *13 bytes (blanks count); a double-spaced, typewritten page, 1500 bytes; this book, 650,000 bytes (approximately).*

Depending on which version of DOS you're using, the type of diskette drives you have, and whether your drives use one or both sides of a diskette, your diskettes can hold anywhere from 163,840 to 368,640 bytes to 1,228,800 (on the PC AT). For convenience, quantities this large are usually given in *kilobytes (K)* or *megabytes (M).* One kilobyte equals 1024 bytes, and one megabyte equals 1024 kilobytes, so the capacity of your diskettes can range from 160K to 360K to 1.2M.

DISPLAYING THE DIRECTORY OF A DISK

To display the directory of the disk in the current drive, you simply type *dir,* the name of the Directory command. Type the command and press Enter:

```
A>dir
```

DOS displays the directory of the current disk. In this example, you see a list of the files on the DOS system diskette. The directory

is longer than the 25 lines the screen can show at one time, so some
of the directory scrolls off the top; you'll see how to handle this
in a moment.

Figure 3-1 shows the Directory-display command.

```
Volume in drive A has no label
Directory of   A:\
ANSI       SYS      1651     3-07-85     1:43p
ASSIGN     COM      1509     3-07-85     1:43p
ATTRIB     EXE     15091     3-07-85     1:43p
BACKUP     COM      5577     3-07-85     1:43p
BASIC      COM     17792     3-07-85     1:43p
BASICA     COM     27520     3-07-85     1:43p
CHKDSK     COM      9435     3-07-85     1:43p
COMMAND    COM     23210     3-07-85     1:43p
COMP       COM      3664     3-07-85     1:43p
DISKCOMP   COM      4073     3-07-85     1:43p
DISKCOPY   COM      4329     3-07-85     1:43p
EDLIN      COM      7261     3-07-85     1:43p
FDISK      COM      8173     3-07-85     1:43p
FIND       EXE      6403     3-07-85     1:43p
FORMAT     COM      9398     3-07-85     1:43p
GRAFTABL   COM      1169     3-07-85     1:43p
GRAPHICS   COM      3111     3-07-85     1:43p
JOIN       EXE     15971     3-07-85     1:43p
KEYBFR     COM      2289     3-07-85     1:43p
KEYBGR     COM      2234     3-07-85     1:43p
KEYBIT     COM      2177     3-07-85     1:43p
KEYBSP     COM      2267     3-07-85     1:43p
KEYBUK     COM      2164     3-07-85     1:43p
LABEL      COM      1826     3-07-85     1:43p
MODE       COM      5295     3-07-85     1:43p
MORE       COM       282     3-07-85     1:43p
PRINT      COM      8291     3-07-85     1:43p
RECOVER    COM      4050     3-07-85     1:43p
RESTORE    COM      5410     3-07-85     1:43p
SELECT     COM      2084     3-07-85     1:43p
SHARE      EXE      8304     3-07-85     1:43p
SORT       EXE      1664     3-07-85     1:43p
SUBST      EXE     16611     3-07-85     1:43p
SYS        COM      3727     3-07-85     1:43p
TREE       COM      2831     3-07-85     1:43p
VDISK      SYS      3307     3-07-85     1:43p
        36 File(s)      61440 bytes free
```

*Figure 3-1. A directory display of the DOS 3.1 diskette on an
IBM personal computer*

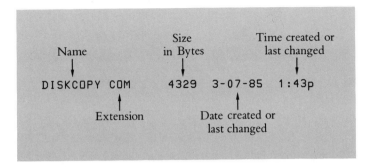

Figure 3-2. A directory entry

Note: The Directory command is used in examples throughout the book. Unless stated otherwise, the Version 3.10 display is shown. If you are using a different version of DOS, your directory listing will differ somewhat from the listing illustrated. The names of the files, their sizes, and the dates vary from one version of DOS to another. Do not be concerned. Such variations do not affect the way you use DOS or the way DOS responds to commands.

The two lines at the top of the directory give information about the disk itself and are explained in detail in Chapter 5, "Managing Your Files." The last line shows how many bytes are unused on the disk, as well as the number of files.

Figure 3-2 shows a breakdown of one entry from a directory. The file name is DISKCOPY; note it is eight letters long, the maximum length of a DOS file name. The next item, COM, is the file's extension. The next item tells you the file is 4329 bytes long — roughly the number of characters you would see on about 3 double-spaced, typed pages. The final two entries give the date and time the file was either created or last changed.

SOME IMPORTANT KEYS

In the examples in the previous chapter, you used the standard typewriter portion of the keyboard—including the Backspace and Enter keys—to enter commands. Several other keys have important meanings to DOS; you'll find yourself using them frequently

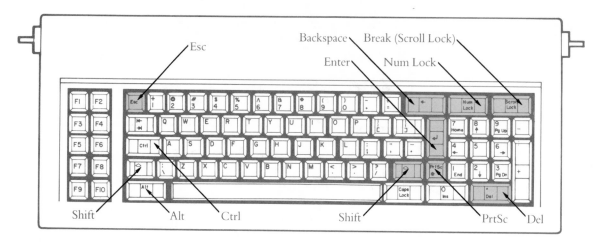

Figure 3-3. Some important keys

while you're using DOS. Figure 3-3 shows where these keys are located on the PC keyboard.

Shift

The Shift keys are labeled with an open arrow. Like the Shift keys on a typewriter, they have no effect by themselves; they shift the keyboard to uppercase letters and special characters.

Esc

Short for *Escape*. This key cancels a line you have typed. To see how it works, type several characters (but don't press Enter):

```
A>Now is the time
```

To erase this line, you could repeatedly press the Backspace key; press the Escape key instead:

```
A>Now is the time\
```

DOS displays a reverse slash (\) to indicate that the line was canceled, and moves the cursor to the beginning of the next line. It doesn't repeat the system prompt, but the cursor indicates DOS is still ready for you to type a command. Press the Enter key, and DOS displays the system prompt and the cursor on the next line:

```
A>_
```

Pressing the Escape key is the quickest way to cancel a line you have typed.

Ctrl

Short for *Control*. This key has no effect by itself, but it is used like the Shift keys to change the effect of pressing another key. The combination of the Control key and some other key is represented in this book by Ctrl- followed by the other key. Ctrl-Break, for example, means "hold down the Control key and press the Break key." The Control key combinations and what they do are described in a moment.

Num Lock

Short for *Numeric Lock*. This key does two things. It switches the effect of the keys in the calculator-style number pad at the right side of the keyboard back and forth between cursor movement and numbers. It is also used in combination with the Control key to freeze the display. To test the first function, press Num Lock and the 4 key in the numeric pad several times:

```
A>444_
```

The keys produce numbers on the screen. Now press Num Lock again and press the same 4 key:

```
A>44_
```

Pressing Num Lock a second time switched the keys to their cursor-movement functions. The 4 key is labeled with a left arrow in addition to the number 4; pressing it moves the cursor left, in the direction of the arrow, and erases a character just as the Backspace key does. Press Num Lock and the same 4 key again:

```
A>44 4_
```

You switched back to numbers. Press Num Lock one more time to switch back to cursor movement, press Esc to cancel the line, and press Enter to return to the system prompt:

```
A>444\

A>_
```

You won't often use the arrow-marked direction keys for cursor movement with DOS, but many application programs, such as word processors, involve frequent cursor movements.

Break

This key is labeled Scroll Lock on the top surface and Break on the front. It has no effect by itself, but it is used with the Control key to cancel a command.

Alt and Del

Short for *Alternate* and *Delete*. These keys have no effect by themselves; they are used with the Control key to restart DOS.

PrtSc

Short for *Print Screen*. This key is used with the Shift and Control keys to print the contents of the screen. You used Shift-PrtSc in the previous chapter; you'll use Ctrl-PrtSc, and see the difference, in a short while.

CONTROL-KEY FUNCTIONS

Figure 3-4 shows the effects produced by holding down the Control key and pressing another key. You'll probably use these

Ctrl-NumLock	Halts whatever the system is doing until you press another key. Typically used to freeze the display when information is scrolling by too fast or scrolling off the top of the screen. Can also be typed Ctrl-S (Ctrl, plus the letter S).
Ctrl-Break	Cancels whatever the system is doing. Use this when you really don't want the computer to continue what it's doing. Can also be typed Ctrl-C (Ctrl, plus the letter C).
Ctrl-PrtSc	Pressing this key combination once causes DOS to start printing every line, as it is displayed; pressing Ctrl-PrtSc a second time stops simultaneous displaying and printing. Can also be typed Ctrl-P (Ctrl, plus the letter P).
Ctrl-Alt-Del	Restarts DOS. This combination is unique; no other keys can be used to do the same thing.

Figure 3-4. Control key combinations

combinations fairly often with DOS, so the next few topics show you examples of each combination. When you are being shown exactly what to type, the names of the keys are separated by hyphens and enclosed in angle brackets to represent pressing a Control key combination. Thus, when you see <Ctrl-Break> in a command, it means "press Ctrl-Break."

Before trying the examples, you should also note that DOS displays the Control key as the symbol ^. DOS does not acknowledge all Control key commands on the screen, but when it does, it uses the symbol ^ in combination with a letter. Control-Break, for example, shows on the screen as ^C and can, actually, be typed by holding down the Control key and typing the letter C.

Freezing the Display

When you displayed the directory earlier, the first few lines scrolled off the screen. To let you read such long displays, DOS lets you temporarily halt the display by pressing Ctrl-Num Lock. When you do this, the display remains frozen, giving you time to read it. To start the display moving again, you simply press any key.

To test this function, type the following to display the directory. When the entries start appearing on the screen, press Ctrl-Num Lock to freeze the display:

```
A>dir
```

Press any key, and the display resumes. You can press Ctrl-Num Lock to stop and start the display as many times as you like, so you can view displays that are many screens long.

Pressing Ctrl-S has the same effect as pressing Ctrl-Num Lock.

Canceling a Command

If you enter a command and then change your mind, or realize you meant to enter some other command, you can cancel the command you entered by pressing Ctrl-Break. To test this function, type the Directory command again. This time, press Ctrl-Break when DOS begins to display the directory entries:

```
A>dir

Volume in drive A has no label
Directory of  A:\

ANSI     SYS     1651    3-07-85   1:43p
ASSIGN   COM     1509    3-07-85   1:43p
ATTRIB   EXE    15091    3-07-85   1:43p
BACKUP   COM     5577    3-07-85   1:43p
BASIC    COM    17792    3-07-85   1:43p
BASICA   COM    27520    3-07-85   1:43p
CHKDSK   COM     9435    3-07-85   1:43p
COMMAND  COM       23^C

A>_
```

Your display may have stopped somewhere else in the directory, but when you press Ctrl-Break, DOS stops what it is doing, displays ^C at the stopping point, and returns to the command level.

Pressing Ctrl-C has the same effect as pressing Ctrl-Break.

Printing and Displaying Simultaneously

In the previous chapter you printed the contents of the screen by pressing Shift-PrtSc. There's another way to print from the

screen: Pressing Ctrl–PrtSc tells DOS to start printing everything it displays. DOS continues to print and display simultaneously until you press Ctrl–PrtSc again.

To test this function, make sure your printer is turned on, press Ctrl–PrtSc, then enter the Directory command:

```
A> <Ctrl-PrtSc>dir
```

DOS again displays the directory of the system disk, but this time each line is printed as it is displayed. The directory is displayed more slowly than when you use the Directory command alone, because DOS waits until a line is printed before displaying and printing the next line. You can cancel the Directory command before the complete directory is printed by pressing Ctrl–Break. Remember to press Ctrl–PrtSc to end the simultaneous displaying and printing.

If you want to print something without printing the command that creates the display, type the command first, then press Ctrl–PrtSc, and then press Enter. For example, when you printed the directory in the preceding example, the Directory command was the first line printed. To avoid printing the command, type the following:

```
A> dir<Ctrl-PrtSc>
```

Now printing begins with the first line of the directory; the Directory command isn't printed. Cancel the command by pressing Ctrl–Break.

Again, after you have pressed Ctrl–PrtSc to start printing, be sure to remember to press it again to stop; otherwise, DOS continues to print everything you display, even if you go on to an entirely different task.

Pressing Ctrl–P has the same effect as pressing Ctrl–PrtSc.

Shift–PrtSc versus Ctrl–PrtSc

These two methods of printing from the screen work differently and have different uses. Shift–PrtSc uninterruptedly prints everything on the screen. Ctrl–PrtSc, as you just saw, alternates displaying and printing, line by line. If everything you want is on the screen, use Shift–PrtSc; it's faster. But, if you want to keep a

running record of a series of commands and responses, or you want
to print something longer than one screenful, use Ctrl-PrtSc.

Ctrl-PrtSc is better for printing long displays because you can
press it once to tell DOS to start simultaneous displaying and printing. Then, you simply enter a command, such as the Directory
command, to create the display, and press Ctrl-PrtSc again when
you want to stop printing. If you use Shift-PrtSc for printing displays more than one screen long, you have to display the first screen,
print it, then display the second screen, print it, and so forth until
everything you want has been printed.

Restarting the System

Suppose you find yourself in a situation where your computer
is not responding as you think it should, or it complains about something you don't know how to handle, or you decide it would be best
to scrap what you're doing and start over from the beginning. You
don't have to turn the power switch off and on to restart your system; you can do it by pressing Ctrl-Alt-Del.

Try it: Hold down both Ctrl and Alt with your left hand and
press Del with your right.

The screen clears, the red light on drive A (or drive C, if you
have a fixed disk) goes on, the system beeps, and DOS is loaded just
as it was when you turned the power on. Restarting with Ctrl-Alt-
Del takes less time, though, because the computer doesn't test all
its devices and memory as it does whenever you switch the power
off and on.

Notice that the date is once again 1-01-1980 and DOS is prompting you to enter the current date; restarting DOS resets the date and
time. Type the following to set the date and time to 4:25 p.m. on
April 27, 1986:

```
Current date is Tue  1-01-1980
Enter new date (mm-dd-yy) 4-27-86
Current time is  0:00:35.09
Enter new time: 16:25
```

DOS displays its start-up message and the system prompt.

A SHORT DIVERSION

The system prompt (A>) is an economical way for DOS to show you the current drive and to let you know that you can enter a command. But the combination of a letter (for the current drive) and the greater-than sign (>) is only one possible system prompt. An advanced DOS command, Prompt, lets you change the system prompt to almost anything you want.

For example, you might prefer a more courteous machine. Type the following and press Enter:

```
A>prompt May I help you? <Enter>
```

Now the system prompt isn't quite so cryptic:

```
May I help you? _
```

Each time DOS returns to the command level, it displays this polite phrase. Try it by pressing the Enter key once or twice to cause DOS to display the system prompt again. Although your new prompt looks quite different from A> (and actually conveys less information), the meaning is the same: DOS is at the command level, ready for you to enter a command.

To see just how much you can cram into the system prompt, type the following example (including a blank after the colon), as a single line. Although the example is shown as two separate lines, don't press the Enter key until you come to <Enter> at the end of the second line:

```
May I help you? prompt The time is $t$_The date is
$d$_The current disk is $n$_Your command: <Enter>
```

Now the system prompt is three lines of data followed by a request for a command:

```
The time is 16:26:03.54
The date is Sun  4-27-1986
The current disk is A
Your command: _
```

You would probably quickly tire of all this, but the exercise shows how much flexibility DOS gives you. You don't have to take advantage of it all, but it's there if you want it.

To return the system prompt to its normal form, type the Prompt command by itself:

```
The time is 16:26:03.54
The date is Sun  4-27-1986
The current disk is A
Your command: prompt
```

It's back to the familiar A> (or C>).

CHAPTER SUMMARY

- Each diskette has a directory that lists the name, extension, and size of each file, and the date and time the file was created or last changed. You can see the directory by typing *dir* and pressing Enter.

- The Esc key cancels a line you have typed.

- Ctrl-Num Lock freezes the display. Ctrl-S has the same effect.

- Ctrl-Break cancels a command. Ctrl-C has the same effect.

- Ctrl-PrtSc turns simultaneous displaying and printing on and off. Ctrl-P has the same effect.

- Ctrl-Alt-Del restarts DOS.

Now that you're more familiar with the keyboard, the next chapter gives you a closer look at diskettes and files.

CHAPTER
4
A LOOK AT
FILES AND DISKETTES

The computer's memory is temporary; it is cleared each time you turn off the computer. The only way you can save data permanently is to store the data in a file on a disk. When DOS needs data that is stored in a file, it reads the data from the disk into memory. If you change the data and want to keep the changed version, you must store the revised version on disk before turning off the system.

TYPES OF FILES

In general, a file contains either a program or data. A program is a set of instructions for the computer. Data is the text and numbers the program needs to do your work, such as a project proposal, a table of tax rates, or a list of customers.

Three types of files, in particular, are important to your work: text files, command files, and application program files. They are all different, so it's important to look more closely at the kind of information these files contain and at how the files are used.

Text Files

Text files are data files that contain characters you can read (everyday letters, numbers, and symbols). Word-processing programs store their documents in text files, as does Edlin, the DOS text editor. Many files you use in your work with the computer — and almost all of the files that you will use in this book — are text files.

The definition of a text file may seem self-evident at first, but it actually introduces you to an important characteristic of computer information storage. Your computer keeps information in two very different forms: one is text, the characters contained in text files; the other is machine-readable code, which looks meaningless to most people, but which is quite meaningful to computers.

Command Files

Command files contain the instructions DOS needs to carry out commands. These instructions can be a program, such as Diskcopy, or, as you will see in Chapter 13, "Creating Your

Own Commands," they can be a series of DOS commands, which you put together to perform a specific task, and which you store in a text file.

Not all DOS commands are command files, however. Some commands, such as the Directory command, are built into the main body of DOS. When you load DOS into memory, you load these commands with it. When you want to use these commands, DOS has them "on tap" for immediate use—it does not need to look up a separate command file to carry them out.

These built-in commands are called *permanent,* or *internal, commands.* In contrast, the commands that are kept in command files until they are requested by you are called *temporary,* or *external, commands.* When you use a permanent command, you simply request the command and DOS carries it out. When you use a temporary command, DOS loads the command file from disk into memory, and then carries out the command.

Application Program Files

An application program, such as a word processor, is stored in a command file; it stores your work, such as documents, in data files.

HOW FILES ARE NAMED

No matter the type of file, however, each file must have a file name. Recall that a file name can be up to eight characters long. You can use almost any character on the keyboard when you name your files, but it's a good idea to give your files names that describe their contents, such as BUDGET or LETTER2.

To identify a file more completely, a three-character suffix called the file extension can be added to the file name; this suffix is separated from the file name by a period. So that you and DOS can tell your files apart, each file on a disk must have either a different name or a different extension (REPORT.JAN and REPORT.FEB, for example, are different files to DOS, even though their file names are the same).

Specifying the Drive

When you name a file in a command, DOS must know which drive contains the disk with the file on it. If you don't specify a drive letter, DOS looks on the disk in the current drive (the drive letter shown in the system prompt). If the disk containing the file is not in the current drive, you can precede the file name with the letter of the drive and a colon. For example, if you specify the file as *b:report.doc*, DOS looks for it in drive B.

PREPARING FOR THE EXAMPLES

The following pages show a number of examples to help you become more comfortable with files and diskettes. With DOS, as with most other computer applications, doing is often the easiest and most effective way of learning.

If you are using a system with diskette drives, insert your working (backup) copy of the DOS system diskette in drive A and start up the computer. Enter the date and time so DOS responds with the system prompt A>.

If you have a fixed disk, DOS is already in drive C, so simply turn on the computer and go through the start-up routine until you see the system prompt C>.

Don't Worry About Memorizing

You use several commands in this chapter, but you needn't remember exactly how to use each one; all the commands are described in more detail in the remaining chapters of the book. The purpose of this chapter is to introduce you to files and diskettes.

QUALIFYING A COMMAND

Up to now, all the commands you have entered consisted of a single word or abbreviation, such as *time* or *dir*. Most commands, however, let you add one or more qualifiers to make the action of the command more specific. These qualifiers are called parameters.

Some commands require parameters; others allow you to add parameters if you want. The Directory command, for example, does not require parameters, but it lets you add the name of the specific file you want to see (you'll use some parameters in the following examples). The descriptions of the commands in later chapters show their parameters, both required and optional.

DISPLAYING SPECIFIC DIRECTORY ENTRIES

In the previous chapter you used the Directory command to display the directory entries of all files on the system disk. You can display the directory entry of a single file, or the directory entries for a selected set of files, by adding a qualifier to the Directory command.

Displaying the Directory Entry Of a Single File

To display the directory entry for a specific file, you simply type the file name (and extension, if there is one) after the command name. For example, you copied the system diskette with the Diskcopy command. Its command file is DISKCOPY.COM. To display the directory entry for DISKCOPY.COM, type the following, including the blank between the command and the file name:

```
A>dir diskcopy.com
```

DOS displays only the directory entry of the file you specified:

```
Volume in drive A has no label
Directory of  A:\

DISKCOPY COM     4329  3-07-85  1:43p
        1 File(s)     61440 bytes free

A>_
```

If the file you name isn't on the disk, or if you don't type the file name exactly as it is stored, DOS responds *File not found*.

Displaying the Directory Entries
Of a Set of Files

What if you remember most of a file name, or the file name but not the extension? DOS helps you out by giving you two *wildcard characters,* * and ?, that you can substitute for actual characters in a file name. Like wild cards in a poker game, the wildcard characters can represent any other character. They differ only in that ? can substitute for one character, while * can substitute for more than one character.

Suppose you can only remember that a file's name begins with the letter C? It takes only a moment to check all the files that begin with C. Use the DOS directory as an example and type the following command:

```
A>dir c*
```

DOS displays the directory entries of all file names that begin with C:

```
Volume in drive A has no label
Directory of  A:\

COMMAND   COM     23210    3-07-85    1:43p
CHKDSK    COM      9435    3-07-85    1:43p
COMP      COM      3664    3-07-85    1:43p
        3 File(s)      61440 bytes free

A>_
```

Wildcard characters can simplify the task of keeping track of your files. Chapter 5, "Managing Your Files," includes several examples of using wildcard characters with different commands.

Now, it's time to stop practicing with the system disk and create some files of your own.

PREPARING A DISKETTE FOR USE

Before DOS can store a file on a new diskette, you must prepare the diskette for use. You do this with the Format command. This preparation, in which DOS writes certain information for its own use on the diskette, is called *formatting.* You'll need two formatted diskettes for the examples in this book. Now is a good

time to format the diskettes, so get out the two blank diskettes and two blank labels you need before proceeding.

Place a blank diskette in drive B (the diskette drive, if you have a fixed disk) with the label up and away from the machine. Close the latch and type the following:

```
A> format b:
```

This command tells DOS to format the diskette in drive B.

Formatting a diskette erases any files that may be stored on it, so DOS gives you a chance to make sure you haven't put the wrong diskette in the specified drive, by displaying a message, then waiting for you to type something:

```
Insert new diskette for drive B:
and strike ENTER when ready_
```

If you discover that you put in the wrong diskette, no problem: Just take out the wrong one and put in the right one before you press the Enter key.

If you can't find a diskette that you want to format, and you want to cancel the command, again, no problem: You don't have to turn the system off, just press Ctrl-Break.

But you do want to format the diskette now, so press Enter. DOS displays *Formatting...,* the red light on drive B goes on, and DOS begins writing on the diskette. When it has finished formatting the diskette, DOS tells you *Format complete,* reports on the amount of available storage on the diskette, and asks if you want to format another:

```
362496 bytes total disk space
362496 bytes available on disk

Format another (Y/N)?_
```

Depending on the type of disk drives you have and the version of DOS you're using, the total disk space in the report might be 1,213,952; 362,496 (as shown); 322,560; 179,712; or 160,256 bytes.

DOS is now waiting for you to say whether you want to format another diskette. Type *y*. The message asking you to put the diskette in drive B is repeated, so go through the same process to format the second diskette. When DOS finishes, it asks you again whether you want to format another.

Now type *n*. DOS displays the system prompt (A>), telling you the Format command is ended and that DOS is waiting for you to type another command.

You now have two formatted diskettes. It's time to put one of them to use by creating a file, so insert one in drive B.

CREATING A TEXT FILE

An easy way to create a text file is by using the DOS Copy command. As you might guess from its name, the Copy command can be used to make a copy of a file. It can also be used to copy from the keyboard into a file.

DOS refers to the parts of your computer, such as the keyboard, display, and printer, as devices. To DOS, devices, like files, have names. The keyboard is known to DOS as CON (for CONsole).

You are going to create a file by telling DOS to copy what you type from the keyboard onto the blank diskette in drive B.

Note: If you're using a fixed disk, DOS treats your diskette drive as both drive A and drive B. In the remaining examples, DOS will sometimes display Insert diskette for drive A: *or* Insert diskette for drive B: *followed by and strike any key when ready. When you see this message, simply press the space bar or any other key and continue with the example.*

To create a file named NOTE.DOC on the diskette in drive B, type the following. End each line by pressing Enter; where you see a blank line, press Enter to tell DOS to insert an extra line:

```
A>copy con b:note.doc
October 16, 1985

Dear Fred,
Just a note to remind you
that our meeting is at 9.

Jack
```

That's the end of the file. To tell DOS that it's the end of the file, type Ctrl-Z (hold down the Control key and press Z), then press Enter:

```
<Ctrl-Z><Enter>
```

When you press Ctrl-Z, DOS displays ^Z (the ^, remember, represents the Control key). After you press Enter, DOS acknowledges that it copied a file:

```
        1 File(s) copied

A>_
```

To verify that the file is there, display the directory of the diskette in drive B:

```
A>dir b:
```

Sure enough, NOTE.DOC is on the diskette:

```
    Volume in drive B has no label
    Directory of  B:\

NOTE      DOC       94 10-16-85   2:54p
          1 File(s)    361472 bytes free

A>_
```

This method of creating a text file is quick and convenient, and it is used in examples throughout the book.

Displaying a Text File

Because you can read the characters in text files, you'll often want to display one on the screen. It's even easier to display a text file than it is to create it. Just use the DOS Type command. To display your file, type the following:

```
A>type b:note.doc
```

DOS quickly displays each line and then returns to the command level:

```
October 16, 1985

Dear Fred,
Just a note to remind you
that our meeting is at 9.

Jack

A>_
```

This is the quickest way to see what's in a file; you'll probably use the Type command frequently.

Displaying a file isn't always helpful, though, because not all files are text files; they don't all contain readable characters. See for yourself. Type the following to display the contents of the DOS command file named SYS.COM:

```
A>type sys.com
```

Yes, the display is correct. It's hard to tell from that jumble what is in the file, because the file contains a program stored in machine code, not as a text file.

Printing a Text File

One of the main reasons you write documents, of course, is to have a printed copy. You can print your file by copying it to the printer. You've already copied from the keyboard to a disk. Now, copy from the disk to the printer. The printer is known to DOS as PRN. Make sure the printer is turned on and type the following:

```
A>copy b:note.doc prn
```

The file is printed. When you print a file, you'll probably want to position the paper by hand first before you enter the command, so the printing will begin where you want it to.

There's an easier way, however, to print a file: the Print command. To print your file with this command, type the following:

```
A>print b:note.doc
```

DOS responds:

```
Name of list device [PRN]: _
```

Press the Enter key. DOS displays the following two messages and prints your file:

```
Resident part of PRINT installed

     B:\NOTE.DOC is currently being printed

A>_
```

These messages are explained in more detail in Chapter 5, "Managing Your Files."

The Print command makes the printer advance to the next page after printing. Although this file is too short to show it, you can continue to use the system to do other work while the Print command is printing a file.

Copying a Text File

The Copy command is one of the more versatile DOS commands. You have already used it to create and print a text file. The Copy command also duplicates files.

To copy the file named NOTE.DOC into another file named LETTER.DOC, type:

```
A>copy b:note.doc b:letter.doc
```

When you press Enter, DOS copies the file; then it acknowledges that it did so:

```
     1 File(s) copied

A>_
```

Display the directory of the diskette in drive B again to verify the copy:

```
A>dir b:
```

Now you have two text files:

```
Volume in drive B has no label
Directory of  B:\

NOTE      DOC        94  10-16-85   2:54p
LETTER    DOC        94  10-16-85   2:54p
          2 File(s)     360448 bytes free

A>_
```

If you wanted, you could make changes to one file and still have a copy of the original version on disk. You'll find the Copy command quite useful when you need several files that differ only slightly, or when you have several small files that can be combined in different ways to create other files: often-used paragraphs, for example, that can be recombined in different letters, contracts, or other documents.

Erasing a Text File

Just as you get rid of paper files, you can erase disk files. To erase NOTE.DOC from the diskette in drive B, type:

```
A>erase b:note.doc

A>_
```

Now check the directory one more time:

```
A>dir b:

Volume in drive B has no label
Directory of  B:\

LETTER    DOC        94  10-16-85   2:54p
          1 File(s)     361472 bytes free

A>_
```

It's gone.

SOME ADVANCED FEATURES

Several commands and features give you much greater control over the way DOS does its work. For example, you can:

- View a long display one screenful at a time, without having to freeze the display by pressing Ctrl-Num Lock.

- Tell DOS to send the results, or output, of a command to the printer instead of the display, simply by adding a few characters to the command.

- Sort lines of data—for example, sort alphabetically the list of directory entries produced by the Directory command.

- Search lines of data for a series of characters.

The examples in this section give you a glimpse of these advanced features; the features are described in detail, with many additional examples, in later chapters.

You'll notice that these advanced features cause more disk activity and take a bit longer than the other DOS commands. That's because DOS creates temporary files to carry out the advanced features. DOS deletes these temporary files before returning to the command level.

Viewing a Long Display
One Screenful at a Time

When you displayed the directory of the system diskette in Chapter 3, the first few lines scrolled off the top of the screen because the display was too long to fit on the screen. You saw that you can freeze the display by pressing Ctrl-Num Lock. There's an easier way to stop scrolling: The More command displays one screenful, with -- *More* -- at the bottom of the screen, then waits for you to press any key to continue to the next screenful. Type the following (type the vertical bar by pressing the right Shift key at the same time you press the key just left of the Z):

```
A>dir | more
```

DOS displays the first screenful; but the last few lines aren't displayed yet (notice -- *More* -- in the last line):

```
Volume in drive A has no label
Directory of  A:\

ANSI      SYS     1651   3-07-85   1:43p
ASSIGN    COM     1509   3-07-85   1:43p
ATTRIB    EXE    15091   3-07-85   1:43p
BACKUP    COM     5577   3-07-85   1:43p
BASIC     COM    17792   3-07-85   1:43p
BASICA    COM    27520   3-07-85   1:43p
CHKDSK    COM     9435   3-07-85   1:43p
COMMAND   COM    23210   3-07-85   1:43p
COMP      COM     3664   3-07-85   1:43p
DISKCOMP  COM     4073   3-07-85   1:43p
DISKCOPY  COM     4329   3-07-85   1:43p
EDLIN     COM     7261   3-07-85   1:43p
FDISK     COM     8173   3-07-85   1:43p
FIND      EXE     6403   3-07-85   1:43p
FORMAT    COM     9398   3-07-85   1:43p
GRAFTABL  COM     1169   3-07-85   1:43p
GRAPHICS  COM     3111   3-07-85   1:43p
JOIN      EXE    15971   3-07-85   1:43p
KEYBFR    COM     2289   3-07-85   1:43p
KEYBGR    COM     2234   3-07-85   1:43p
-- More --
```

To see the rest of the directory, press any key. DOS displays the remaining lines:

```
KEYBIT    COM     2177   3-07-85   1:43p
KEYBSP    COM     2267   3-07-85   1:43p
KEYBUK    COM     2164   3-07-85   1:43p
LABEL     COM     1826   3-07-85   1:43p
MODE      COM     5295   3-07-85   1:43p
MORE      COM      282   3-07-85   1:43p
PRINT     COM     8291   3-07-85   1:43p
RECOVER   COM     4050   3-07-85   1:43p
RESTORE   COM     5410   3-07-85   1:43p
SELECT    COM     2084   3-07-85   1:43p
SHARE     EXE     8304   3-07-85   1:43p
SORT      EXE     1664   3-07-85   1:43p
SUBST     EXE    16611   3-07-85   1:43p
SYS       COM     3727   3-07-85   1:43p
TREE      COM     2831   3-07-85   1:43p
VDISK     SYS     3307   3-07-85   1:43p
02111E23                 01-01-80   2:17a
02111F22                 01-01-80   2:17a
       38 File(s)     59392 bytes free
```

The More command displays long output one screenful at a time, giving you a chance to view it all at your convenience.

Note: The files named 02111E23 and 02111F22 are temporary files that DOS creates for the More command to use. The file names are based on the date and time you enter the More command, so your display will probably show different names. When the More command is finished, DOS erases the files. You can confirm this by displaying the directory again without using the More command; the files aren't shown. (If you're not using Version 3 of DOS, the names of these temporary files begin with a percent sign—%PIPE1.$$$ and %PIPE2.$$$.)

Sending Command Output to the Printer

In earlier examples you printed the output of the Directory command by pressing Shift-PrtSc and Ctrl-PrtSc. There's a more direct way to print the output of a command: Simply follow the command with a greater-than symbol (>) and the name of the printer, PRN. To print the directory of the disk in drive A, make sure the printer is turned on and type:

```
A>dir > prn
```

If you don't want to wait for the whole directory, cancel the printing by pressing Ctrl-Break.

This same technique can be used to send the output of a command to some other device or to a file, by substituting the device name or file name for PRN.

Sorting Lines of Data

You have probably arranged card files or lists in some sequence, such as alphabetic or numeric order. The Sort command sorts, or arranges, lines of data such as a list of names, for you. To see how this works, sort the lines of the text file B:LETTER.DOC. Type:

```
A>sort < b:letter.doc
```

The less-than symbol (<) tells DOS to send a copy of the file B:LETTER.DOC to the sort program. The file is displayed, but it is now arranged in alphabetic order:

```
Dear Fred,
Jack
Just a note to remind you
October 16, 1985
that our meeting is at 9.

A>_
```

Although you may not want to sort the lines of your letters, you can put whatever you like in a text file—such as a list of customers or employees. The Sort command is a powerful addition to your kit of computer tools.

Finding a Series of Characters in a File

How many times have you searched through a pile of letters or notes, looking for a particular item or reference? If you have to look through DOS files or the output of DOS commands, the Find command will do the looking for you. For example, suppose you want to see the directory entries of all DOS files with SK in their names. Type the following (the quotation marks tell DOS which letters— known technically as a *character string,* or just *string*—to look for):

```
A>dir | find "SK"
```

DOS displays just the entries with SK in their names:

```
CHKDSK    COM      9435    3-07-85   1:43p
DISKCOMP  COM      4073    3-07-85   1:43p
DISKCOPY  COM      4329    3-07-85   1:43p
FDISK     COM      8173    3-07-85   1:43p
VDISK     SYS      3307    3-07-85   1:43p

A>_
```

The Find command is even more useful when you use it to search for a series of characters in a text file. If a file contains a list of names and telephone numbers, for example, you can quickly display one particular entry, or all entries that contain a particular series of

characters (such as an area code), or even all entries that *don't* contain a particular series of characters. Chapter 14, "Taking Control of Your System," shows you how to create such an automated index of names and telephone numbers with nothing but DOS commands.

Combining Features

These advanced features of DOS can also be used together in a single command, giving you even more flexibility in controlling DOS. Combining these features makes it possible to do a great deal with just one command. For example, suppose you want to print the directory entries of all files on the disk in the current drive whose names include SK; further, you want the entries sorted according to the size of the files. Type the following:

```
A>dir ¦ find "SK" ¦ sort /+16 > prn
```

This whole command translates easily into: Go to drive A, look at the directory, find all files with the letters SK in their names, sort those files at the 16th column (where the size begins), and send the results to the printer. DOS does as it is told; it prints the sorted files in order, from the smallest (3307 bytes) to the largest (9435 bytes):

```
VDISK      SYS     3307     3-07-85   1:43p
DISKCOMP   COM     4073     3-07-85   1:43p
DISKCOPY   COM     4329     3-07-85   1:43p
FDISK      COM     8173     3-07-85   1:43p
CHKDSK     COM     9435     3-07-85   1:43p
```

You may rarely search your directories this carefully, but such combinations make DOS a powerful tool for handling text files.

CHAPTER SUMMARY

This chapter concludes the portion of the book designed to give you a feel for running DOS, including some of its advanced features. The key points to remember include:

- The computer's memory is cleared each time you turn the system off. To save your work permanently, you must store it in a file on disk.

- A text file contains ordinary characters you can read.

- A command file contains instructions that DOS uses to carry out a command.

- A file name can be up to eight characters long; an extension of up to three characters can be added, separated from the file name by a period.

- Each file on a disk must have a different name or a different extension.

The remainder of the book shows you how to use DOS to manage your files, disks, and devices; use the text editor; and create your own commands.

PART

2

LEARNING
TO USE DOS

Part 2 shows you how to use DOS to manage your work with the computer. The chapters in Part 2 include extensive examples that use real-life situations to illustrate each DOS command, but the information is organized so that you can quickly find a particular topic to refresh your memory.

The material in these chapters covers all versions of DOS. Chapter 8 discusses using DOS with other languages.

Chapters 13 through 17 show you how to use the advanced features of DOS. Chapter 18 introduces you to networks.

CHAPTER
5

MANAGING
YOUR FILES

The previous chapters defined a file as a named collection of related information stored on a disk, and showed you several ways to create, copy, display, print, and otherwise work with your computer files. This chapter describes the DOS filing system in detail, showing you more about how files are named and how you can use DOS to manage your computer files.

Note: A few of the examples in the remaining chapters of this book may look familiar, because they repeat some of the examples in Chapters 2, 3, and 4. This repetition is intentional, to make Chapters 5 through 18 a complete reference section. You won't have to refer back to Chapters 2, 3, or 4 for command descriptions.

THE DOS FILE COMMANDS

To be useful, a filing system—whether it contains disk files or paper files—must be kept orderly and up to date. Using the DOS file commands, you can manage your disk files much as you manage your paper files. This chapter covers the DOS commands you use most often on a day-to-day basis. It shows you how to:

- Display specific directory entries with the Directory command.

- Display a file with the Type command.

- Copy a file with the Copy command.

- Combine files with the Copy command.

- Send a copy of a file to a device with the Copy command.

- Dispose of a file with the Erase command.

- Change the name of a file with the Rename command.

- Compare two files with the Compare command.

- Print a file with the Print command.

- Control whether a file can be changed with the Attribute command.

FILE NAMES AND EXTENSIONS

As Chapter 4 pointed out, files are named so that you (and DOS) can tell them apart; each file on a disk must have a different name. You know that a file name can be up to eight characters long, made up of any letter or number; you can also use the following symbols with any version of DOS:

! @ # $ % & ( ) - _ { } ''

You can add a suffix—called an extension—to the file name to describe its contents more precisely. The extension can be up to three characters long, using the same characters that are valid for the file name; it must be separated from the name by a period. The extension distinguishes one file from another just as the name does: REPORT and REPORT.JAN, for example, are two different files, as are REPORT.JAN and REPORT.FEB. Figure 5-1 shows some valid and invalid file names.

Try to make file names and extensions as descriptive as possible. A short file name may be easy to type, but you may find it difficult to remember what the file contains if you haven't used it for awhile. The more descriptive the name, the more easily you can identify the contents of the file.

These file names are valid	These are invalid . . .	because
B	1986BUDGET	Name too long
85BUDGET	BUDGET.1986	Extension too long
BUDGET.85	.86	No file name
BUDGET.86	SALES 85.DAT	Blank not allowed
BDGT(86)	$1,300.45	Comma not allowed

Figure 5-1. Valid and invalid file names

Special Extensions

Figure 5-2 describes some extensions that have special meanings to DOS. These extensions are either created by DOS or cause DOS to assume the file contains a particular type of program or data. You should avoid giving your files any of these extensions.

Some application programs also use special extensions. For example, Microsoft Word, the Microsoft word processor, uses DOC to identify a document, BAK to identify a backup version of a document, and STY to identify a file containing a style sheet of print specifications. You should avoid using extensions that have special

Extension	Meaning to DOS
COM	Short for *Command*. Identifies a command file that contains a program DOS runs when you type the file name.
EXE	Short for *Executable*. Like COM, identifies a command file that contains a program DOS runs when you type the file name.
BAS	Short for *BASIC*. Contains a program written in the BASIC programming language. You can't run this program by typing its name; you can run it only while using the BASIC language.
SYS	Short for *System*. Identifies a file for use by DOS only.
BAK	Short for *Backup*. Contains an earlier version of a text file. Edlin, the DOS text editor, and many word processors automatically make a backup copy of a file and give it this extension at the start of an editing session.
BAT	Short for *Batch*. Identifies a text file you can create that contains a set of DOS commands that are run when you type the name of the file.

Figure 5-2. Special DOS file name extensions

meaning for your application programs; these extensions are usually listed in the documentation that comes with each program.

Specifying the Drives

You can tell DOS to look for a file in a specific drive by typing the drive letter and a colon before the file name. If you specify a file as *b:report,* for example, DOS looks in drive B for a file named *report;* if you specify the file as REPORT, DOS looks in the current drive.

PREPARING FOR THE EXAMPLES

The examples in this chapter require formatted diskettes and some sample files. Follow the instructions under the heading that describes your system, then complete the preparation by creating the sample files, as shown.

If You're Not Using a Fixed Disk

You need two formatted diskettes for the examples in this chapter. Put one of the formatted diskettes in drive B, and type the following to create a sample text file named REPORT.DOC on the diskette in drive B (recall from Chapter 4 that Ctrl-Z tells DOS it's reached the end of the file):

```
A>copy con b:report.doc
This is a dummy file.
^Z
```

DOS responds:

```
        1 File(s) copied

A>
```

Change the current drive to B by typing:

```
A>b:
```

DOS changes the system prompt to show that drive B is now the current drive:

```
B>_
```

Go on to the heading "Creating the Sample Files."

If You Are Using a Fixed Disk

The examples in this and the remaining chapters assume that you have copied DOS to the fixed disk (drive C). You need one formatted diskette for the examples in this chapter. Put the formatted diskette in the diskette drive, and type the following to create a sample text file named REPORT.DOC on the diskette:

```
C>copy con b:report.doc
This is a dummy file.
^Z
```

DOS asks you to make sure the correct diskette is in the diskette drive:

```
Insert diskette for drive B: and strike
any key when ready
```

The correct diskette is in the drive, so just press the space bar or any other key. DOS acknowledges:

```
1 File(s) copied
```

```
C>_
```

Change the current drive to B by typing:

```
C>b:
```

DOS changes the system prompt to show that drive B is now the current drive:

```
B>_
```

Now you can go on to the following examples.

Note: DOS is on the fixed disk, in drive C, so remember: (1) where the examples show the drive letter as A, you see C; (2) be sure to type c: *wherever the examples tell you to type* a:.

Creating the Sample Files

Use the Copy command, which is described in detail later in the chapter, to create some other sample files:

```
B>copy report.doc report.bak
          1 File(s) copied

B>copy report.doc bank.doc
          1 File(s) copied

B>copy report.doc budget.jan
          1 File(s) copied

B>copy report.doc budget.feb
          1 File(s) copied

B>copy report.doc budget.mar
          1 File(s) copied
```

Now check the directory.

```
B>dir
```

It should list six files:

```
Volume in drive B has no label
Directory of  B:\

REPORT    DOC        23  10-16-85    9:16a
REPORT    BAK        23  10-16-85    9:16a
BANK      DOC        23  10-16-85    9:16a
BUDGET    JAN        23  10-16-85    9:16a
BUDGET    FEB        23  10-16-85    9:16a
BUDGET    MAR        23  10-16-85    9:16a
          6 File(s)      356352 bytes free
```

Remember, the time and date will vary according to the information you enter when you start DOS, but the files and file sizes (23 bytes) should match exactly.

WILDCARD CHARACTERS

To make it easier to manage your disk files, most file commands let you use wildcard characters to handle several files at once. That way, when you want to do the same thing to several files—change their names, perhaps, or erase them—you don't have to enter a separate command for each file. You can use wildcard characters to tell DOS you mean a set of files with similar names or extensions. Just as a wild card in a poker game can represent any other card in the deck, a wildcard character can represent any other character in a file name or extension.

There are two wildcard characters, the asterisk (*) and the question mark (?). The following examples use the Directory command to illustrate ways you can use wildcard characters to specify groups of files.

Using the Asterisk Wildcard Character: *

The asterisk makes it easy to carry out commands on sets of files with similar names or extensions; it can represent up to all eight characters in a file name or up to all three characters in an extension. If you use the asterisk to represent the name or extension, you are specifying all file names or all extensions.

The following examples illustrate several ways to use the asterisk to find selected directory entries. You can use the asterisk with other DOS commands as well.

To specify all files named BUDGET, regardless of extension, type the following:

```
B>dir budget.*
```

DOS displays the directory entry of each sample file named BUDGET, regardless of its extension:

```
Volume in drive B has no label
Directory of   B:\

BUDGET    JAN        23   10-16-85    9:16a
BUDGET    FEB        23   10-16-85    9:16a
BUDGET    MAR        23   10-16-85    9:16a
        3 File(s)       356352 bytes free
```

To specify all file names beginning with B, type the following:

```
B>dir b*
```

If you don't specify an extension, the Directory command displays the entry for each file that matches the name, regardless of extension (it's the equivalent of specifying the extension as *). There are four such files:

```
Volume in drive B has no label
Directory of  B:\

BANK      DOC      23  10-16-85   9:16a
BUDGET    JAN      23  10-16-85   9:16a
BUDGET    FEB      23  10-16-85   9:16a
BUDGET    MAR      23  10-16-85   9:16a
          4 File(s)     356352 bytes free
```

To specify all files with the same extension, regardless of name, you replace the name with *. For example, to specify each file with the extension DOC, type:

```
B>dir *.doc
```

DOS displays just those entries:

```
Volume in drive B has no label
Directory of  B:\

REPORT    DOC      23  10-16-85   9:16a
BANK      DOC      23  10-16-85   9:16a
          2 File(s)     356352 bytes free
```

Using the Question Mark Wildcard Character: ?

The question mark replaces only one character in a file name or extension. You'll probably use the asterisk more frequently, using the question mark only when one or two characters in the middle of a name or extension vary.

To see how the question mark works, type the following:

```
B>dir budget.?a?
```

This command specifies all files named BUDGET that have extensions beginning with any character, followed by an A, and ending with any character. DOS displays two entries:

```
Volume in drive B has no label
Directory of  B:\

BUDGET   JAN       23  10-16-85    9:16a
BUDGET   MAR       23  10-16-85    9:16a
         2 File(s)      356352 bytes free
```

A Warning About Wildcard Characters

Be careful using wildcard characters with commands that can change files. Suppose you spent several days entering a year's worth of budget data into 12 files named BUDGET.JAN, BUDGET.FEB, and so on. On the same disk you also have three files you don't need named BUDGET.OLD, BUDGET.TST, and BUDGET.BAD. The disk is getting full, so you decide to delete the three unneeded files. It's 2 a.m., you're tired, and you're in a hurry, so you quickly type *erase budget.** and press Enter.

You may realize immediately what you have done, but the files are gone. Or, it may not dawn on you until you try to use one of the 12 good budget files and DOS replies *File not found.* You display the directory; there isn't a single file named BUDGET.

With commands that can change a file (Erase or Copy), use wildcard characters with extreme caution.

DISPLAYING DIRECTORY ENTRIES

dir <filename> /W /P   As you have seen in many examples, the Directory command (dir) displays entries from the directory that DOS keeps on each disk. Each entry includes the name and extension of the file, its size in bytes, and the date and time it was created or last updated. You can use the Directory command to display all entries, or just the entries of selected files.

In the descriptions of the commands here and throughout the remaining chapters, you are shown the general form of the command—the name of the command and all its parameters—before you try the hands-on examples. If a parameter has an exact form,

such as /W, the form is shown. If a parameter is something you specify, such as a file name, it is named and shown enclosed in angle brackets: for example, <filename>.

The Directory command has three qualifiers, or parameters: filename, /W, and /P. Written out, the command format, including the parameters, looks like this:

dir <filename> /W /P

When using the Directory command, if you:

• Include a <filename>, for example, *dir budget.jan,* DOS searches the disk in the current drive and displays the entry for that file.

• Include both a drive letter and a <filename>, for example, *dir b:budget.jan,* DOS displays the directory entry for the file you specify from the disk in the drive you specify.

• Include a <filename> with wildcard characters, DOS displays the entries for all files whose name and extension match the wildcard characters (for example, you used *dir budget.** earlier to display the entries for BUDGET.JAN, BUDGET.FEB, and BUDGET.MAR).

• Omit a <filename>, but include a drive letter, for example, *dir b:,* DOS displays all the entries from the disk in the drive you specify.

• Omit a <filename>, for example, *dir,* DOS displays all directory entries on the disk in the current drive.

Because a list of directory entries can be quite long, the Directory command includes two options you can use to keep the list from scrolling off the top of the screen:

• /W *(Wide)* tells DOS to display only the file names and extensions in five columns across the screen. This display contains less information, because it omits the file sizes, dates, and times, but it makes a long list of entries more compact.

- /P *(Pause)* tells DOS to display the entries one screenful at a time; a message at the bottom of the screen tells you to strike a key to continue.

Examples of Displaying Directory Entries

Because you have already used the Directory command several times, only the options are shown here. (Remember, if you are using a fixed disk, type *c:* where the example shows *a:*.)

To display the directory of the system disk in the wide format, type the following:

```
B>dir a: /w
```

DOS arranges just the name and extension of each file, in columns across the screen (you can see three of the five columns in the following display):

```
Volume in drive A has no label
Directory of  A:\

ANSI      SYS    ASSIGN   COM ... BASIC    COM
BASICA    COM    CHKDSK   COM ... DISKCOMP COM
DISKCOPY  COM    EDLIN    COM ... FORMAT   COM
GRAFTABL  COM    GRAPHICS COM ... KEYBGR   COM
KEYBIT    COM    KEYBSP   COM ... MODE     COM
MORE      COM    PRINT    COM ... SELECT   COM
SHARE     EXE    SORT     EXE ... TREE     COM
VDISK     SYS
        36 File(s)      61440 bytes free
```

Such a display doesn't contain as much information as the standard directory display, but it packs a lot of entries onto the screen. It's particularly handy when you just want a quick look at the files on a crowded disk.

To display the directory of the system disk one screenful at a time by using the /P option, type:

```
B>dir a: /p
```

DOS displays the first 23 entries, then *Strike a key when ready . . . .* To see the next screenful, press any key. This option lets you view the entire directory without using Ctrl-Num Lock to freeze the display periodically.

type <filename>

DISPLAYING A FILE

Many of the files you use are text files, and there will be times when you want to check the contents of a file but don't need a printed copy. DOS gives you a quick way to see what's in a file: the Type command. (The name Type is a carryover from the days when most computers had only typewriter-like consoles.)

When you use the Type command, DOS displays the file without stopping; if the file is longer than one screenful and you want to read the entire file, freeze the display by pressing Ctrl-Num Lock.

The Type command has one parameter:

type <filename>

<filename> is the name of the file to be displayed. The Type command displays just one file at a time, so you can't use wildcard characters in the file name. If you do use a wildcard character, or if the file you name doesn't exist, DOS displays *Invalid filename or file not found* and returns to command level.

An Example of Displaying a File

To display the file named REPORT.DOC on the diskette in the current drive, type:

```
B>type report.doc
```

DOS displays the file:

```
This is a dummy file.
```

You'll probably use the Type command frequently to check the contents of your text files.

MAKING COPIES OF FILES

copy <file1> <file2>

Just as you sometimes make copies of your paper files, you'll find yourself needing copies of your disk files. You may want to share a file with a colleague who has a computer, you may want to alter the copy slightly to produce a different version, or you may want to store a copy for safekeeping. The Copy command can make a copy of a file on the same disk (with a different file name) or on a different disk (with the same file name, if you wish).

When used to make copies of files, the Copy command has two major parameters, <file1> and <file2>. There are three others (/A, /B, and /V), but they are seldom used, except by programmers. The format of the Copy command is:

copy <file1> <file2>

<file1> is the name of the file to be copied (the source file) and <file2> is the name of the copy to be made (the target file). You can use wildcard characters to copy a set of files.

When copying files, if you:

- Specify a drive other than the current drive as part of <file1>, and you omit <file2>, the file is copied to the disk in the current drive and is given the same name as <file1>. Example: *B>copy a:report.jan.*

- Specify only a drive letter as <file2>, the file is copied to the disk in the drive you specify and is given the same name as <file1>. Example: *B>copy report.feb a:*

- Specify a <file1> that doesn't exist, DOS responds <FILENAME> *File not found* and *0 File(s) copied* and returns to command level.

- Specify a <file1> that is not on the disk in the current drive and omit <file2>, DOS copies <file1> to the disk in the current drive and gives the copy the same name as the original. Example (note, the current drive is B): *B>copy a:report.mar.*

- Specify a <file2> that doesn't exist, DOS creates it.

- Specify a <file2> that does exist, DOS replaces its contents with <file1>. This is the same as erasing the existing target file, so be careful not to give a copy the same name as an existing file you want to keep.

The following practice session illustrates different ways to copy files; it also indicates the type of situation in which you might want to use each form of the command.

Examples of Copying Files

You want to change a document you already have on disk, but you want to keep the original, as well as the changed version. For example, to make a copy of the file REPORT.DOC on the same diskette and to name the copy RESULTS, type:

```
B>copy report.doc results
```

DOS acknowledges *1 File(s) copied.*

To verify that both files, REPORT.DOC and RESULTS are on the diskette, display the directory by typing:

```
B>dir
```

DOS now shows seven files on the diskette:

```
Volume in drive B has no label
Directory of  B:\

REPORT    DOC      23  10-16-85    9:16a
REPORT    BAK      23  10-16-85    9:16a
BANK      DOC      23  10-16-85    9:16a
BUDGET    JAN      23  10-16-85    9:16a
BUDGET    FEB      23  10-16-85    9:16a
BUDGET    MAR      23  10-16-85    9:16a
RESULTS            23  10-16-85    9:16a
        7 File(s)     355328 bytes free
```

Any time you want to verify the results of an example, use the Directory command to see what files are on the diskette.

Suppose you want to copy a file from another diskette and store it, under the same file name, on the diskette in the current drive.

For example, your current drive is drive B. To copy a file from drive A to the diskette in drive B, all you need to specify is the drive letter and name of the source file, because DOS assumes you want to copy the source file to the disk in the current drive and give the target file the same name. Drive A (C if you have a fixed disk) contains the DOS system disk. On it are a number of external DOS commands, including FORMAT.COM, the file for the Format command. Copy FORMAT.COM to the disk in the current drive, by typing the following:

```
B>copy a:format.com
```

DOS copies FORMAT.COM to the diskette in drive B and gives it the same name.

Or suppose you want to update or modify a file; store the new version under the same file name and on the same diskette as the original; and be able to distinguish between the two versions. Make a copy of a file on the same diskette, with the same file name but a different extension. You can use the asterisk wildcard character to tell DOS to use the same file name. For example, type the following:

```
B>copy budget.mar *.apr
```

DOS copies the file and names the copy BUDGET.APR.

You have several files stored on disk. Suppose you want to keep the originals, but use copies of them all for a new project; and, to avoid confusion, you want to give the copies a new file name. For example, make a copy of each file named REPORT, giving each copy the name FORECAST; type:

```
B>copy report.* forecast.*
```

DOS displays the name of each source file as it makes the copies:

```
REPORT.DOC
REPORT.BAK
        2 File(s) copied
```

You can copy all the files on a diskette by specifying the source file as *.* and specifying the target as just a drive letter. This procedure is not the same as copying the diskette with the Diskcopy command; the difference is explained under the heading "Copying a Complete Diskette" in Chapter 6, "Managing Your Diskettes."

**copy <filename>
<device>**

SENDING FILES TO DEVICES

In Chapter 4, you printed a file by using the Copy command to send a copy of the file to the printer. You can also send a copy of a file to any other output device. If, for example, you copy a file to a communications connection, or *port,* on the computer, the file goes to whatever is attached to the port, such as a telecommunications line to another computer.

When it is used to send a copy of a file to a device, the Copy command has two parameters:

copy <filename> <device>

<filename> is the name of the file to be sent; <device> is the name of the device to which the file is to be sent.

Be sure <device> exists; if you try to send a file to a device that doesn't exist or isn't ready, DOS may stop running and you must then restart the system.

An Example of Sending Files to a Device

To send a copy of each sample file with the extension DOC to the printer, type:

```
B>copy *.doc prn
```

DOS displays the name of each file as it sends the file to the printer:

```
REPORT.DOC
BANK.DOC
FORECAST.DOC
        1 File(s) copied
```

The files are printed with no separation between them. DOS reports only one file copied because, in effect, only one output file was created: the printed copy of the files.

COMBINING FILES

copy <source>
<target>

Sometimes, it's useful to combine several files. Perhaps you have several short documents, and you decide it would be easier and more convenient to work with one document that includes all the shorter ones. If you have several sets of files with similar names or extensions, you can combine each set into a new file, creating several new files. The Copy command lets you copy several files into a new file without destroying the original versions.

When it is used to combine files, the Copy command has two parameters:

    copy <source> <target>

<source> represents the files to be combined. You can use wildcard characters to name the source files to be combined, or you can specify a list of several file names separated by a plus sign (+). If any file in a list separated by plus signs doesn't exist, DOS goes on to the next name without telling you the file doesn't exist.

<target> represents the file that results from combining the source files. If you specify a target, DOS combines the source files into the target file. If you omit the target, DOS combines the source files into the first source file you specify.

Examples of Combining Files

You have two files and you want to use them together as the basis for a single new file, while keeping the originals intact. For example, to combine BANK.DOC and REPORT.DOC into a new file named BANKRPT.DOC, type:

```
B>copy bank.doc+report.doc bankrpt.doc
```

DOS displays the names of the source files as it copies them:

```
BANK.DOC
REPORT.DOC
        1 File(s) copied
```

Again, DOS reports one file copied because the command created only one file.

You can also copy several files into one existing file. For example, to combine the three source files BUDGET.JAN, BUDGET.FEB, and BUDGET.MAR into the first source file, BUDGET.JAN, type:

```
B>copy budget.jan+budget.feb+budget.mar
```

DOS displays the name of each source file as it copies:

```
BUDGET.JAN
BUDGET.FEB
BUDGET.MAR
        1 File(s) copied
```

Now, suppose you've been keeping monthly budget files. It's the end of the year. You still need separate monthly files for comparison with next year's figures, but right now, you want to work with all the files together. To combine all files named BUDGET into a file named ANNUAL.BGT, type:

```
B>copy budget.* annual.bgt
```

DOS responds:

```
BUDGET.JAN
BUDGET.FEB
BUDGET.MAR
BUDGET.APR
        1 File(s) copied
```

Or, suppose you want to combine pairs of files with the same file names, but different extensions. You can combine them under the same file names, with new extensions, and end up with both the original and combined versions.

If you have entered all the examples in this chapter, among the files on the diskette in drive B are REPORT.DOC and REPORT.BAK, FORECAST.DOC, and FORECAST.BAK. To combine each pair of files with the same name and the extensions DOC and BAK into a single file with the same name and the extension MIX, type:

```
B>copy *.bak+*.doc *.mix
```

DOS displays the files as it copies them:

```
REPORT.BAK
REPORT.DOC
FORECAST.BAK
FORECAST.DOC
        2 File(s) copied
```

This time DOS reports two files copied because the command created two files: REPORT.MIX and FORECAST.MIX.

ERASING FILES

erase <filename>

Just as you have to clean out a file drawer once in a while, you'll occasionally have to clear your disks of files you no longer need. The Erase command (you can type it either as *erase* or as *del*) erases one or more files from a disk.

The Erase command has one parameter:

erase <filename>

<filename> is the name of the file to be erased. If you use wildcard characters, DOS erases all files that match <filename>. If the file doesn't exist, DOS displays *File not found* and returns to command level.

Warning: Whenever you type an Erase command that uses wildcard characters, double-check the command on the screen before you press the Enter key, because you don't get a second chance. Make sure you have specified the correct drive letter (if necessary), file name, and extension; be certain that you know exactly which files will be erased and that you want all of them to be erased.

There is one exception to this warning: If you tell DOS to erase all the files on a disk by typing *erase *.**, DOS prompts *Are you sure (Y/N)?* before erasing the files. If you respond with anything other than *y*, DOS then cancels the Erase command and returns to command level.

Examples of Erasing Files

To erase the file named BUDGET.APR on the diskette in the current drive, type:

```
B>erase budget.apr
```

As soon as you press the Enter key, the file's gone.

To erase all files with an extension of BAK on the diskette in the current drive, type:

```
B>erase *.bak
```

DOS erases REPORT.BAK and FORECAST.BAK and displays the system prompt. Remember, you don't get a second chance, so make sure you have typed the correct file name, and the correct drive letter and extension (if they are necessary) whenever you use wildcard characters with the Erase command.

CHANGING FILE NAMES

rename <oldname> <newname>

There are times when you'll want to change the name of a file. You may simply change your mind, or perhaps you have changed the contents of a file so much that you want to give it a new name that more closely describes its new contents. The Rename command (you can type it as *ren* if you like) changes a file's name, extension, or both. You can use wildcard characters to rename a set of files.

The Rename command has two parameters:

rename <oldname> <newname>

<oldname> is the name of an existing file. If the file doesn't exist, DOS displays *Duplicate file name or File not found* and returns to command level.

<newname> is the new name you want to give to the file specified by <oldname>. If there is already a file with the new name, DOS displays *Duplicate file name or File not found* and returns to command level. Two files on the same disk can't have the same name, and DOS would have to erase the existing file to carry out the command, so this safeguard keeps you from inadvertently erasing one file in the process of renaming another.

The Rename command simply changes the name of a file; it doesn't copy a file to a different disk. Both the old name and new name must refer to the same drive. If they specify different drives, DOS ignores the drive letter specified in the new name.

Examples of Changing File Names

To change the name of the file ANNUAL.BGT to FINAL on the disk in the current drive, type:

```
B>rename annual.bgt final
```

DOS changes the name and displays the system prompt.

To change the extension of the file named BUDGET.MAR from MAR to 003, on the disk in the current drive, you can use the * for the new file name. Type the following:

```
B>rename budget.mar *.003
```

The file is now named BUDGET.003.

To change the extension DOC to TXT for all files on the disk in the current drive, use the * for both the old and new file names. Type the following:

```
B>rename *.doc *.txt
```

Verify this change with the Directory command by typing:

```
B>dir *.txt
```

DOS shows four files, all of which used to have the extension DOC:

```
Volume in drive B has no label
Directory of  B:\

REPORT   TXT      23  10-16-85   9:16a
BANK     TXT      23  10-16-85   9:16a
FORECAST TXT      23  10-16-85   9:16a
BANKRPT  TXT      47  10-16-85  10:51a
         4 File(s)     340992 bytes free
```

If you use the Directory command now to display the entries of all files with the extension DOC, DOS responds *File not found*.

CONTROLLING WHETHER
A FILE CAN BE CHANGED

attrib +R −R
<filename>

Your disks will contain many files. Some, such as program files (including DOS, application programs, and programs you write yourself), you will seldom, if ever, erase. Although you probably have backup copies, some of these files may exist only on your working disks; erasing them could represent a serious loss.

Similarly, you will probably have other files, such as spreadsheets for periodic calculations or reports, and word-processing style sheets or form letters, that you seldom change. Because these files can represent a significant investment of time and information, inadvertently changing them could also be a serious loss.

The Attribute (attrib) command lets you protect yourself from inadvertently erasing or changing a file by making it *read-only*, which means that you (or anyone else using the file) can read it but cannot erase or change it. Before a read-only file can be changed or erased, the protection must be removed with the Attribute command.

Because it takes only one command to affect the read-only status of a file, it takes little time to temporarily protect files that may change later—the most recent version of a text file or spreadsheet, for example. This protection can be particularly useful if someone else is going to use the same disk or computer you do.

You can also use the Attribute command to display the read-only status of a file or set of files.

The Attribute command has three parameters:

attrib +R −R <filename>

+R tells DOS to deny all attempts to change or erase <filename> (make it read-only).

−R tells DOS to let <filename> be changed or erased.

<filename> is the name of the file whose read-only status is to be displayed or changed. If you enter the command with just <filename>, DOS displays the name of the file and, if the file is read-only, an R in the first column. You can check or change the read-only status of a series a files by using wildcard characters.

The display of the Directory command doesn't show whether a file is read-only; you must use the Attribute command.

Example of Controlling Whether a File Can Be Changed

Attribute is an external DOS command. DOS must read the program file, ATTRIB.EXE, into memory from the system disk. Because your system disk is not in the current drive, type the following to tell DOS to look in drive A for the Attribute command file, as well as to check the current drive (B) for the status of all files whose extension is TXT (remember to type *c:* instead of *a:* if DOS is on your fixed disk):

```
B>a:attrib *.txt
```

DOS responds:

```
                    B:\REPORT.TXT
                    B:\BANK.TXT
                    B:\FORECAST.TXT
                    B:\BANKRPT.TXT
```

Now make BANK.TXT read-only by typing:

```
B>a:attrib +r bank.txt
```

DOS responds by displaying the system prompt. Now, when you check the status again, DOS shows that BANK.TXT is read-only. Type the following:

```
B>a:attrib *.txt

                    B:\REPORT.TXT
         R          B:\BANK.TXT
                    B:\FORECAST.TXT
                    B:\BANKRPT.TXT
```

If you try to erase BANK.TXT, DOS displays an error message:

```
B>erase bank.txt
Access denied
```

The result would be the same if you edited the file with a word processor; when you tried to store the revised version, DOS would issue the error message. You could, however, save the revised version with a different name.

Remove the read-only protection and verify that it is gone by typing the following:

```
B>a:attrib -r bank.txt

B>a:attrib bank.txt
        B:\BANK.TXT
```

COMPARING FILES

comp <file1><file2>   *Note: The command for comparing files is in IBM's version of MS-DOS. If you are not using an IBM personal computer, go on to the heading "Printing Files."*

Sometimes you'll want to know whether two files are the same. Suppose you have two files named BUDGET on different disks. Are they different budgets, or two copies of the same one? You could display or print both files and compare them, but that could take quite a while and you still might miss some small difference. It's quicker and more accurate to use the Compare (comp) command.

The Compare command has two parameters:

comp <file1> <file2>

<file1> and <file2> are the file names of the files to be compared. If you omit <file2>, DOS prompts you for it. If you omit both <file1> and <file2>, DOS prompts you for both.

If the files are different lengths, DOS displays *Files are different sizes* and asks you if you want to compare any more files. If the files are the same length, the Compare command compares them byte-by-byte. If the files are identical, DOS displays *Files compare OK.*

If the files are the same length but DOS finds a difference, DOS displays a message that shows the characters that differ, and how far they are from the start of the file. If DOS finds ten mismatches, it displays *10 Mismatches - ending compare,* and asks if you want to compare any more files.

Compare is an external DOS command. Before DOS can carry out the command, it must be able to find the command file on disk.

When you use the Compare command, and the system diskette isn't in the current drive, you must either copy the command file to the diskette in your current drive or, as with the Attribute command example, precede the command name with the letter of the drive containing your DOS system disk.

Examples of Comparing Files

To compare REPORT.TXT with BUDGET.FEB, type:

```
B>a:comp report.txt budget.feb
```

The files are identical, so DOS replies as follows (do not be concerned by *Eof mark not found*—DOS is simply telling you it did not include your ^Z end-of-file indicator as a character in the file):

```
B:REPORT.TXT and B:BUDGET.FEB

Eof mark not found

Files compare ok

Compare more files (Y/N)? _
```

Type *y.* DOS prompts you for the names of the files. To compare the sample file REPORT.TXT on the disk in drive B with the DOS file SYS.COM on drive A, type the file names as follows:

```
Enter primary file name
report.txt

Enter 2nd file name or drive id
a:sys.com
```

DOS determines that the files are different lengths, and it doesn't even begin to compare them:

```
B:REPORT.TXT and A:SYS.COM

Files are different sizes

Compare more files (Y/N)? _
```

Type *n* and DOS returns to command level.

You can use wildcard characters to compare two sets of files with one command. To compare all files with the extension TXT and all files with the same file name but the extension MIX, type:

```
B>a:comp *.txt *.mix
```

There are four files with the extension TXT, but only two with the extension MIX. DOS tells you which files don't exist and which ones it tried to compare:

```
B:REPORT.TXT and B:REPORT.MIX

Files are different sizes


B:BANK.TXT and B:BANK.MIX

B:BANK.MIX - File not found


B:FORECAST.TXT and B:FORECAST.MIX

Files are different sizes


B:BANKRPT.TXT and B:BANKRPT.MIX

B:BANKRPT.MIX - File not found

Compare more files (Y/N)? _
```

Type *n* to return DOS to command level.

Because all the sample files are identical, you'll have to create one that is different, but still the same length (23 bytes), to see how DOS notifies you about differences. To create a different file, named DIFF, type the following:

```
B>copy con diff
This is not the same.
^Z
          1 File(s) copied
```

Now compare REPORT.TXT with DIFF by typing:

```
B>a:comp report.txt diff
```

DOS quickly finds and reports ten errors:

```
B:REPORT.TXT and B:DIFF

Compare error at OFFSET 8
File 1 = 61

File 2 = 6E

Compare error at OFFSET 9
File 1 = 20

File 2 = 6F

Compare error at OFFSET A
File 1 = 64

File 2 = 74

Compare error at OFFSET B
File 1 = 75

File 2 = 20

Compare error at OFFSET C
File 1 = 6D

File 2 = 74

Compare error at OFFSET D
File 1 = 6D

File 2 = 68

Compare error at OFFSET E
File 1 = 79

File 2 = 65

Compare error at OFFSET 10
File 1 = 66

File 2 = 73

Compare error at OFFSET 11
File 1 = 69

File 2 = 61

Compare error at OFFSET 12
File 1 = 6C

File 2 = 6D
```

```
10 Mismatches - ending compare

Compare more files (Y/N)? _
```

Type *n* to return DOS to command level.

The message that shows the differing characters and their locations uses numbers that are combinations of the digits 0 through 9 and the letters A through F. These characters are from the base-16 number system usually called hexadecimal, in which A through F are used to represent the decimal numbers 10 through 15. If you must know what the differing characters are or must calculate their exact locations, you'll need a chart of the American Standard Code for Information Interchange (ASCII), which shows how characters are encoded, and you'll need a guide to hexadecimal arithmetic. The manuals that came with your computer probably contain both.

PRINTING FILES

print <filename>
/P /C /T

You can print files at the same time you're using the computer to do other things. DOS keeps a list of files to be printed —called the *print queue*—and prints the files in the order in which they appear in the queue. The print queue normally can hold up to ten files.

In addition to printing files, the Print command lets you change two characteristics of its operation: the size of the print queue and the printer that DOS uses. For a description of these uses of the Print command, see "Changing Operation of the Print Command" following this section.

Because the computer can really do only one thing at a time, DOS prints when nothing else is happening, such as when you pause to think between keystrokes. You'll notice that printing slows, and sometimes even stops, when other things are going on—especially when DOS is using a disk drive.

You use the Print command to add a file to the print queue; delete a file from the queue; cancel all printing; and display the file names in the queue. When used to print a file, the Print command has four parameters:

    print <filename> /P /C /T

<filename> is the name of the file to be added to or deleted from the print queue. You can enter more than one file name with a Print command; just type the list of file names, separating each with a blank.

/P *(Print)* tells DOS to add <filename> to the print queue. DOS assumes this parameter if all you specify is <filename>.

/C *(Cancel)* tells DOS to remove <filename> from the print queue. If the file is being printed, printing stops and the paper is advanced to the top of the next page.

/T *(Terminate)* stops all printing. If a file is being printed, printing stops and the paper is advanced to the top of the next page. All files are removed from the print queue.

If you enter the Print command with no parameters, DOS displays the list of files in the print queue.

Examples of Printing a File

DOS advances the paper to the next page each time it prints a new file, so the examples here use several sheets of printer paper. Familiarize yourself with the examples before you try them, so that you know ahead of time when to be prepared to terminate the printing process. You'll save both time and paper.

First, a bit of preparation is required for the examples.

You'll be using some DOS command files that aren't on the current disk, so tell DOS to look on your system disk for commands; type:

```
B> path a:\
```

The Path command is described in Chapter 9, "A Tree of Files."

Most of the sample files you created in this chapter consist of a single line and would print too quickly for you to try using all the Print parameters in the following examples. Increase the size of the file REPORT.TXT using Edlin, the DOS text editor (it's described in Chapters 11 and 12). Type the following lines:

```
B> edlin report.txt
End of input file
*1,1,2,99c
*e
```

The Edlin command copies the first (and only) line 99 times, so REPORT.TXT now consists of 100 identical lines.

Command files don't contain printable characters, so erase FORMAT.COM from the diskette in drive B by typing:

```
B>erase format.com
```

Finally, make sure the printer is turned on and that the paper is adjusted to the top of a page. This completes the preparation for the Print command examples.

To print the file REPORT.TXT, type:

```
B>print report.txt
```

The first time you enter the Print command after starting the system, DOS prompts you for the name of the printer to use:

```
Name of list device [PRN]: _
```

The brackets around PRN mean that DOS will use the device named PRN if you press the Enter key. Unless you have more than one printer attached to your system, or you are using a printer with a serial interface, just press the Enter key. If you have never printed with your printer, press the Enter key. If nothing is printed, read the documentation that came with your printer.

When you respond to the prompt, DOS loads the Print command file, PRINT.COM, from the system disk and keeps it in memory until you either turn the system off or restart DOS. PRINT.COM increases the amount of memory that DOS uses by about 3200 bytes. DOS reports that the program is loaded:

```
Resident part of PRINT installed
```

And it displays the names and print status of the files in the print queue:

```
B:\REPORT.TXT is currently being printed
```

There is one file in the print queue (REPORT.TXT), and it's now being printed.

When you printed a file in Chapter 4 by copying it to the printer, DOS didn't display the system prompt—and you couldn't use the system—until the file was printed. This time, the system prompt returned as soon as printing started. As soon as DOS starts printing a file with the Print command, DOS is ready to accept another command.

If you decide you don't want to print a file after all, you can remove it from the print queue with the /C parameter; type the following while REPORT.TXT is being printed:

```
B>print report.txt /c
```

DOS stops printing the file and prints the following message on the page:

```
File B:\REPORT.TXT Canceled by operator
```

It then advances the paper to the next page and sounds the printer's alarm.

You can put more than one file in the print queue with a single Print command. To tell DOS to print both REPORT.TXT and BUDGET.JAN, type:

```
B>print report.txt budget.jan
```

DOS starts printing REPORT.TXT and displays the print queue:

```
        B:\REPORT.TXT is currently being printed
        B:\BUDGET.JAN is in queue
```

If you want to stop printing entirely, you can remove all files from the print queue with the /T parameter. Type the following, again while REPORT.TXT is being printed:

```
B>print /t
```

DOS stops printing the current file, prints *All files canceled by operator* at the point it stopped printing, advances the paper to the

next page, removes all remaining files from the queue, and sounds the alarm. It displays a terse acknowledgment:

```
PRINT queue is empty
```

You can also put several files in the print queue at once by using wildcard characters. To print all the files whose extension is TXT, type:

```
B>print *.txt
```

Now there are four files in the queue:

```
B:\BANK.TXT is currently being printed
B:\REPORT.TXT is in queue
B:\FORECAST.TXT is in queue
B:\BANKRPT.TXT is in queue
```

DOS prints the files in the order shown. Stop all printing again by typing:

```
B>print /t
```

Again, DOS stops printing the current file, prints the cancellation message, advances the paper to the next page, sounds the alarm, removes all remaining files from the queue, and acknowledges on the screen:

```
PRINT queue is empty
```

The following example uses several sheets of paper. If you are not using continuous form paper or an automatic sheet feeder, you shouldn't try this example, because it will print on the platen of your printer.

The print queue normally holds up to ten files. To fill it, tell DOS to print all the files on the diskette in drive B; there are 13 files, so DOS puts the first 10 in the queue. Type the following:

```
B>print *.*
```

DOS tells you the queue is full and displays the list of files in the queue:

```
PRINT queue is full

        B:\REPORT.BAK is currently being printed
        B:\DIFF is in queue
        B:\BANK.TXT is in queue
        B:\BUDGET.JAN is in queue
        B:\BUDGET.FEB is in queue
        B:\BUDGET.003 is in queue
        B:\RESULTS is in queue
        B:\REPORT.TXT is in queue
        B:\FORECAST.TXT is in queue
        B:\BANKRPT.TXT is in queue
```

There's really no point to actually printing all these sample files. Terminate all printing by typing:

```
B>print /t
```

DOS empties the queue and alerts you as before:

```
PRINT queue is empty
```

Changing Operation of the Print Command

**print /D:<printer>
/Q:<size>**

DOS initially limits the print queue to 10 files, but you can increase the size of the queue and can also tell DOS to use a printer other than the standard printer, PRN (more details on printers are in Chapter 7, "Managing Your Devices").

You can only change Print command operations once during a session at your computer; if you try to use these options again before restarting DOS or turning the computer off, DOS displays the message *Invalid parameter* and ignores the command.

When used to change the size of the print queue or the name of the printer, the Print command has two parameters:

print /D:<printer> /Q:<size>

/D:<printer> tells DOS to use the printer named <printer>. If you omit /D:<device>, DOS uses the standard printer named PRN.

/Q:<size> tells DOS the number of files the print queue can hold; the maximum number is 32. If you omit /Q:<size>, the print queue holds 10 files.

If you wanted to increase the size of the print queue to 15 files, you would type *print /q:15*. If you wanted to tell DOS to use the printer named COM1, you would type *print /d:com1*. You can combine the /D and /Q parameters in the same Print command, but you cannot combine them with other parameters unless you are entering the Print command for the first time since starting DOS.

The Print command lets you print text files without losing the use of your system during printing; it can make both you and your system more productive.

CHAPTER

MANAGING
YOUR DISKETTES

D iskettes are the computer's filing cabinets. Managing your computer filing system includes not only keeping track of your files, as described in the previous chapter, but also taking care of your diskettes. There are many ways to prepare and store information on diskettes; the concepts underlying diskette handling, however, apply to all microcomputers.

To avoid generalities, the material in this chapter focuses on the version of MS-DOS that runs on the IBM personal computers. If your computer is not totally compatible with the IBM personal computers, the practice examples may not work exactly as described. If you find that any of the examples do not run on your computer, refer to your DOS manual for the specific instructions or parameters you must use.

Several DOS commands deal with entire diskettes, not individual files. For example, you must prepare a new diskette for use; this process is called formatting (or, less commonly, initializing). Or, if you want a copy of a diskette, you needn't copy each file separately; instead, you can copy the entire diskette with one command.

This chapter suggests ways to handle your diskettes, briefly describes how DOS stores files on diskettes, and shows you how to do the following:

- Prepare a diskette with the Format command.

- Create another system diskette with the Format command.

- Duplicate a diskette with the Diskcopy command.

- Compare the contents of two diskettes with the Diskcomp command.

- Analyze and report on the use of diskette storage space with the Check Disk command.

- Assign, change, or delete the volume label of a disk with the Label command.

- Display the volume label of a disk with the Volume command.

The Label and Volume commands can be used with either diskettes or a fixed disk.

Two additional commands, Backup and Restore, can also be used with diskettes or a fixed disk to make backup copies of files and to restore them if need be. Because Backup and Restore are typically used to deal with the large number of files on a fixed disk, these commands are described in Chapter 10, "Managing Your Fixed Disk."

HANDLING DISKETTES

Diskettes are remarkably durable. Their useful life depends on how often you use them, of course, but even more important is the way you treat them. Handle your diskettes with the same care you use when handling valuable recording tapes or photographs:

- Avoid touching the diskette surfaces that show through the openings in the protective jacket. Dirt, fingerprints, or dust can shorten the life of a diskette and can damage or destroy the data.

- Keep diskettes away from magnets and other sources of magnetic influence, such as telephones, electric motors, and television sets.

- Keep food and drinks away from diskettes. The same goes for cigarettes, cigars, pipes, and ashtrays.

- Don't fold, spindle, or mutilate diskettes. Don't pile other objects on them.

- Don't write on diskette labels with a pencil, ballpoint pen, or other sharp instrument; use a felt-tipped marker.

- Store your diskettes in a safe place when you're not using them. Protect them from extreme heat or cold, humidity, or contact with other objects.

Many products are available for storing diskettes, including plastic cases, vinyl pockets that fit a three-ring binder, and hanging file folders. All offer good protection; they aren't necessary, but they make it easier for you to store your diskettes safely, rather than leaving them scattered around your desk.

Although an office is a mild environment compared to a factory or a shop floor, data on a diskette can be damaged by such innocuous objects as a paper clip that has been stored in a magnetic paper-clip holder, a magnetized letter opener, an electric pencil sharpener, or a telephone answering machine. If you put a letter down on top of a diskette lying on your desk, it's all too easy to put a hot coffee cup or heavy object on the letter without realizing that the diskette is underneath.

The safest places for a diskette are in the computer and in protective storage. Information and time are two of your most valuable assets: A damaged diskette can cost you both, so protect your diskettes accordingly.

BACK UP YOUR DISKETTES

Even though you treat your diskettes with care, they can still be mislaid or damaged by accident, and files can be inadvertently changed or erased. Making backup copies of your diskettes limits the amount of information and time you lose if something goes wrong. The time it takes to make these copies could be one of your better investments.

Unless a program diskette is copy protected so that you cannot duplicate the original, make a copy of the program before you ever use it. Store the original diskette in a safe place, and use the copy. If something happens to the copy, make another copy from the original. Always keep the original stored safely.

Your collection of data files will grow as you use application programs, such as a word processor or spreadsheet. Back up a data diskette whenever the value of the information it contains—or the time it would take to re-create it—is greater than the value of a blank diskette and the few minutes it takes to make a copy.

As you found in Chapter 2, when you copied the DOS diskettes, it's easy to make a backup copy of a diskette. Keep your backup copies in a safe place and use your computer with the comforting thought that, should something unforeseen happen, you're protected.

HOW INFORMATION IS STORED ON A DISKETTE

Information is stored on a diskette much like music or video is recorded on tape. A description of how DOS uses a diskette helps you understand the commands you use to manage your diskettes.

What Is a Diskette?

What we call a diskette actually consists of two parts: a disk of thin plastic coated with magnetic material, usually brown; and a protective plastic jacket, usually black. Figure 6-1 shows a diskette and its main features.

The dashed line in Figure 6-1 shows how the coated disk lies inside the protective jacket. The magnetic coating (shaded in the figure) is visible through the openings in the jacket. The hole in the center of the disk goes around the drive motor, which spins the disk so that data can be recorded (written) or played back (read).

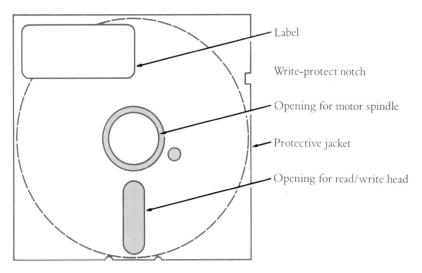

Label

Write-protect notch

Opening for motor spindle

Protective jacket

Opening for read/write head

Figure 6-1. A diskette

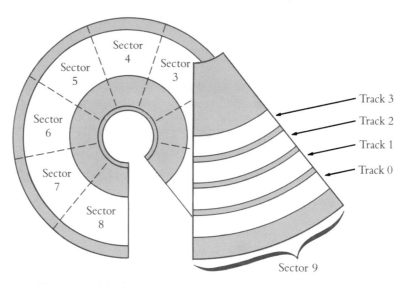

Figure 6-2. Tracks and sectors on a diskette

If you cover the write-protect notch with a piece of tape or one of the self-stick tabs usually included in a package of diskettes, nothing on the diskette can be changed. Cover the write-protect notch of each of the DOS system diskettes and each of your application program diskettes, unless the application program manual tells you otherwise.

How Does DOS Keep Track of Files?

Information is recorded on a diskette in narrow concentric circles called tracks; there are 40 such tracks on a standard diskette and 80 tracks on the high-capacity diskette used on the IBM Personal Computer AT. A track is divided into smaller areas called sectors, each of which can hold 512 bytes of information (½ K). Figure 6-2 shows how tracks and sectors are laid out on a diskette. For simplicity's sake the illustration shows only four of the tracks.

The side, track, and sector numbers of the beginning of a file are stored as part of the directory entry for the file. You don't see this information when you use the Directory command, but DOS can find any sector on a diskette by its side, track, and sector numbers, just as you can find any seat in a theater by its row and seat numbers.

Diskette Capacity

Tracks on a standard diskette are numbered 0 through 39 (making 40 in all); sectors are numbered 1 through 9, for a total of 360 sectors (40 tracks times 9 sectors per track) on each side. Most IBM personal computers have double-sided drives, which use both sides of a diskette, but earlier models had single-sided drives, which used only one side. A double-sided diskette can store 360K (368,640 bytes); a single-sided diskette can store 180K (184,320 bytes).

The high-capacity diskettes used on the IBM Personal Computer AT have 80 tracks (numbered 0 through 79), each of which has 15 sectors. A sector still stores 512 bytes, so a high-capacity diskette can store 1.2 megabytes (1,228,800 bytes).

Volume Label

Any diskette or fixed disk can be assigned a name, or *volume label*, to identify its contents. The volume label can be up to 11 characters long, and can use the same characters allowed in a file name plus a space. DOS stores the volume label on the disk, and displays it when you use the Directory, Check Disk, Label, or Volume command. The volume label is for identification only; you can't use it in a command to specify a disk.

PREPARING FOR THE EXAMPLES

The examples in this chapter require one diskette that doesn't contain any files you want to keep (the examples erase any data on the diskette). Put the diskette in drive B or, if you're using a fixed disk or a one-drive system, put the diskette in your diskette drive.

PREPARING A DISKETTE FOR USE

As mentioned earlier, the Format command prepares a diskette for use. The diskette can either be new or previously formatted. However, formatting erases any existing files, so be sure not to format a diskette that contains files you need.

In carrying out the Format command, DOS also checks for flaws on the recording surface of the diskette, and marks any bad sectors so they won't be used. After formatting, DOS displays a message that tells you the maximum number of bytes the diskette could hold, how many bytes (if any) are defective, and how many bytes are available for storing files.

DOS knows whether drives are single sided or double sided and formats the diskette accordingly. If you have double-sided drives but want to copy some files to a diskette for a colleague who has single-sided drives, you can tell DOS to format only one side of a diskette.

If you are using high-capacity drives, you can tell DOS to read and write 360K double-sided diskettes, but the diskettes you write can only be used in another high-capacity drive; the tracks are too narrow to be read reliably by a standard double-sided drive.

DOS automatically formats a diskette for nine sectors per track, but you can tell it to format a diskette with eight sectors per track so the diskette can be used with any version of DOS.

The Format command reserves space on the diskette for the directory, thus reducing the amount of storage available for files. Because the directories of single-sided and double-sided diskettes are different sizes, and because early versions of DOS created only eight (rather than nine) sectors per track, the storage capacity of your diskettes depends on both the type of diskette drive and the version of DOS you use. Figure 6-3 shows the number of bytes available for all combinations of drives and number of sectors per

Sectors Per Track Drive Type	Eight	Nine	Fifteen
Single-sided	160,256 format /1 /8	179,712 format /1	
Double-sided	322,560 format /8	362,496 format	
High-capacity		362,496 format /4	1,213,952 format

Figure 6-3. Storage capacity of different diskettes

track, and it shows the corresponding Format command options (described in the following sections) that can be used with each type of diskette.

Format Parameters

format <drive>
/V /1 /4 /8

When used to prepare a non-system diskette, the Format command has five parameters:

format <drive> /V /1 /4 /8

<drive> is the letter, followed by a colon, of the drive that contains the diskette to be formatted (such as B:). If you omit <drive>, DOS formats the diskette in the current drive.

/V tells DOS you want to give the diskette a volume label.

/1 formats only one side of a diskette in a double-sided drive.

/4 formats only nine sectors per track on a double-sided diskette in a high-capacity drive.

/8 formats the diskette with eight sectors per track.

Warning: If you don't specify <drive>, and the current drive contains your system diskette, DOS tries to format the system diskette; if you haven't covered the write-protect notch, this erases everything on your system diskette. Even more serious, if the current drive is a fixed disk, DOS formats the fixed disk and erases everything on it. Although newer versions of DOS may ask you if you're sure you want to format a fixed disk, the consequences of inadvertent formatting are severe enough that you should be certain you know which disk is going to be formatted before you press the Enter key after typing a Format command.

Examples of Preparing a Diskette

If you're using a fixed disk, your system prompt is C>, not A>, as shown in the examples. This difference has no effect on what you type or how DOS responds, so go ahead and follow the examples as printed; just remember the difference in the system prompt.

Format the diskette in drive B and give it a volume label by typing the following:

```
A>format b: /v
```

DOS asks you to put the diskette in drive B:

```
Insert new diskette for drive B:
and strike ENTER when ready_
```

Make sure the diskette you plan to use for the examples is in the drive, then press a key. DOS responds *Formatting...Format complete*, then prompts you for the volume label:

```
Volume label (11 characters, ENTER for none)? _
```

Name this diskette DOSDISK by typing the following:

```
dosdisk
```

DOS displays the report of available storage on the diskette and asks if you want to format another. Reply *n*.

Display the directory of the disk: It's empty, but you see the volume label on the first line.

```
A>dir b:

 Volume in drive B is DOSDISK
 Directory of  B:\

File not found
```

You have already formatted several diskettes, so the remaining examples merely describe how to use some of the options of the Format command. You needn't do these examples.

If you have double-sided diskette drives and want to format just one side of a diskette in drive B, you would type *format b: /1*. A diskette formatted in this way can be used on a system with either single-sided or double-sided drives.

If DOS discovers bad sectors while formatting a diskette, it displays the number of bytes not available; the bytes available are reduced by the number of bytes in bad sectors. For example, if DOS

were to find eight bad sectors on a nine-sectored, double-sided diskette, the report would be:

```
362496 bytes total disk space
  4096 bytes in bad sectors
358400 bytes available on disk
```

If you wanted to format a diskette in drive B for eight sectors, instead of nine, you would type *format b: /8*. This diskette could be used in a system running any version of DOS.

If you were using a high-capacity drive and wanted to format a diskette in drive A for nine sectors, you would type *format a: /4*. This diskette could be used in a high-capacity drive, but not reliably in a double-sided drive.

MAKING ANOTHER SYSTEM DISK

format <drive> /S

You used the Diskcopy command to make backup copies of the DOS diskettes. The copies contained exactly the same files as the original. Sometimes, however, to leave room for a large application program, you might need a system diskette that doesn't include all the DOS command files.

You could copy your system diskette and erase the files you don't need, but there's a simpler way: The /S option of the Format command formats a diskette and copies the files that must be on a system diskette. These are COMMAND.COM, plus several hidden files which are necessary for DOS to operate and which must be stored in specific locations on the diskette. A system diskette created in this way contains none of the command files for the DOS external commands, such as Format, but you can use this diskette to start DOS and to use any of the internal commands, such as the Directory command.

Examples of Creating a System Diskette

To create a system diskette in drive B, type:

```
A>format b: /s
```

When DOS prompts you to, insert a diskette and press Enter. DOS formats the diskette, and when it displays the report of diskette storage, it shows the space taken by the system:

```
362496 bytes total disk space
 62464 bytes used by system
300032 bytes available on disk
```

You don't want to create another system diskette now, so type *n* when DOS asks if you want to format another. The directory of the system diskette you just created shows one file (COMMAND.COM), but the diskette also contains the two hidden system files DOS needs.

You can combine the /S option with any of the other Format command parameters described earlier.

COPYING A COMPLETE DISKETTE

diskcopy <**source**> <**target**> **/1**

The Diskcopy command makes an exact duplicate of any diskette, including the hidden and system files on a system diskette. If the target diskette isn't formatted, IBM's version of DOS formats it before copying; Diskcopy in other versions of DOS may require formatted diskettes. Diskcopy works only with diskettes; you cannot use it to copy to or from a fixed disk.

The Diskcopy command has three parameters:

diskcopy <source> <target> /1

<source> is the letter, followed by a colon, of the drive that contains the diskette to be copied (such as A:).

<target> is the letter, followed by a colon, of the drive that contains the diskette that is to receive the copy (such as B:).

If you omit <target>, DOS copies from the diskette in <source> to the diskette in the current drive; if you omit <target> and specify the current drive as <source>, DOS assumes you want to use only the current drive and prompts you to switch diskettes during the copy.

If you don't specify <source> or <target>, DOS assumes you want to use only the current drive and prompts you to switch diskettes during the copy.

/1 copies only the first side of a diskette if you have a system with double-sided drives.

DOS gives the target diskette the same number of sides and sectors as the source diskette. If the source diskette, for example, has nine sectors per track and the target diskette was formatted with eight, DOS formats the target diskette with nine sectors per track before copying.

Examples of Copying a Diskette

You copied the system diskette in Chapter 2, but make another copy here; you'll need it in a moment for another example. Follow the instructions under the heading that describes your system.

If you have two diskette drives

To copy the system diskette in drive A to the diskette in drive B, type:

```
A>diskcopy a: b:
```

DOS prompts you to put in the diskettes. The diskette you just formatted is in drive B, so just press a key. DOS tells you how many tracks, sectors, and sides it's copying (sectors and sides in Version 2), then asks if you want to copy another; reply *n*.

If you wanted to copy only the first side of a diskette in drive B to the current drive, you would type *diskcopy b: /1.*

DOS would prompt and report as in the previous example.

If you have one diskette drive

Because you have only one diskette drive, DOS must use it for both the source and target diskettes, prompting you to exchange diskettes as required.

If you're using a fixed disk, you probably have only one diskette drive. DOS will prompt you to swap the source and target diskettes in and out of the diskette drive during the Diskcopy procedure. The diskette you just formatted with a volume label is in the diskette drive. Remove it and put in your copy of the DOS system diskette.

If you're using a single-drive system, the system diskette is already in drive A.

To copy the system diskette, type:

```
A>diskcopy
```

DOS prompts you to put in the source diskette:

```
Insert SOURCE diskette in drive A:

Press any key when ready . . .
_
```

You want to copy the system diskette, so just press a key. DOS tells you how many tracks, sectors, and sides it's copying (sectors and sides, if you're using Version 2), then prompts you to put the target diskette in the drive:

```
Insert TARGET diskette in drive A:

Press any key when ready . . .
_
```

Remove the system diskette and put in your practice diskette, then press a key. DOS continues to prompt you to exchange diskettes until it has copied the diskette. Then it asks if you want to copy another:

```
Copy another diskette (Y/N)?_
```

Reply *n*.

If you're using a fixed disk, suppose that all you need is a copy of each file on the source diskette—in other words, the diskette doesn't contain hidden or system files, and the copied files can be stored anywhere on the target diskette. It's probably more convenient to use the Copy command to do the following: Copy the files from the source diskette to the fixed disk, then copy the files from the fixed disk to the target diskette, and finally, erase the copied files from the fixed disk.

**diskcomp <drive1>
<drive2> /1 /8**

COMPARING TWO DISKETTES

*Note: The command for comparing two diskettes is in IBM's version of
MS-DOS. If you are not using an IBM personal computer, skip to the heading
"Checking the Condition of a Disk."*

You want to know whether two diskettes are identical—for
example, you have copied a diskette with the Diskcopy command,
and you want to be certain your duplicate is an exact copy of the
original. Diskcomp compares two diskettes sector-by-sector. The
Diskcomp command can only be used with diskettes; you cannot
use it to compare a fixed disk to a diskette.

*Note: Just because two diskettes contain the same files doesn't mean they're
identical, because the files may be stored in different sectors. If you want to
compare the files on two diskettes, rather than the diskettes themselves, use
the Compare (comp) command (described in Chapter 5) and specify all
files (*.*).*

The Diskcomp command has four parameters:

diskcomp <drive1> <drive2> /1 /8

<drive1> and <drive2> are the drive letters, each followed by
a colon, of the diskettes to be compared (such as A: and B:). If you
omit <drive2>, DOS compares the diskette in <drive1> to the
diskette in the current drive.

If you omit both <drive1> and <drive2>, DOS assumes you
want to use only the current drive and prompts you to switch
diskettes during the comparison.

/1 compares only the first side of double-sided diskettes. /8
limits the comparison to eight sectors, even if <drive1> contains a
nine-sector diskette.

If DOS finds any differences, it displays the side and track of
each; for example:

```
Compare error on side 0, track 33
```

Examples of Comparing Two Diskettes

To try these examples, follow the instructions under the heading that describes your system.

If you have two diskette drives

To compare the diskette in drive B (the copy of the system diskette) to the diskette in drive A (the system diskette), type:

```
A>diskcomp a: b:
```

DOS prompts you to put in the diskettes:

```
Insert FIRST diskette in drive A:

Insert SECOND diskette in drive B:

Press any key when ready . . .
```

The diskettes are already in the drives, so press a key. DOS reports how many tracks, sectors, and sides it is comparing, then reports the results of the comparison and asks if you want to compare more diskettes:

```
Comparing 40 tracks
9 sectors per track, 2 side(s)

Compare OK


Compare another diskette (Y/N) ?_
```

Reply *n*.

If you had double-sided drives and wanted to compare only the first side of the diskettes, you would type *diskcomp a: b: /1.*

DOS would prompt and report as in the previous example, noting that it was comparing only one side.

If you have one diskette drive

To compare the system diskette to the copy you just made, type:

```
A>diskcomp
```

DOS prompts you to put in the first diskette:

```
Insert FIRST diskette in drive A:

Press any key when ready . . .
```

The copy you made of the system diskette is already in the drive, so press a key. DOS reports how many tracks, sectors, and sides it's comparing, then prompts you to put in the second diskette:

```
Comparing 40 tracks
9 sectors per track, 2 side(s)

Insert SECOND diskette in drive A:

Press any key when ready . . .
```

Remove the copy of the system diskette, put the DOS diskette in the diskette drive, and then press a key. DOS continues to prompt you to exchange diskettes until it finally tells you it's done and asks if you want to compare more diskettes:

```
Compare OK


Compare another diskette (Y/N) ?_
```

Reply *n*.

CHECKING THE CONDITION OF A DISK

chkdsk <**drive**>
<**filename**> **/V/F**

Computers aren't infallible; malfunctions can produce errors in the directory of a disk. Such errors are rare, but the Check Disk (chkdsk) command helps by making sure that all files are recorded properly. Check Disk analyzes the directory on a disk, comparing the directory entries with the locations and lengths of the files, and reports any errors it finds. The Check Disk report includes the following:

- The total amount of space on the disk.

- The number of files and directories and how much space they take up.

- How much space on the disk remains available for files.

- The size of the computer's memory and how many bytes remain free for use.

You can also ask the command to display the name of each file on the disk (including subdirectories), and to check whether any files are stored inefficiently.

If possible, DOS stores files in adjacent, or contiguous, sectors. As files are deleted and new files are stored, however, they can become fragmented (stored in non-adjacent sectors). A fragmented file isn't a cause for worry; the worst that can happen is that DOS will take slightly longer to read the file. If several files on a diskette are fragmented, you can restore them to contiguous sectors by copying all the files to an empty, formatted diskette with the Copy command. (Remember, don't use the Diskcopy command, because it makes a faithful sector-by-sector copy of the diskette, storing the files in exactly the same—non-contiguous—sectors in which they are stored on the original diskette.)

The Check Disk command has four parameters:

chkdsk <drive><filename> /V /F

<drive> is the letter, followed by a colon, of the drive that contains the disk to be checked. If you omit <drive>, DOS checks the disk in the current drive.

<filename> is the name of the file whose storage you want DOS to check. DOS displays a message if the file is stored in non-contiguous sectors. You can use wildcard characters to check a set of files.

/V displays the name of each directory and file on the disk.

/F tells DOS to correct any errors it finds in the directory if you so specify when the error is found.

Examples of Checking a Disk

To check the diskette in drive B (the copy of the system disk), type:

```
A>chkdsk b:
```

DOS displays its report:

```
362496 bytes total disk space
 38912 bytes in 3 hidden files
262144 bytes in 36 user files
 61440 bytes available on disk

524288 bytes total memory
487248 bytes free
```

To check the diskette in drive B (the copy of the system diskette), and to check whether all files on it are stored in contiguous sectors, type:

```
A>chkdsk b:*.*
```

DOS displays the same report as the preceding, but adds the following message:

```
All specified file(s) are contiguous
```

If any files were stored in non-contiguous sectors, DOS would display their names in place of this message.

To check the diskette in drive B and, at the same time, display the name of each directory and file on it, type:

```
A>chkdsk b: /v
```

DOS displays the name of each file and directory on the diskette, then appends its usual report of disk space and memory available. Because you are checking the copy of your system disk in this example, the list of files scrolls off the top of the screen; to view it all, you can freeze the display by pressing Ctrl-Num Lock.

You can combine the Check Disk parameters in one command; for example, *chkdsk b: *.* /v* would check the diskette in drive B, check all files on it for fragmentation, and display the names of all files and directories.

If the Check Disk command finds an error, it displays a message, such as *Disk error reading drive B* or *Allocation error for file, size adjusted*, followed by a file name and a prompt asking you whether to correct the error. If you specified the /F parameter, you can reply *y* to tell DOS to try to correct the error. Depending on the type of error, this may cause the loss of some data.

ASSIGNING OR CHANGING A DISK'S VOLUME LABEL

label <drive> <label>

The Label command assigns, changes, or deletes the volume label of a diskette or fixed disk. It has two parameters:

label <drive> <label>

<drive> is the letter, followed by a colon, of the drive that contains the disk whose volume label is to be altered (such as B:).

<label> is the volume label to be assigned to the disk in the drive specified by <drive>.

If you omit <drive>, DOS assumes you want to alter the label of the disk in the current drive. If you omit <label>, DOS prompts you to enter the new label.

Examples of Changing a Disk's Volume Label

Earlier, in the Format command example, you assigned the volume label DOSDISK to the diskette in drive B. To change its volume label to DOSCOPY, type the following:

```
A>label b:

Volume in drive B is DOSDISK

Volume label (11 characters, ENTER for none)? _
```

Type *doscopy* to change the volume label (you'll verify the change in a moment).

To delete a volume label, you would reply to the prompt by pressing the Enter key without typing a name. DOS would then ask *Delete current volume label (Y/N)?*. You would reply *y* to delete the volume label.

vol <drive>

DISPLAYING A DISK'S VOLUME LABEL

The Volume (vol) command displays the volume label of a fixed disk or a diskette. If you assign descriptive volume labels to your diskettes when you format them, you can use the Volume command to make sure that you're using the correct diskettes: It's faster and easier than checking the directory.

The Volume command has one parameter:

vol <drive>

<drive> is the letter, followed by a colon, of the drive that contains the diskette whose volume label is to be displayed (such as B:). If you omit <drive>, DOS displays the volume label of the disk in the current drive.

To display the volume label of the diskette in drive B, type:

```
A>vol b:
```

DOS displays the volume label:

```
Volume in drive B is DOSCOPY
```

If the diskette has no volume label, DOS responds *Volume in drive B has no label.*

CHAPTER
7
MANAGING
YOUR DEVICES

Data flows into and out of a computer system through pieces of equipment called *devices*. Devices are categorized by whether they handle data coming in (input) or going out (output), or both. The keyboard, for example, is an input device; the computer gets information from it. A printer is an output device; the computer sends information to it. A disk drive is both an input device and an output device; the computer can either read a file from a disk or write a file onto a disk.

Some devices, such as the keyboard, don't need much attention from you, because DOS requires no special instructions to operate them. Other devices, however, such as a color display or a printer, sometimes require you to tell DOS how you want to use them. If you have both a monochrome display and a color display, for example, each time you start DOS it uses the monochrome display unless you tell it otherwise.

Color displays, printers, and the computer's communications channels, called ports, can all be used in a variety of ways. This chapter shows you how to do the following with the DOS device commands:

- Clear the screen with the Clear Screen command.

- Switch displays and control the color display with the Mode command.

- Control the width and line spacing of your printer with the Mode command.

- Define the settings of the communications ports with the Mode command.

- Copy from a device to a file or to another device with the Copy command.

- Make DOS able to print graphics with the Graphics command.

- Make DOS able to display special graphics characters on a color/graphics display in graphics mode with the Graftabl (Load Graphics Table) command.

DOS also includes a group of commands that let you change the keyboard layout, available characters, and other operating characteristics to match the requirements of several different languages and countries. If you need to use your computer with more than one language, Chapter 8, "DOS Is an International System," and the section "Changing Your System Configuration" in Chapter 18 show you how to use these commands.

DEVICE NAMES

Just as files have names, so do devices. You can use a device name in many DOS commands just as you would use a file name. DOS assigns all device names, however; you can't name a device yourself. Figure 7-1 on the next page shows the devices that make up a typical system, with the names assigned to them by DOS.

CON is short for *Console*. It is both an input device and an output device, and refers to both the keyboard (input) and the display (output). Because the keyboard is input only and the display is output only, DOS can tell which one to use by the way you use the name CON in a command.

PRN is short for *Printer*. It is an output device, and refers to the parallel printer that DOS uses unless you specify otherwise (much as DOS looks for files on the current drive unless you specify otherwise). You can attach as many as three parallel printers (named LPT1, LPT2, and LPT3); DOS assumes that PRN means LPT1 unless you or a program specify otherwise.

AUX is short for *Auxiliary*. It is for both input and output, and refers to the communications port that DOS uses unless you instruct otherwise. You can attach one or two communications ports, named COM1 and COM2; unless you or a program specify otherwise, DOS assumes that AUX means COM1. On a typical system, COM1 could, perhaps, be used for a modem; COM2 could be used for a serial printer. Or vice versa.

DOS reserves these names for devices only; you cannot give any of these names to a file.

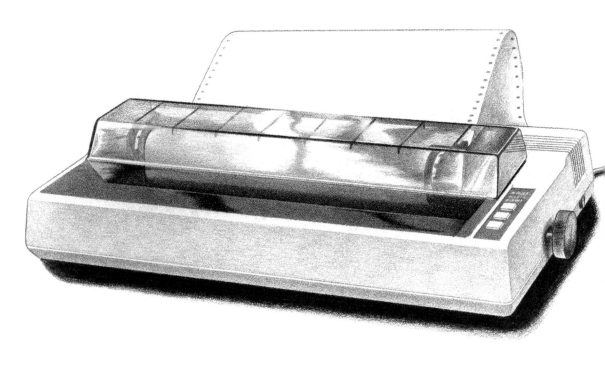

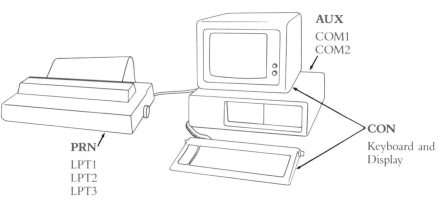

Figure 7-1. DOS *device names*

PREPARING FOR THE EXAMPLES

Devices often need very specific set-up instructions and operating parameters. Most of the examples in this chapter are designed to work with the IBM personal computers. The Mode command, in particular, is for the version of DOS that runs on IBM systems. If you're not using an IBM or IBM-compatible personal computer, you probably use different instructions to manage your devices. Refer to your documentation for specific information.

When you try the examples, be sure the devices you name are attached to the system and are turned on. You won't hurt anything by entering a command naming a device that isn't ready, but the command may cause an error that requires you to restart DOS.

CLEARING THE SCREEN

cls

Sometimes you may want to erase distracting entries from the screen. You can clean things up with the Clear Screen (cls) command, which erases everything and then displays the system prompt in the upper left corner.

The Clear Screen command has one form:

cls

To test it, type its name:

```
A>cls
```

The screen is cleared, except for the system prompt.

CONTROLLING THE DISPLAY

mode <method>

The Mode command has several display-related options. Which one you choose depends on the type of display and how much you want to see on-screen.

If you have a non-IBM monochrome or color display attached to the IBM Color/Graphics Adapter, you can use the Mode command to specify whether it displays 40 or 80 columns across the screen.

When used to control a display attached to the color/graphics adapter, the Mode command has one form:

mode <method>

<method> is either 40 or 80.

Example of Controlling a Non-IBM or Color Display

To display 40 columns on a display attached to the color/graphics adapter, type:

```
A>mode 40
```

DOS clears the screen and displays the system prompt in the upper left corner.

ADJUSTING A NON-IBM DISPLAY

**mode <method>,
R or L,T**

If you are using a non-IBM display with the color/graphics adapter, the image may not be centered on the screen. One option of the Mode command lets you shift the image right or left. To help you judge when the display is centered, you can tell DOS to display a test pattern that fills the top row on the screen with a repeating pattern of the numbers 0 through 9.

When used in this way, the Mode command has two additional parameters:

mode <method>,R or L,T

mode <method> is the Mode command that selects or controls a display (as described in the previous topic). In addition, to shift the image right or left, type a comma, followed by *r* or *l,* after the Mode command. DOS clears the screen and shifts the image either two columns in the specified direction, if 80 columns are displayed, or one column in the specified direction, if 40 columns are displayed.

To display the test pattern, type a comma, followed by *t,* at the end of the Mode command. DOS clears the screen, shifts the image in the direction you specified, and displays the test pattern followed by a prompt that asks whether you can see the complete test pattern. If you respond *n,* DOS shifts the image again in the same direction and repeats the test pattern and the prompt; this lets you adjust the display several times without entering several Mode commands. When you respond *y,* the command is completed.

Example of Adjusting a Non–IBM Display

To specify 80 columns, shifted two columns to the right, type:

```
A>mode 80,r
```

DOS clears the screen, sets the width to 80, shifts the image two columns to the right, and displays the system prompt.

To specify 40 columns, shifted one column left, and to display a test pattern, type:

```
A>mode 40,l,t
```

DOS clears the screen, sets the width to 40, shifts the image one column left, then displays the test pattern and prompt:

```
01234567890123456789012345678901234567890123456789

Do you see the rightmost 9? (Y/N)
_
```

If you can't see the 9 at the right edge, type *n;* DOS clears the screen and displays the test pattern and prompt, shifted one more column left; each time you type *n,* DOS shifts the image left another column. When you see the entire test pattern, type *y;* DOS clears the screen and displays the system prompt.

SWITCHING AND CONTROLLING TWO DISPLAYS

mode <method>

If you have both an IBM Monochrome Display and a color display attached to your system, DOS uses the monochrome display when you start the system. The Mode command lets you switch from one display to the other; specify the number of columns displayed on a color display; and specify whether or not DOS tries to

display in color. If you're using a non-IBM monochrome display, it must be attached to the color/graphics adapter. Disabling color in this situation often makes the display easier to read.

When used to switch and control displays, the Mode command has one form:

mode <method>

<method> in this case is one of the following:

mono   IBM Monochrome Display
bw40   color display, 40 columns, color disabled
bw80   color display, 80 columns, color disabled
co40   color display, 40 columns, color enabled
co80   color display, 80 columns, color enabled

Examples of Switching and Controlling Displays

If you're using the color display, type the following to switch to the IBM Monochrome Display:

```
A>mode mono
```

DOS displays the system prompt on the monochrome display. The color display is now inactive.

To specify the color display, 40 columns, and color, type:

```
A>mode co40
```

DOS clears the screen and displays the system prompt in the upper left corner in large characters.

CONTROLLING THE PRINTER WIDTH AND SPACING

mode <printer>
<width>,<spacing>

The printer normally prints a maximum of 80 characters per line, and six lines per inch. It can also print in a smaller type, called *condensed,* that fits 132 characters on a line. This ability to change line widths is often useful for printing spreadsheets and other documents wider than 80 characters. The printer can also print eight lines per inch, to fit more lines on a page.

If you have a letter-quality printer, such as an NEC 3550, the documentation that came with the printer tells you how to define the printer to DOS and how to control the printer's characteristics, such as line and character spacing.

You can use the Mode command to specify the line width (80 or 132) and spacing (6 or 8).

When used to control the printer, the Mode command has three parameters:

mode <printer> <width>,<spacing>

<printer> is the name of the printer, followed by a colon (LPT1:, LPT2:, or LPT3:). <width> is either 80 or 132. <spacing> is either 6 or 8, and must be preceded by a comma.

You must always include <printer>. If you omit <width>, DOS leaves the current width unchanged, but you must still type the comma before <spacing> to tell DOS that you omitted <width>. If you omit <spacing>, DOS leaves the current spacing unchanged.

Examples of Controlling the Printer

Make sure the printer is turned on before entering the following examples.

To cause LPT1: to print in small type (up to 132 characters per line if the printer can do so), type the following:

```
A>mode lpt1: 132
```

DOS replies:

```
LPT1: set for 132
```

To test the setting, print and display the directory simultaneously by typing:

```
A><Ctrl-PrtSc>dir
```

The directory is printed with the new line width. (You can cancel the Directory command by pressing Ctrl-Break.) Press Ctrl-PrtSc to stop simultaneous printing.

To set the spacing of LPT1: to eight lines per inch and leave the width unchanged, type:

```
A>mode lpt1: ,8
```

DOS replies:

```
Printer lines per inch set
```

To see the effect of this setting, again start printing and displaying the directory simultaneously by typing:

```
A><Ctrl-PrtSc>dir
```

This time the directory is printed in both small type (from the previous example) and closer line spacing. Press Ctrl-PrtSc again to stop simultaneous printing.

To restore the printer to normal width and line spacing, type:

```
A>mode lpt1: 80,6
```

DOS replies:

```
LPT1: set for 80

Printer lines per inch set
```

The printer is back to its normal settings.

CONTROLLING THE SERIAL COMMUNICATIONS PORT

mode <port>
<baud>,<parity>,
<databits>,
<stopbits>

Serial communications is controlled by several characteristics, or *parameters,* that define how fast and in what form data is transmitted. Different devices often require different parameter settings; the communications parameters of your serial port must match those of the device or computer service with which you want to communicate. Before you can use a communications port, you must set these parameters with the Mode command.

The communications parameters you can set include:

- *Baud,* how many characters per second are sent or received.

- *Parity,* the kind of error-checking technique used.

- *Databits,* the number of electrical signals required to define a character.

- *Stopbits,* the number of electrical signals that mark the end of a character.

A more complete definition of these parameters is beyond the scope of this book. Figure 7-2 lists the parameters you can set with the Mode command. The documentation of the device or computer service you want to use shows the required setting; compare these settings with Figure 7-2 to see which parameters you must change.

Name	Valid Settings	How You Specify	Value DOS Assumes
Baud	110,150,300, 600,1200,2400, 4800,9600	You can abbreviate to first two digits (11 for 110, 24 for 2400)	None (you must set a value)
Parity	None Odd Even	N O E	Even (E)
Databits	7 or 8	7 or 8	7
Stopbits	1 or 2	1 or 2	2 if baud = 110, 1 otherwise

Figure 7-2. Serial communications parameters

When used to initialize a serial communications port, the Mode command has one form:

mode <port> <baud>,<parity>,<databits>,<stopbits>

<port> is the name, followed by a colon, of the communications port (COM1: or COM2:). The remaining parameters, separated by commas, are those described in Figure 7-2.

You must specify a value for <baud> each time you enter this Mode command. DOS assumes the values for the other parameters listed in the last column of Figure 7-2 unless you specifically change them; you needn't specify these parameters unless the device or service with which you want to communicate requires values different from those that DOS assumes.

If you omit any parameter from the Mode command, you must still type the comma that precedes it, to show DOS you omitted the parameter.

Examples of Controlling the Serial Communications Port

These examples show you different uses of the Mode command. Don't enter them unless you have a serial communications port.

To set the baud rate for COM1: to 1200 and accept the default values for the other parameters, you would type:

```
A> mode com1: 1200
```

DOS replies by reporting the current setting of each parameter:

```
COM1: 1200,e,7,1,-
```

This report shows that <baud> is 1200, <parity> is even, <databits> is 7, and <stopbits> is 1. The hyphen at the end tells you DOS will not keep trying to send to a device that isn't ready, but will stop after a brief time.

To set <baud> for COM2: to 300, <parity> to odd, leave <databits> set to 7, and set <stopbits> to 2, you would type:

```
A> mode com2: 300,o,,2
```

Note the two commas before the 2, telling DOS that you omitted <databits>. DOS confirms the settings:

```
COM2: 300,o,7,2,-
```

CONNECTING A SERIAL PRINTER

mode <printer> = <port>

If you want to use a serial printer attached to a communications port, you must use the Mode command to tell DOS to send printer output to the communications port instead of the regular (parallel) printer port; this is called *redirecting* the printer output.

Before you redirect the printer output, you must first set the parameters of the serial communications port to the values required by the printer, as described in the preceding topic.

When used to redirect printer output to a serial communications port, the Mode command has one form:

mode <printer>=<port>

<printer> is the name of the printer whose output is to be redirected (LPT1:, LPT2:, or LPT3:). <port> is the name of the serial communications port (COM1: or COM2:). You must enter both parameters.

Example of Connecting a Serial Printer

To redirect printer output from LPT1: to serial port COM1:, you would first set the serial port to match the communications parameters of your printer, then you would type:

```
A>mode lpt1:=com1:
```

DOS would acknowledge:

```
LPT1: redirected to COM1:
```

Now all output that would normally go to LPT1: would be sent to COM1: instead. To cancel the redirection, restoring the printer output to LPT1:, you would type:

```
A>mode lpt1: 1,1
```

The two numbers following LPT1: correspond to the digit in the name of the communications port (COM1:) and printer (LPT1:), respectively. If you had redirected LPT1: to COM2:, you would cancel the redirection by typing *mode lpt1: 2,1.*

COPYING FROM A DEVICE
TO A FILE OR ANOTHER DEVICE

copy \<source\>
\<target\>

As you saw in earlier examples, you can use the Copy command to copy from a device to a file. You have used this technique several times to create sample files by copying from the keyboard to a file, and will find it handy for creating short text files.

You can also copy from one device to another. Copying from the keyboard to the printer, for example, is a quick and convenient way to print short notes or lists.

When you copy from one device to a file or another device, DOS continues to copy until it comes to the character (Ctrl-Z) that marks the end of a file. When you copy from the keyboard, you can send this end-of-file character by pressing the key labeled F6 and the Enter key (or, as you've done before, by pressing Ctrl-Z).

When used to copy from a device to a file or another device, the Copy command has two parameters:

    copy \<source\> \<target\>

\<source\> is the name of the source device. \<target\> is the name of the target file or device.

Examples of Copying From a Device
To a File or Another Device

To copy from the keyboard (CON) to the printer (PRN), make sure the printer is turned on and type:

```
A>copy con prn
```

Now everything you type is both displayed and sent to the printer. Type a few lines, and then end the copy by pressing F6 or Ctrl-Z (shown as ˆZ in the example because that's how DOS displays it):

```
These lines are being
copied from the
keyboard to the printer.
^Z
        1 File(s) copied

A>_
```

To copy from the serial communications port (AUX) to the printer (PRN), you would first set the serial port to match the communications parameters of whatever is attached to it, then you would type:

```
copy aux prn
```

Everything received at the communications port would be printed until the end-of-file character was received.

PRINTING GRAPHICS IMAGES

graphics <printer>
/R /B

Pressing Shift-PrtSc prints the text displayed on either a monochrome or color display, but it does not print graphics images from a display attached to the color/graphics adapter. The Graphics command enables DOS to print these graphics images on any of several different printers.

You need only enter the Graphics command once. After you enter it, pressing Shift-PrtSc prints everything on the screen of the active display, including graphics images. Low-resolution graphics images are printed across the paper; color on non-color printers is simulated with shading. High-resolution graphics images are printed sideways (rotated 90 degrees) and enlarged.

The Graphics command loads a program that increases the amount of memory that DOS uses by about 1000 bytes.

The Graphics command has three parameters:

graphics <printer> /R /B

<printer> is one of the IBM printers, or a compatible model:

- For the IBM Personal Computer Color Printer, the options are: *color1* for a black ribbon; *color4* for a red-green-blue ribbon; *color8* for a cyan-magenta-yellow ribbon.

- For the IBM Personal Computer Compact Printer, you specify *compact*.

- For the IBM Personal Graphics Printer (or an Epson printer with the Graftrax option), you specify *graphics*.

If you do not specify <printer>, DOS assumes *graphics*.

/R tells DOS to print the screen as you see it—in other words, light characters on a dark background.

/B tells DOS to print the background color if you have specified *color4* or *color8* for <printer>. If you don't specify /B, DOS doesn't print the background color.

When you enter the Graphics command, DOS loads the program, adds it to the system kept in memory, and displays the system prompt. You needn't enter the command again until the next time you start DOS.

If you are using a color display and have a printer that can print graphics, you can test the Graphics command by entering the command and appropriate parameters, then displaying a graphics image and pressing Shift-PrtSc.

DISPLAYING GRAPHICS CHARACTERS

graftabl

Even when the color/graphics adapter is in graphics mode, it normally cannot display the 128 special characters that include accented characters, Greek letters, box-drawing graphics, and others. The Graftabl command enables DOS to display these characters when the color/graphics adapter is in graphics mode.

Like the Graphics command, you need only enter the Graftabl command once. After you enter it, the additional characters can be displayed on the screen. The Graftabl command loads a small program that increases the amount of memory that DOS uses by about 1200 bytes.

The Graftabl command has no parameters:

graftabl

You don't need the Graftabl command in normal DOS operation, but there are certain times it can come in handy. For example, suppose you would like to display accented French or Spanish characters on the screen. If your display is connected to the color/graphics adapter, you would simply type *graftabl*. DOS would respond *GRAPHIC CHARACTERS LOADED*, and all 128 special graphics characters would be available until you reset or turned off your computer. (For more information on using foreign-language characters with DOS, see Chapter 8, "DOS Is an International System.")

CHAPTER

8

DOS IS AN
INTERNATIONAL SYSTEM

Even though many languages share the basic Roman alphabet, they use different characters. These differences include both accented Roman characters, such as è, é, ë, or ê, and those that are altogether different, such as ¿ or £.

Different countries, regardless of language, also represent the numeric form of a date in different ways. In most North American and European countries, the numeric form of a date is shown in a day-month-year sequence (for example, 16-10-85 for October 16, 1985). In the United States, however, the sequence is month-day-year (10-16-85), and in Japan it is year-month-day (85-10-16).

Different countries with different traditions also have their own methods of writing the time. And, of course, there are many different currency symbols and more than one way of separating large or decimal numbers.

Depending on the country for which your computer was manufactured, DOS assumes a keyboard arrangement and country code that determine how date, time, currency symbols, and decimals are handled. Starting with Version 3.0, DOS lets you change these characteristics. The language that DOS itself uses—its command names and the messages it displays—remains unchanged, but you can tailor many of its operating qualities to the linguistic and monetary traditions of a particular country. This capability can be particularly useful if you use your computer for work with different languages or currencies, or if persons with different language requirements use the same computer.

This chapter shows you how to:

- Choose a keyboard layout with one of the Keyboard commands.

- Set the country code with the Country command.

- Create a DOS system diskette tailored to a particular country with the Select command.

CHOOSING A KEYBOARD LAYOUT

Keyboards used in different countries must accommodate different characters and often use a different arrangement of common

keys. The Keyboard commands change the keyboard layout to match a specific country. All the command names begin with *keyb*; two additional letters identify the country. The Keybfr command, for example, establishes the French keyboard layout.

The Keyboard command for each country loads a small program that combines with the part of DOS kept in memory, decreasing the amount of available memory by about 2000 bytes. The actual size of the program depends on the number of changes the new layout requires.

If you enter a Keyboard command, then enter another Keyboard command without restarting DOS, the second keyboard program is loaded to reconfigure the keyboard. The program loaded by the first Keyboard command remains in memory but you cannot return to it, so issuing a series of Keyboard commands reduces the amount of available memory.

Switching Keyboards While DOS is Running

If your computer was manufactured for use in the United States, the configuration of the United States keyboard is stored in the computer's permanent memory. After changing the keyboard layout with a Keyboard command, you can switch back and forth between the United States configuration and the new one: Press Ctrl-Alt-F1 (hold down both the Ctrl and Alt keys and press the F1 function key) for the United States layout, and Ctrl-Alt-F2 for the other layout. If your word processor or spreadsheet program accepts characters other than standard keyboard characters—you'll have to try it to see—this lets you switch back and forth while editing a document to include information for either country and to use the more familiar keyboard layout to operate the application.

If your computer was manufactured for multilingual operation, you may be able to switch among several keyboard configurations without using a Keyboard command. See your computer's documentation (the *Guide to Operations* if the computer was manufactured by IBM) for a description of how to switch among different keyboards.

Note: Not all printers can print accented or other characters not in the standard set. Check your printer's documentation to see if it can print the IBM graphics characters.

Typing Accented Characters with Dead Keys

In non-English-speaking countries, many of the characters that a language requires are accented, combining an accent mark and a common character (such as Å or ñ). Some of these accented characters are assigned locations on the keyboard; on the French keyboard, for example, you type *è* by pressing the 7 key in the top row of the keyboard (to type the number 7, you press Shift-7).

Often there aren't enough available keys to provide all the accented characters, however, so DOS also uses dead keys to combine accent marks and characters. Some typewriters use this same technique, so using dead keys might be a familiar procedure for you.

A dead key is one that represents just an accent mark. Pressing a dead key doesn't produce any apparent result, but it tells DOS to combine the accent mark with the next key pressed. On the French keyboard, for example, you type ô by pressing the dead key for the circumflex (^), then pressing the key labeled O.

If you press a dead key, then press a character that cannot be combined with the accent mark represented by the dead key, DOS does one of the following:

- In most cases, it beeps and displays the accent mark, followed by the key you pressed, to show you it couldn't combine them as an accented character.

- If the dead key represents the diaeresis (¨), DOS displays a small, filled-in square (■) followed by the second key you pressed.

To correct the error, backspace to erase the two characters and type the correct dead-key sequence.

Keyboard Layouts

keybxx

Each language DOS supports has its own Keyboard command. The Keyboard commands have no parameters (the country names in the right column of the following table are for information only):

keybuk	United Kingdom
keybgr	Germany
keybfr	France
keybit	Italy
keybsp	Spain

Because entering a Keyboard command changes the location of common keys (especially punctuation marks), the character that results from pressing a key won't always match the United States label on the key. You may want to keep a chart of the keyboard layout handy, mark the keys, or even move the keys to the new location.

Figures 8-1 through 8-6 show the keyboard layouts for France, Germany, Spain, the United Kingdom, Italy, and the United States. The figures show the shifted and unshifted characters produced by each key in the main typewriter portion of the keyboard, and identify any dead keys.

```
1 2 3 4 5 6 7 8 9 0 °  _           Dead keys
& é " ' (   è ! ç à ) -

A Z E R T Y U I O P ■ ★           Diaeresis (¨)
a z e r t y u i o p ^ $
                                  Circumflex (^)
Q S D F G H J K L M % £
q s d f g h j k l m ù µ

> W X C V B N ? . / +
< w x c v b n , ; : =
```

Figure 8-1. French keyboard (keybfr)

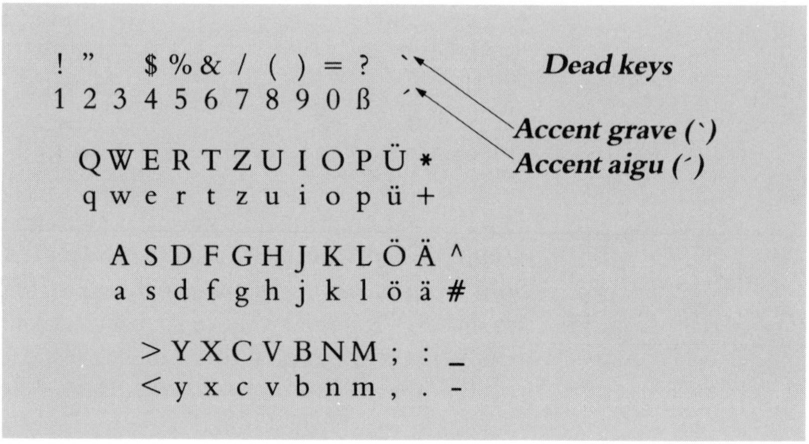

Figure 8-2.   German keyboard (keybgr)

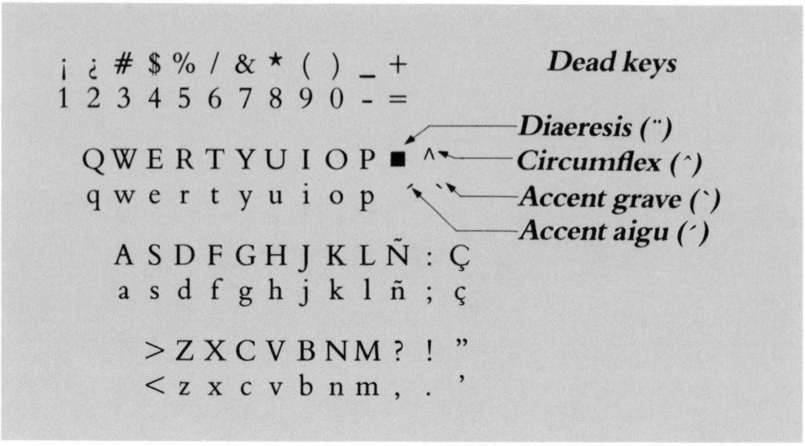

Figure 8-3.   Spanish keyboard (keybsp)

```
! " £ $ % ^ & ⋆ ( ) _ +          No dead keys
1 2 3 4 5 6 7 8 9 0 - =

Q W E R T Y U I O P { }
q w e r t y u i o p [ ]

  A S D F G H J K L : @ ˜
  a s d f g h j k l ; ' #

    ¦ Z X C V B N M < > ?
    \ z x c v b n m , . /
```

Figure 8-4. United Kingdom keyboard (keybuk)

```
! " £ $ % & / ( ) = ? ^          No dead keys
1 2 3 4 5 6 7 8 9 0 ' ì

Q W E R T Y U I O P é ⋆
q w e r t y u i o p è +

  A S D F G H J K L @ #
  a s d f g h j k l ò à ù

    > Z X C V B N M ; : _
    < z x c v b n m , . -
```

Figure 8-5. Italian keyboard (keybit)

```
! @ # $ % ^ & * ( ) _ +        No dead keys
1 2 3 4 5 6 7 8 9 0 - =

QWERTYUIOP { }
q w e r t y u i o p [ ]

  A S D F G H J K L : "  ˜
  a s d f g h j k l ;  ´  `

    ¦ Z X C V B N M < > ?
    \ z x c v b n m , . /
```

Figure 8-6. United States keyboard

Example of Using the Keyboard Command

To change the keyboard arrangement to French, type the following:

```
A>keybfr
```

If you are accustomed to the United States layout, here are the most obvious changes with the French layout: You must hold down the Shift key to type a number; the locations of two pairs of letter keys are reversed (Q-A and W-Z); M is to the right of L and most symbols and punctuation marks are in different places.

Now that you have switched keyboards, you must follow the new layout. For example, the command to display a directory in wide format is *dir /w.* If you don't follow the French keyboard layout, you'll type *dir /z,* because the W and Z have changed places.

Suppose you wanted to type the sentence *L'hôtel célèbre est grand* (The famous hotel is big). Both the é and è are on the keyboard, but the ô is not, so you must use the dead key for the circumflex. And

remember, the Q and the A keys have changed places. Here, step-by-step, is how you would type the phrase:

```
A>L
```

For the apostrophe, press the 4 key in the top row. After the apostrophe, type *h:*

```
A>L'h
```

Now, you have to use the circumflex dead key, which is to the right of the French p. Press the circumflex dead key. Nothing happens yet. Now type *o;* DOS displays *ô*. Continue by typing *tel c:*

```
A>L'hôtel c
```

For é, press the 2 key in the top row; then type *l:*

```
A>L'hôtel cél
```

For è, press the 7 key in the top row; then type *bre est gr:*

```
A>L'hôtel célèbre est gr
```

And finally, press Q to get the French a, and type *nd:*

```
A>L'hôtel célèbre est grand
```

Although that's a painfully long list of instructions just to type a simple sentence, in fact it goes quite quickly after just a bit of practice. Press Esc to clear the line, and press Ctrl-Alt-F1 to return to the United States keyboard layout.

CREATING A LANGUAGE-SPECIFIC DOS SYSTEM DISKETTE

select <code>
<keyboard>

If you use more than one language, or several users with different languages share the computer, DOS offers a simple way to handle multilingual operation: the Select command, which creates a country- and language-specific system diskette.

Country	Country Code	Keyboard Code
United States	001	US
France	033	FR
Spain	034	SP
Italy	039	IT
United Kingdom	044	UK
Germany	049	GR

Figure 8-7. Country and keyboard codes for the Select command

The Select command makes a copy of the DOS system diskette that includes files that automatically configure DOS for a specific country. If you create several such diskettes, you can change languages simply by restarting DOS after putting the appropriate system diskette in drive A.

The Select command has two parameters:

select <code> <keyboard>

<code> is the three-digit country code you want set in the new DOS diskette. You must include all three digits of the country code, including any zeroes at the beginning. The codes are easy to remember, because they correspond to each country's long-distance telephone prefix.

<keyboard> is the two-letter abbreviation of the country whose keyboard layout is to be selected for the new DOS diskette (these are the last two letters of the corresponding Keyboard command).

Figure 8-7 shows the code and keyboard values allowed with the Select command. You can enter the keyboard code in either upper- or lowercase.

Example of Creating a Language-Specific System Diskette

The Select command uses the Diskcopy command to make the copy of the system diskette, then it compares the two diskettes with the Diskcomp command, to make sure the copy was accurate. The

prompts and sequence of steps are the same as if you had entered a Diskcopy command, then a Diskcomp command.

If you're using a computer with a fixed disk, you must start DOS with the system diskette in the diskette drive, even if you normally start DOS from the fixed disk. If you have only one diskette drive, DOS may prompt you to switch diskettes; the number of times you must switch diskettes depends on the amount of memory your computer has.

Throughout the Select procedure, DOS refers to the original system diskette as the source diskette and refers to the language-specific system diskette you're creating as the target diskette.

To create a French system diskette on a computer with one diskette drive, you perform the following steps:

1. Start DOS with the system diskette in drive A, even if you normally start DOS from a fixed disk.

2. Type *select 033 fr* (033 is the country code for France, and fr is the keyboard code). DOS prompts you to put the source diskette in drive A and press any key.

3. The source diskette is in drive A, so press any key. DOS reads from the system diskette, then prompts you to put the target diskette in drive A.

4. Put a blank diskette, formatted or unformatted, in drive A and press any key. If the new diskette isn't formatted, DOS formats it, then notifies you how many tracks, sectors, and sides it's copying and starts to copy the system to the new diskette. After copying the system diskette, DOS asks *Copy another diskette (Y/N)?*. Type *n*.

5. Now DOS compares the two diskettes to make sure the copy was accurate. It prompts you to *Insert FIRST diskette in drive A* and press any key.

6. Leave the new (French) diskette in drive A and press a key. DOS tells you how many tracks, sectors, and sides it's comparing, reads the files from the diskette, and prompts you to *Insert SECOND diskette in drive A* and press any key.

7. Put the original DOS system diskette in drive A and press a key. After comparing the diskettes, DOS displays *Compare OK* and asks *Compare another diskette? (Y/N)*. (If it displays a different message, start again at step 1.) Type *n*.

8. Now DOS prompts you to *Insert TARGET diskette in drive A* and press a key.

9. Put the new French-specific system diskette in drive A and press a key. To make sure it is correct, restart DOS by pressing Ctrl-Alt-Del, check whether the date is displayed in the day-month-year (not month-day-year) sequence, and see if the keyboard follows the French layout (press the Q and A keys to see if they are interchanged from the United States layout).

That's it. You have a system diskette configured for France.

CHAPTER

9

A TREE OF FILES

A s you have seen, when DOS formats a disk, one thing it does is create a directory that describes each of the files on the disk. The directory holds a fixed number of entries: 64 on a single-sided diskette, 112 on a double-sided diskette, 224 on a high-capacity diskette, and 512 or more on a fixed disk (the number varies with the size of the disk).

To make your computer filing system more flexible, DOS lets you create additional directories, called *subdirectories*, on a disk. The subdirectories divide the disk into different storage areas, each of which you can use as if it were a different disk.

To distinguish the main directory that DOS creates from the subdirectories that you create, the main directory is known as the *root directory* because, as you will see, a multi-level directory structure can grow from it.

As you add levels to your file structure, a block diagram would show it spreading from the root directory and branching to other directories, like a tree branches from its root. This type of file structure is often called a tree-structured file system, and is the reason for the name root directory. Despite this multi-level directory structure, you can still use a disk created with Version 1 of DOS, because the later versions interpret the Version 1 disk as one with a root directory only.

DEFINING A SUBDIRECTORY

A subdirectory is simply a file that contains directory entries; these entries are identical in form to the entries in the main directory, but there is no limit to the number of entries there can be in a subdirectory.

You name a subdirectory as you name any other file, but because the subdirectory defines other files, you cannot use the normal file commands to copy or erase a subdirectory. This chapter shows you how to use several commands that enable you to do the following:

• Create a subdirectory with the Make Directory command.

• Delete a subdirectory with the Remove Directory command.

- Change or display the current directory with the Change Directory command.

- Display all the directories on a disk with the Tree command.

- Tell DOS where to look for a command file, if it's not in the current directory, with the Path command.

Using these features of the DOS filing system, you can create and manage a computer filing system that is tailored to the way you work.

PREPARING FOR THE EXAMPLES

The examples in this chapter require one formatted diskette. To start, put the diskette in drive B (if you're using a fixed disk or have a one-drive system, put the diskette in the only diskette drive). If any files from earlier examples are stored on the diskette, erase them by typing the following (make certain you include the *b:,* or you will erase all the files on the current disk):

```
A>erase b:*.*
```

Note: If you're using a fixed disk, DOS asks you to make sure the correct diskette is in the drive:

```
Insert diskette for drive B: and strike
any key when ready
```

Press any key.

DOS then asks you to confirm that you want to erase all the files:

```
Are you sure (Y/N)?_
```

Before you respond, check the command you entered and be certain that you typed the drive letter (b:). If you didn't, press Ctrl-Break to cancel the Erase command, and re-enter the command correctly. If you did type the drive letter, respond *y.* Because a mistake here could cause the loss of valuable files, you must also press the Enter key before DOS carries out the command.

After you have erased the files, change the current drive to B by typing:

```
A>b:
```

This completes the preparation.

CREATING A MULTI-LEVEL FILE STRUCTURE

Suppose you work at a small company and provide services to two departments: Marketing and Engineering. You keep all your papers in a file drawer. You keep miscellaneous items in the front of the drawer, and dividers labeled MKT and ENG separate the parts where you store papers that relate to each department. Figure 9-1 shows how the file drawer might look.

Now suppose you start using a computer. You can set up your computer filing system to match your paper files by creating two subdirectories named MKT and ENG. You can store all your miscellaneous files—such as DOS command files—in the main, or root, directory of the disk, and you can store the files relating to each department in separate subdirectories. Figure 9-2 shows the filing cabinet and a block diagram of this corresponding DOS file structure.

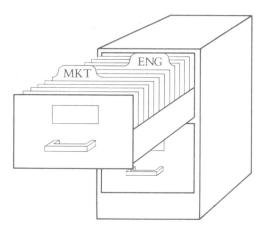

Figure 9-1. File drawer with dividers

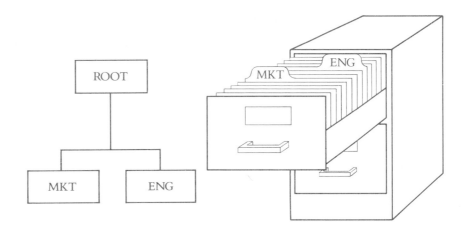

Figure 9-2. Two-level file systems

Creating a Subdirectory

The Make Directory (mkdir, or md) command creates a subdirectory. The only parameter you must include is the subdirectory name. The command is described later in more detail; for now, type the following to create two subdirectories named MKT and ENG:

```
B>mkdir mkt

B>mkdir eng
```

You can see the subdirectories you just created by displaying the entries in the root directory. Type:

```
B>dir
```

DOS shows two files, named MKT and ENG:

```
Volume in drive B has no label
Directory of  B:\

MKT           <DIR>      10-16-85    8:14a
ENG           <DIR>      10-16-85    8:14a
        2 File(s)     360448 bytes free
```

Note that the directory identifies the files as subdirectories by displaying <DIR> after their names.

The backslash (\) in the second line of the display is what DOS uses to refer to the root directory of a disk. You've seen the backslash in earlier directory displays; you'll see more of it and its uses in later examples.

Because MKT is a subdirectory, you can display its contents with the Directory command, just as you display the contents of the root directory. Type the following:

```
B>dir mkt
```

DOS displays the contents of MKT:

```
Volume in drive B has no label
Directory of  B:\MKT

.               <DIR>       10-16-85    8:14a
..              <DIR>       10-16-85    8:14a
        2 File(s)      360448 bytes free
```

Even though you just created it, MKT seems to contain subdirectories named . (one period) and .. (two periods). These really aren't subdirectories; they're abbreviations you use to refer to other directories. You'll see how these abbreviations are used a bit later.

The Path to a Directory

The second line of the preceding directory display tells you that you're looking at the directory of B:\MKT. The \ (backslash) refers to the root directory, and MKT is the name of the subdirectory whose contents you're displaying. Together, they are called the path name of the directory, or just the path, because they describe the path DOS follows through directories. The path names of the two subdirectories you created, \MKT and \ENG, tell DOS that the subdirectories are in the root directory.

You can also include a path name with a file name, to tell DOS where to find a file. The path name goes just before the file name (after the drive letter, if one is included) and is separated from the file name by a backslash. For example, if the subdirectory \MKT contained a file named BUDGET.JAN, the full path and file name would be \MKT\BUDGET.JAN.

The Current Directory

Just as DOS keeps track of the current drive, it also keeps track of the current directory. When you start DOS, the current drive is the drive from which the DOS programs were loaded; the current directory is the root directory of the current drive.

Just as you can change the current drive, you can change the current directory, so that you don't have to type the path name each time you want to work with a directory other than the current directory.

The Change Directory (chdir, or cd) command displays the name of, or changes, the current directory. If you enter the command with no parameters, it displays the name of the current directory. To see what the current directory is, type:

```
B>cd
```

The current directory is the root directory, so the response is short:

```
B:\
```

It tells you that any command you enter will apply to the root directory of the diskette in drive B. Change the current directory to the subdirectory named MKT by typing:

```
B>cd mkt
```

DOS acknowledges merely by displaying the system prompt, but display the current directory again by typing:

```
B>cd
```

DOS responds:

```
B:\MKT
```

Now any command you enter applies to the subdirectory MKT in the root directory. Type the Directory command again:

```
B>dir
```

DOS displays the entries in the subdirectory \MKT:

```
Volume in drive B has no label
Directory of  B:\MKT

.            <DIR>      10-16-85   8:14a
..           <DIR>      10-16-85   8:14a
        2 File(s)     360448 bytes free
```

This is the same display you saw earlier when you typed *dir mkt;* but this time you didn't have to name the subdirectory, because you had changed the current directory to \MKT.

Using Subdirectories

Your diskette now has the directory structure shown in Figure 9-2. You can use each of these directories as if it were a separate disk. The current directory is \MKT. Create a file in the *root* directory by typing the following lines:

```
B>copy con \sample.txt
This is a sample file.
^Z
        1 File(s) copied
```

Notice that you included the backslash to tell DOS to put the file in the root directory. You also use the backslash to display the contents of the root directory when it's not the current directory. Type the following:

```
B>dir \
```

Again DOS displays the entries in the root directory:

```
Volume in drive B has no label
Directory of  B:\

MKT          <DIR>      10-16-85   8:14a
ENG          <DIR>      10-16-85   8:14a
SAMPLE   TXT      24    10-16-85   8:17a
        3 File(s)     359424 bytes free
```

The root directory contains two subdirectories and the file you just created.

Copying from one directory to another

You can treat directories as if they were separate disks, so you can copy a file from one directory to another. Copy SAMPLE.TXT from the root directory to a file named ACCOUNT in the current directory (\MKT) by typing:

```
B>copy \sample.txt account
         1 File(s) copied
```

You included the path (the backslash, meaning the root directory) with SAMPLE.TXT to tell DOS where to find the file; you did not include a path for ACCOUNT, because you were putting it in the current directory. Now display the current directory by typing:

```
B>dir
 Volume in drive B has no label
 Directory of  B:\MKT

.               <DIR>       10-16-85    8:14a
..              <DIR>       10-16-85    8:14a
ACCOUNT             24  10-16-85    8:17a
         3 File(s)     358400 bytes free
```

The file is there. You can copy files from one directory to another as easily as you can copy them from one disk to another.

Just as DOS doesn't confuse two files with the same name on different disks, it doesn't confuse two files with the same name in different directories. DOS can tell the latter apart because their paths are dissimilar. You can demonstrate this by copying the file named ACCOUNT from \MKT to the subdirectory \ENG, giving it the same file name. Type the following:

```
B>copy account \eng
```

You didn't include the file name in the target directory because you want to give the copy the same name as the original. You can

assure yourself that the file was copied; display the directory of
\ENG by typing:

```
B>dir \eng

 Volume in drive B has no label
 Directory of  B:\ENG

.                <DIR>       10-16-85    8:14a
..               <DIR>       10-16-85    8:14a
ACCOUNT                  24  10-16-85    8:17a
         3 File(s)     357376 bytes free
```

You now have two files named ACCOUNT on the same disk;
but they are in two different subdirectories, and their different path
names make them as different to DOS as if you had given them
different file names.

Time Out for a Quick Review

Before completing your multi-level file structure, take a few
minutes to review the following definitions. They summarize the
terms and concepts introduced in the preceding examples.

Directory entry: A description of a file that includes the name,
extension, and size of the file, and the date and time it was created
or last updated.

Directory: A list of directory entries. You'll also see it used with
a sense of place: "Which directory am I in?"

Root directory: The list of directory entries that DOS creates and
maintains on each disk, just as in earlier versions of DOS. It is called
the root directory (or simply the root) because the entire directory
structure on the disk grows from it. Because the root has no name,
it is represented by a backslash (\).

Subdirectory: A file that contains directory entries. Like directory, it is also sometimes used with a sense of place: "Which
subdirectory did I put that file in?"

Path name: The list of directory names that defines the path to a
subdirectory. The directory names are separated by a backslash (\).

The root directory is represented by a backslash at the beginning of the path. If a file name is included, it is separated from the path name by a backslash.

Current directory: The directory that DOS assumes unless you specify another in a command. The current directory is similar in concept and effect to the current drive.

Adding More Levels to Your File Structure

The subdirectories you create can contain any type of file, including other subdirectories. Like putting dividers between dividers in a file drawer, this further structuring narrows the subject of a storage area. Suppose you do the following type of work for the Marketing and Engineering departments:

MARKETING	ENGINEERING
Word processing	Word processing
Budgets	Budgets
Customer lists	Project scheduling
Sales forecasts	

You decide to set up your file structure to match your work. The following list shows the additional subdirectories you could create to match your computer files to the work you do (MKT and ENG are the departmental subdirectories you created earlier):

MKT	ENG
WP	WP
BUDGET	BUDGET
CUSTOMER	SCHEDULE
SALES	

You would then have created the file structure shown on the next page in Figure 9-3.

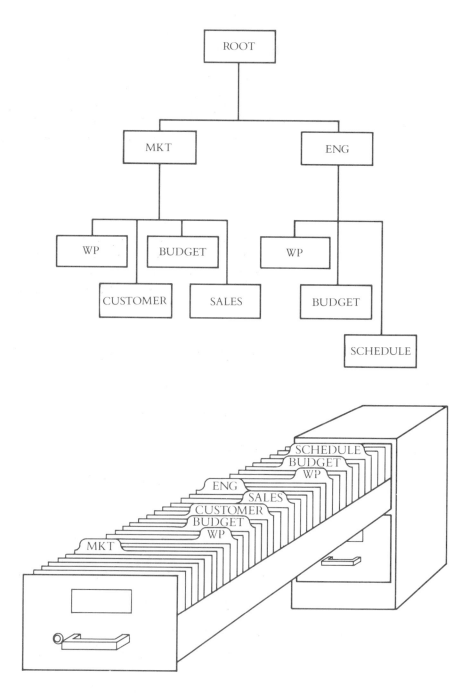

Figure 9-3. Three-level file systems

mkdir
<drive><path>

Making a Subdirectory—
The MKDIR Command

As you saw earlier, the Make Directory (mkdir, or md) command creates a subdirectory. The Make Directory command has two parameters:

mkdir <drive><path>

<drive> is the letter, followed by a colon, of the drive that contains the disk on which the subdirectory is to be created (such as B:). If you omit <drive>, DOS creates the subdirectory on the disk in the current drive.

<path> is the path name of the directory in which the subdirectory is to be created. If you omit <path>, the subdirectory is created in the current directory.

The current directory is \MKT. Check this by typing:

```
B>cd
```

DOS shows you the current directory:

```
B:\MKT
```

For the example in this chapter, you want four subdirectories in \MKT. They are: WP, BUDGET, CUSTOMER, and SALES. Type the following Make Directory commands to create the subdirectories:

```
B>md wp
```

```
B>md budget
```

```
B>md customer
```

```
B>md sales
```

Display the directory by typing:

```
B>dir

Volume in drive B has no label
Directory of  B:\MKT

.               <DIR>       10-16-85   8:14a
..              <DIR>       10-16-85   8:14a
ACCOUNT            24       10-16-85   8:17a
WP              <DIR>       10-16-85   8:21a
BUDGET          <DIR>       10-16-85   8:21a
CUSTOMER        <DIR>       10-16-85   8:21a
SALES           <DIR>       10-16-85   8:21a
        7 File(s)       353280 bytes free
```

The directory shows the file you copied a few minutes ago (ACCOUNT) and the four subdirectories you just created.

Your file structure calls for subdirectories named WP and BUDGET in both \MKT and \ENG. Remember, DOS can distinguish between \MKT\WP and \ENG\WP, \MKT\BUDGET and \ENG\BUDGET, because their paths are different.

To create the subdirectory \ENG\WP, type:

```
B>md \eng\wp
```

You included the path (\ENG) because the current directory is \MKT. The Make Directory command doesn't change the current directory, so it's still \MKT, but you can verify that the subdirectory \ENG\WP was created by displaying the contents of \ENG. Include the path here, too, by typing:

```
B>dir \eng

Volume in drive B has no label
Directory of  B:\ENG

.               <DIR>       10-16-85   8:14a
..              <DIR>       10-16-85   8:14a
ACCOUNT            24       10-16-85   8:17a
WP              <DIR>       10-16-85   8:22a
        4 File(s)       352256 bytes free
```

Now you're going to start moving around from subdirectory to subdirectory, so before creating the last two subdirectories in \ENG, here's a closer look at your navigator, the Change Directory command.

chdir **<drive><path>**

Changing the Current Directory — The CHDIR Command

You have already used the Change Directory (chdir, or cd) command to change and display the current directory. The Change Directory command has two parameters:

chdir <drive><path>

<drive> is the letter, followed by a colon, of the drive that contains the disk on which the current directory is to be changed (such as B:). If you omit <drive>, DOS changes the current directory on the disk in the current drive.

<path> is the path name of the directory that is to become the current directory. If you omit <path>, DOS displays the current directory on <drive>.

If you omit both <drive> and <path> (enter the command with no parameters), DOS displays the current directory of the disk in the current drive.

Changing the system prompt

Although the Change Directory command lets you quickly check the current directory, there is a way to avoid having to check it at all. The system prompt shows the current drive, but you can change it to display other information, such as the current directory.

The Prompt command, which you met briefly in Chapter 3, is described more fully in Chapter 17, "Tailoring Your System." But for now, type the following (include a blank at the end of the line, just before you press the Enter key):

```
B>prompt Current Directory is $p$_Command: <Enter>
```

Now the system prompt tells you the current drive and the current directory:

```
Current Directory is B:\MKT
Command: _
```

You could restore the system prompt to its more familiar form (the letter of the current drive followed by >) by entering the Prompt command with no parameters (prompt), but why not leave it this way for the rest of this chapter? The prompt takes up a bit more space, but it helps you keep track of where you are.

Using the subdirectory markers

Remember those markers listed in each subdirectory? They're designed to let you move quickly up and down a directory structure, particularly when several levels make the path names long.

The .. represents the directory that contains the current directory (sometimes called the parent of the current directory). The current directory is \MKT; to move the current directory up (toward the root directory) one level, type:

```
Current Directory is B:\MKT
Command: cd ..

Current Directory is B:\
Command: _
```

Now the system prompt shows you the current directory; as you can see, it has changed to the root directory, which is one level above \MKT.

To complete your file structure, you need two more subdirectories in \ENG. Change the current directory to \ENG and create \ENG\BUDGET and \ENG\SCHEDULE by typing the following:

```
Current Directory is B:\
Command: cd eng

Current Directory is B:\ENG
Command: md budget

Current Directory is B:\ENG
Command: md schedule
```

This completes the structure of your multi-level file system. You have nine subdirectories, plus the root directory, any of which you can use as if it were a separate disk. To show you how easy it is, the next few examples have you put sample files in several of the subdirectories. Figure 9-4 shows how your final file system will look, including the path names of all directories (above the boxes) and the names of the files you'll add (inside the shaded boxes).

```
                                  \
                         ┌──────────────────┐
                         │ MKT  <DIR>       │
                         │ ENG  <DIR>       │
                         │ SAMPLE.TXT       │
                         └──────────────────┘
```

```
           \MKT                                      \ENG
  ┌──────────────────────┐              ┌──────────────────────┐
  │ WP          <DIR>     │              │ WP           <DIR>    │
  │ BUDGET      <DIR>     │              │ BUDGET       <DIR>    │
  │ CUSTOMER <DIR>        │              │ SCHEDULE <DIR>        │
  │ SALES       <DIR>     │              │ ACCOUNT               │
  │ ACCOUNT               │              └──────────────────────┘
  └──────────────────────┘
```

```
   \MKT\WP            \MKT\BUDGET              \ENG\WP
  ┌────────────┐     ┌────────────┐          ┌────────────┐
  │ LET1.DOC   │     │            │          │ LET1.DOC   │
  │ LET2.DOC   │     │ BGT1.PLN   │          │ LET2.DOC   │
  │ LET3.DOC   │     │ BGT2.PLN   │          │ LET3.DOC   │
  │ RPT1.DOC   │     │ BGT3.PLN   │          │            │
  │ RPT2.DOC   │     │            │          └────────────┘
  │ RPT3.DOC   │     └────────────┘
  │ LET1.STY   │        \MKT\CUSTOMER            \ENG\BUDGET
  │ LET2.STY   │      ┌────────────┐          ┌────────────┐
  │ LET3.STY   │      │            │          │            │
  └────────────┘      │            │          │            │
                      │            │          │            │
                      └────────────┘          └────────────┘
                         \MKT\SALES               \ENG\SCHEDULE
                      ┌────────────┐          ┌────────────┐
                      │            │          │            │
                      │            │          │            │
                      └────────────┘          └────────────┘
```

Figure 9-4. Two-department file structure

To create the sample files in \ENG\WP, first change the current directory to \ENG\WP and copy ACCOUNT from \ENG, naming it LET1.DOC, by typing the following:

```
Current Directory is B:\ENG
Command: cd wp

Current Directory is B:\ENG\WP
Command: copy \eng\account let1.doc
         1 File(s) copied
```

Note that you must use \ENG in the command, even though \ENG\WP is a subdirectory of \ENG.

Now copy LET1.DOC twice, to create LET2.DOC and LET3.DOC, and display the directory by typing:

```
Current Directory is B:\ENG\WP
Command: copy let1.doc let2.doc
         1 File(s) copied

Current Directory is B:\ENG\WP
Command: copy let1.doc let3.doc
         1 File(s) copied

Current Directory is B:\ENG\WP
Command: dir

 Volume in drive B has no label
 Directory of  B:\ENG\WP

 .            <DIR>       10-16-85    8:22a
 ..           <DIR>       10-16-85    8:22a
 LET1    DOC        24    10-16-85    8:17a
 LET2    DOC        24    10-16-85    8:17a
 LET3    DOC        24    10-16-85    8:17a
         5 File(s)    347136 bytes free
```

From this subdirectory, you can copy all three of these files to \MKT\WP with one command. Type the following:

```
Current Directory is B:\ENG\WP
Command: copy *.* \mkt\wp
```

DOS lists the source files as it copies them:

```
LET1.DOC
LET2.DOC
LET3.DOC
         3 File(s) copied
```

These files could be word-processing files that contain letters. Now create three additional files in \MKT\WP that could represent word-processing files that contain reports. First, change the directory to \MKT\WP, then copy the three files whose names begin with LET, changing their names so they begin with RPT. Type the following:

```
Current Directory is B:\ENG\WP
Command: cd \mkt\wp

Current Directory is B:\MKT\WP
Command: copy let?.doc rpt?.doc
```

DOS lists the source files as it makes the copies:

```
LET1.DOC
LET2.DOC
LET3.DOC
        3 File(s) copied
```

To complete the files in this subdirectory, copy the same three files again, this time changing their extension to STY, which could identify word-processing files that contain style sheets for formatting and printing documents. Type the following:

```
Current Directory is B:\MKT\WP
Command: copy let?.doc let?.sty
```

Now display the directory to verify that all nine files are there by typing:

```
Current Directory is B:\MKT\WP
Command: dir

 Volume in drive B has no label
 Directory of  B:\MKT\WP

.              <DIR>      10-16-85    8:21a
..             <DIR>      10-16-85    8:21a
LET1     DOC       24     10-16-85    8:17a
LET2     DOC       24     10-16-85    8:17a
LET3     DOC       24     10-16-85    8:17a
RPT1     DOC       24     10-16-85    8:17a
RPT2     DOC       24     10-16-85    8:17a
RPT3     DOC       24     10-16-85    8:17a
LET1     STY       24     10-16-85    8:17a
LET2     STY       24     10-16-85    8:17a
LET3     STY       24     10-16-85    8:17a
       11 File(s)      337920 bytes free
```

To complete the file system, you need three files in
\MKT\BUDGET named BGT1.PLN, BGT2.PLN, and BGT3.PLN.
Use the Copy command to copy the files and change their
names by typing the following:

```
Current Directory is B:\MKT\WP
Command: copy let?.doc \mkt\budget\bgt?.pln
```

DOS lists the source files as it makes the copies:

```
LET1.DOC
LET2.DOC
LET3.DOC
        3 File(s) copied
```

Your file system now has the directories and files shown in
Figure 9-4.

Removing a Subdirectory — The RMDIR Command

rmdir
<drive><path>

As you work with a multi-level filing system, you may find
that you no longer need a particular subdirectory, or that you want
to combine the files from several subdirectories into one and then
delete the unneeded subdirectories from your file structure. The
Remove Directory (rmdir, or rd) command removes a subdirectory.
A subdirectory cannot be removed if it contains any files or subdirectories.

The Remove Directory command has two parameters:

rmdir <drive><path>

<drive> is the letter, followed by a colon, of the drive that
contains the disk with the subdirectory to be removed. You can
omit <drive> if the subdirectory is on the disk in the current drive.

<path> is the path name of the subdirectory to be removed.
You must specify <path> because DOS will not remove the current
directory.

Suppose you decide you don't need the subdirectory \ENG\WP.
Tell DOS to remove it by typing:

```
Current Directory is B:\MKT\WP
Command: rd \eng\wp
```

DOS responds *Invalid path, not directory, or directory not empty* because \ENG\WP isn't empty: You put three files in it, LET1.DOC, LET2.DOC, and LET3.DOC. You don't need them any longer, so you can erase them and then remove the directory.

This example points out the difference in the ways you handle files and subdirectories. As you saw in earlier chapters, you use the Erase command to erase a file from a disk. To remove a directory, however, you use the Remove Directory command.

In the next example, you will erase three files with the Erase command, and then remove a directory with the Remove Directory command. First, change the current directory to \ENG and delete the files with the Erase command by typing:

```
Current Directory is B:\MKT\WP
Command: cd \eng

Current Directory is B:\ENG
Command: erase wp\*.doc
```

You changed the current directory to \ENG, rather than to \ENG\WP, because DOS won't remove the current directory.

Now that \ENG\WP is empty, enter the Remove Directory command and verify the change by displaying the directory. Type the following:

```
Current Directory is B:\ENG
Command: rd wp

Current Directory is B:\ENG
Command: dir

 Volume in drive B has no label
 Directory of  B:\ENG

 .             <DIR>      10-16-85   8:14a
 ..            <DIR>      10-16-85   8:14a
 ACCOUNT          24      10-16-85   8:17a
 BUDGET        <DIR>      10-16-85   8:24a
 SCHEDULE      <DIR>      10-16-85   8:24a
         5 File(s)    338944 bytes free
```

The subdirectory \ENG\WP is gone.

If you want to remove a directory but need some of the files it contains, copy the files you need to another subdirectory, then erase all the files and remove the directory.

Displaying the Directory Structure— The TREE Command

tree <drive> /F

Note: The Tree command is in IBM's version of MS-DOS. If you are not using an IBM personal computer, skip to the heading "The Path to a Command."

If you create a file structure with several levels, you may not remember exactly what subdirectories you created or exactly where they are. You could display the contents of each directory and subdirectory on the disk to find the files marked <DIR>, but there's a quicker way.

The Tree command displays the path of each subdirectory on a disk and includes an option that lets you tell DOS to display the name of each file in each subdirectory, for a complete list of everything on the disk.

The Tree command has two parameters:

tree <drive> /F

<drive> is the letter, followed by a colon, of the drive containing the disk whose directory structure is to be displayed (such as B:). If you omit <drive>, DOS displays the directory structure of the disk in the current drive.

/F displays the name of each file in the root directory and each subdirectory. This can be a long list, especially for a fixed disk.

To display the directory structure of the diskette in drive B (the current drive), type:

```
Current Directory is B:\ENG
Command: tree
```

DOS responds:

```
Bad command or file name

Current Directory is B:\ENG
Command: _
```

What happened? DOS looked for a command file named TREE in the current directory (\ENG), and didn't find it because the DOS command files are in the root directory of the diskette in drive A

(or drive C if you are using a fixed disk). You could change the current drive, use the command, then change the drive back, but that could get inconvenient. DOS gives you a solution: the Path command.

The Path to a Command

path <drive><path> ;

In a multi-level filing system, you'll probably change the current directory as you use different files in the subdirectories. But you'll use command files, too, such as the external DOS commands and application programs. When you type a command, DOS looks for the command file in the current directory; if you have changed the current directory to a subdirectory, chances are it doesn't contain the command files you need.

The Path command lets you tell DOS where to look for a command file if it's not in the current directory. You can name one or more directories—the root directory or any subdirectory—on any disk drive. This command lets you work in any subdirectory you want and still be able to use any command file.

The Path command has three parameters:

path <drive><path> ;

<drive> is the letter, followed by a colon, of the drive with the disk that contains the command files (such as B:). If you omit <drive>, DOS looks in the directory specified by <path> on the current drive.

<path> is the path name of the directory that contains the command files.

The semicolon, used without <drive> or <path>, cancels any command paths you may have defined.

You can specify several command paths in one command, separating them with semicolons. If you enter the command with no parameters (just type the word *path*), DOS displays the command paths you have defined.

This example uses the Tree command described in the previous section. If your version of DOS does not have the Tree command, go on to the Chapter Summary.

If you're using diskettes, tell DOS to look in the root directory of drive A for command files by typing:

```
Current Directory is B:\ENG
Command: path a:\
```

If you're using a fixed disk, tell DOS to look in the root directory of drive C for command files by typing:

```
Current Directory is B:\ENG
Command: path c:\
```

Enter the Tree command again to display the directory structure of the diskette in the current drive; the report is long and part of it will scroll off the screen, but you're going to print it in a moment so just let it go. Type the following:

```
Current Directory is B:\ENG
Command: tree
```

Now, DOS finds the command file. The last few lines of the report are on the screen; here is the complete report (some blank lines you see on-screen have been omitted here):

```
DIRECTORY PATH LISTING

Path: \MKT
Sub-directories:   WP
                   BUDGET
                   CUSTOMER
                   SALES

Path: \MKT\WP
Sub-directories:   None

Path: \MKT\BUDGET
Sub-directories:   None

Path: \MKT\CUSTOMER
Sub-directories:   None

Path: \MKT\SALES
Sub-directories:   None

Path: \ENG
Sub-directories:   BUDGET
                   SCHEDULE
```

```
Path: \ENG\BUDGET
Sub-directories:  None

Path: \ENG\SCHEDULE
Sub-directories:  None
```

As the description of the Tree command pointed out, the /F option tells DOS to include in the report the name of each file in each subdirectory. A printed copy of such a report can be helpful, especially if your filing system has several levels.

Using a technique described in Chapter 14, "Taking Control of Your System," you can send the output of a command to the printer. Try it; make sure your printer is turned on and type the following (notice that a slash, not a backslash, precedes the f):

```
Current Directory is B:\ENG
Command: tree /f > prn
```

This printed guide to your filing system can help you keep track of the files and subdirectories and use the system more effectively. If you're going to continue using your system, type the following to restore the system prompt:

```
Current Directory is \ENG
Command: prompt

B>_
```

CHAPTER SUMMARY

Although this chapter introduced several new terms and concepts, it doesn't take many commands to set up a multi-level file system. The structure shown in Figure 9-3, for example, required only the following 11 commands (don't enter them, this list is just to show you the commands you entered):

md mkt	md sales
md eng	md \eng\wp
cd mkt	cd \eng
md wp	md budget
md budget	md schedule
md customer	

You might not create a file structure with this many levels on a diskette. As you noticed, subdirectories require a great deal of work from the diskette drive. But you might find that two or three subdirectories reduce the number of diskettes you use, or let you use your system more efficiently. The examples in this chapter showed you how to use all the commands you need to create and manage a multi-level filing system.

If you're using a fixed disk, save the diskette that contains the file system you created in this chapter. You'll use it to copy sample files in the next chapter, "Managing Your Fixed Disk."

CHAPTER
10
MANAGING YOUR FIXED DISK

The fixed disk holds 10 or 20 million bytes of information and operates much more quickly than a diskette. As its name implies, you don't remove the disk; it is permanently fixed in the drive. Like a diskette, a fixed disk stores data in tracks and sectors. In this case, however, data is stored on several coated metal, rather than plastic, disks that are enclosed in a nonremovable case. The fixed disk commonly used with the IBM Personal Computer XT contains four separate disks, each of which has 306 tracks of 17 sectors. The total capacity of this fixed disk is 20,808 sectors, or 10,653,696 bytes—commonly referred to as 10 megabytes. The fixed disk normally installed in the IBM Personal Computer AT uses a similar arrangement of several disks, but has a total capacity of 20 megabytes.

Managing your fixed disk consists primarily of two tasks: setting up a filing system that lets you take advantage of the disk's capacity without losing track of all the files, and backing up the files to protect yourself against loss of data in the event your fixed disk is inadvertently erased or damaged.

Setting up a multi-level filing system was covered in the previous chapter. This chapter shows you how to back up and restore files. The Volume and Label commands described in Chapter 6, "Managing Your Diskettes," can also be used with a fixed disk. If you don't have a fixed disk, you can go to Chapter 11, "Creating and Editing Files of Text."

In most ways, you treat a fixed disk as if it were a large diskette, using the DOS file commands to copy, erase, rename, and otherwise work with your files. But two diskette commands—Diskcopy and Diskcomp—don't work with the fixed disk because they are specifically designed to work only with entire diskettes.

Warning: It's possible to erase all the files on the fixed disk by inadvertently formatting it. A way to protect yourself against this is described under "Renaming the Format Command" in Chapter 17, "Tailoring Your System."

The Backup and Restore commands let you develop a backup procedure that matches your directory structure and work flow. Although they work with fixed disks or diskettes, they are intended primarily to manage the large number of files possible on a fixed

disk. This chapter suggests some guidelines to simplify the job of backing up files from your fixed disk, and shows you how to:

- Back up files from one disk to another with the Backup command.

- Restore files from a backup disk with the Restore command.

PUTTING APPLICATION PROGRAMS ON THE FIXED DISK

The examples in this chapter use part of the directory structure and sample data files you created in the previous chapter. When you actually set up a directory structure, you'll undoubtedly want to copy the command and data files of your application programs onto the fixed disk. Depending on how you set up your directories and how many application programs you use, you might put the application programs in the root directory, another subdirectory, or perhaps in a separate subdirectory for each application.

Some application programs are copy protected and cannot be copied to the fixed disk. To use such an application program, you put the program diskette in drive A and use the Path command to tell DOS to look for command files on drive A, in addition to using the fixed disk. Check each application program's documentation for instructions on using the program with a fixed disk.

PREPARING FOR THE EXAMPLES

Note: If you haven't yet prepared your fixed disk, turn to Appendix A and follow the instructions there before continuing.

The examples in this chapter require a formatted diskette, plus the diskette you used for the examples in the previous chapter.

If your system isn't running, turn it on and set the time and date as usual.

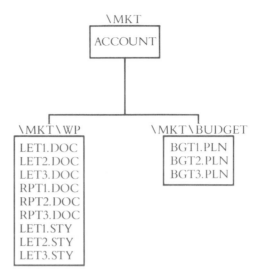

Figure 10-1. Subdirectories and files for fixed-disk examples

The examples in this chapter require the sample subdirectories and files in Figure 10-1. You will create these on the fixed disk.

Creating the Directories

To create the subdirectories, type the following:

```
C>md mkt
C>md mkt\wp
C>md mkt\budget
```

You probably recognize these as part of the file structure you created in the previous chapter. Now, however, you are creating these subdirectories on your fixed disk.

Copying the Files

The files you need are on the diskette you used for the examples in the previous chapter. To copy the files to the fixed disk, put the

diskette in the diskette drive and type the following (press any key when DOS prompts you for the diskette for drive A):

```
C>copy a:\mkt\account \mkt

Insert diskette for drive A: and strike
any key when ready
        1 File(s) copied

C>copy a:\mkt\wp\*.* \mkt\wp
A:\MKT\WP\LET1.DOC
A:\MKT\WP\LET2.DOC
A:\MKT\WP\LET3.DOC
A:\MKT\WP\RPT1.DOC
A:\MKT\WP\RPT2.DOC
A:\MKT\WP\RPT3.DOC
A:\MKT\WP\LET1.STY
A:\MKT\WP\LET2.STY
A:\MKT\WP\LET3.STY
        9 File(s) copied

C>copy a:\mkt\budget\*.* \mkt\budget
A:\MKT\BUDGET\BGT1.PLN
A:\MKT\BUDGET\BGT2.PLN
A:\MKT\BUDGET\BGT3.PLN
        3 File(s) copied
```

This completes the preparation.

DEVELOPING A BACKUP PROCEDURE

It could take a drawerful of diskettes to back up all the files on a fixed disk: If your average file were 10,000 bytes long (about 6½ double-spaced, typed pages), a full 10-megabyte fixed disk would have more than 1000 files, and you would need almost 30 double-sided diskettes to back them all up. A full 20-megabyte fixed disk could require almost 60 double-sided diskettes, and about a third as many high-capacity diskettes.

But you don't have to back up all your files. You needn't back up program files, for example, because you've already got the original DOS and application-program diskettes. Some data files, such as a spelling dictionary, don't usually change, so it isn't necessary to back them up, either.

How often you back up your other data files, such as word-processed documents and spreadsheets, depends on how often they change. Spreadsheets may change often while the budget is being prepared, for example, but remain unchanged the rest of the year.

Your backup procedures depend on how you use your computer. But no matter how you decide to back up your files, be sure to do so regularly. A system failure can happen, but if you back up your files regularly, such a failure will be an inconvenience, rather than a disaster.

BACKING UP FILES

backup
<path><filename>
<drive> /A /S /M /D:
<date>

The Backup command lets you select files on the basis of their path name, their file name, whether they have been changed since the last backup, or whether they have been changed since a particular date. The options can be combined, so you can back up files in just about any way you like.

The Backup command has seven parameters:

backup <path><filename> <drive> /A /S /M /D:<date>

<path> is the path name of the directory from which files are to be backed up. If you don't specify <path>, DOS backs up files from the current directory.

<filename> is the name of the file to be backed up. You can use wildcard characters to back up a set of files. If you don't specify <filename>, DOS backs up all files.

<drive> is the letter, followed by a colon, of the drive that contains the diskette that receives the backup files (such as A:). You must specify <drive>.

/A adds the backup files to the backup diskette, rather than erasing all files on the backup diskette, as the command usually does, before making the backup copies.

/S backs up files from all subdirectories.

/M backs up only the files that have been modified since the last backup.

/D:<date> backs up all files that have changed since <date>. Enter <date> just as you would for the Date command (numbers that represent the month, date, and year, separated by hyphens, such as 10-16-85). You can combine the /A, /S, /M, and /D:<date> options in one Backup command.

If you're using a network or other multi-user DOS system and the Backup command responds *Not able to backup at this time,* someone else is using the file. Try again later.

Backing Up All the Files in a Directory

The simplest way to back up files is by directory. You back up all files in a directory by entering the Backup command, followed by the path of the directory and the letter of the diskette drive that contains the backup diskette. To back up all the files in \MKT\BUDGET for example, type the following:

```
C>backup \mkt\budget a:
```

DOS beeps and displays a warning:

```
Insert backup diskette 01 in drive A:

Warning! Files in the target drive
A:\ root directory will be erased
Strike any key when ready
```

If you don't use the /A option, DOS erases any files on the backup diskette before it makes the backup copies. This warning gives you a chance to make sure the right diskette is in the drive. Put your formatted blank diskette in drive A and press any key. DOS displays the name of each file as it makes the copies:

```
*** Backing up files to drive A: ***
Diskette Number: 01

\MKT\BUDGET\BGT1.PLN
\MKT\BUDGET\BGT2.PLN
\MKT\BUDGET\BGT3.PLN
```

The directory of the backup diskette shows one file you might not expect. Type the following:

```
C>dir a:

 Volume in drive A has no label
 Directory of  A:\

BACKUPID @@@      128  10-16-85  3:19p
BGT1    PLN      152  10-16-85  8:17a
BGT2    PLN      152  10-16-85  8:17a
BGT3    PLN      152  10-16-85  8:17a
         4 File(s)   358400 bytes free
```

BACKUPID.@@@ is a small file that DOS stores on a backup diskette to identify it. Also, note that the files you backed up are larger than the originals on the fixed disk; confirm this by typing:

```
C>dir \mkt\budget

 Volume in drive C is FIXEDDISK
 Directory of  C:\mkt\budget

.             <DIR>       10-17-85 12:11p
..            <DIR>       10-17-85 12:11p
BGT1    PLN       24  10-16-85  8:17a
BGT2    PLN       24  10-16-85  8:17a
BGT3    PLN       24  10-16-85  8:17a
         5 File(s)   9658400 bytes free
```

DOS adds 128 bytes at the beginning of each backup file. This addition contains the path and file name of the file that was backed up, and is used by the Restore command when it restores files to the fixed disk. The Restore command deletes the path and file-name information, so the restored version of the file is identical to the one you originally backed up. You'll work with the Restore command later in the chapter.

If a Backup command fills the diskette before backing up all the files you specified, DOS prompts you to put in another diskette. It displays the same warning, but refers to the second diskette as BACKUP DISKETTE 02. If another diskette is required, DOS prompts again, increasing the diskette number each time.

If you were actually backing up files, you would label the diskette you just used with the contents and date and store it away in a safe place.

Backing Up All Subdirectories

You can back up the files in a directory and all its subdirectories with the /S option. For example, to back up all the files in \MKT and its subdirectories (\MKT\WP and \MKT\BUDGET) on drive C, specify \MKT as the path and include the /S parameter by typing the following (be sure to use the backslash in \MKT, but use the forward slash in /S):

```
C>backup \mkt a: /s
```

Again, DOS displays the warning; press any key to start the backup. DOS displays the file names as it makes the copies:

```
*** Backing up files to drive A: ***
Diskette Number: 01

\MKT\ACCOUNT
\MKT\WP\LET1.DOC
\MKT\WP\LET2.DOC
\MKT\WP\LET3.DOC
\MKT\WP\RPT1.DOC
\MKT\WP\RPT2.DOC
\MKT\WP\RPT3.DOC
\MKT\WP\LET1.STY
\MKT\WP\LET2.STY
\MKT\WP\LET3.STY
\MKT\BUDGET\BGT1.PLN
\MKT\BUDGET\BGT2.PLN
\MKT\BUDGET\BGT3.PLN
```

This backup diskette contains all your marketing files, not just the files from one of the subdirectories. Note that you again backed up BGT1.PLN, BGT2.PLN, and BGT3.PLN, even though your previous Backup command applied to those files. As the warning indicated, your prior backups were erased.

Backing Up Specific Files

You can back up specific files by including a file name with the Backup command. A word-processing directory, for example, might contain both documents, which change frequently, and style sheets, which seldom change. You would back up the documents much more frequently than you would the style sheets. Type the following to change the current directory to \MKT\WP and back up only the documents (files with an extension of DOC):

```
C>cd \mkt\wp
C>backup *.doc a:
```

DOS displays its usual warning, but wait a moment before you press any key to back up the files. It's good practice to store a printed list of the files on a backup diskette along with the diskette itself. That's easy; make sure your printer is on, and press Ctrl-PrtSc to start simultaneous printing.

Now press any key to start the backup. As usual, DOS displays the file names as it backs them up, but this time it prints the file names, too:

```
*** Backing up files to drive A: ***
Diskette Number: 01

\WP\MKT\LET1.DOC
\WP\MKT\LET2.DOC
\WP\MKT\LET3.DOC
\WP\MKT\RPT1.DOC
\WP\MKT\RPT2.DOC
\WP\MKT\RPT3.DOC
```

The files with an extension of STY were not backed up because you specified only those with an extension of DOC.

You can store the printed list with the backup diskette. Remember to press Ctrl-PrtSc again to stop simultaneous printing.

Backing Up Only Files That Have Changed

As your files increase, you may want to be even more selective about the ones you back up. For example, a word-processing directory might contain hundreds of documents; backing them all up could take quite a bit of time and several backup diskettes.

Two options of the Backup command let you back up only the files that have changed since a directory was last backed up, or only the files that have changed since a particular date.

Selecting files that have changed since the last backup

The /M (*Modify*) option of the Backup command backs up only files that have changed since the directory was last backed up. To see this, you need a file that has changed since you backed up \MKT\WP in the last example. Create a short file by copying from the console:

```
C>copy con new.doc
This file has changed
since the last backup.
^Z
          1 File(s) copied
```

Now tell DOS to back up only the files with an extension of DOC that have changed since the directory was last backed up:

```
C>backup *.doc a: /m
```

DOS beeps its usual warning and, when you press a key, displays the files backed up:

```
*** Backing up files to drive A: ***
Diskette Number: 01

\MKT\WP\NEW.DOC
```

Only the new file is backed up.

Selecting files that have changed since a particular date

The /D:<date> option backs up only those files that have changed since a particular date. To see this, you'll need a file with a different date. Change the system date with the Date command. Type the following:

```
C>date
Current date is Tue 10-16-1985
Enter new date (mm-dd-yy): 1-1-90
```

Now create a file named DATE.DOC by copying from the console:

```
C>copy con date.doc
This file was last changed
on 1-1-90.
^Z
        1 File(s) copied
```

Use the /D:<date> option to back up the files that have changed since December 31, 1989 by typing:

```
C>backup *.doc a: /d:12-31-89
```

After the warning, DOS displays the file it backs up:

```
*** Backing up files to drive A: ***
Diskette Number: 01

\MKT\WP\DATE.DOC
```

Only the file changed after the date you specified is backed up.

Adding Files to a Backup Diskette

Each form of the Backup command you have used so far starts by erasing any files on the backup diskette. There may be times, however, when you would like to back up files from several different directories on one diskette, or add a file or two to an existing backup diskette. The /A option adds a file to a backup diskette.

Your backup diskette now contains \MKT\WP\DATE.DOC. To back up the files in \MKT\BUDGET, adding them to the backup diskette, type the following:

```
C>backup \mkt\budget a: /a
```

This time DOS doesn't need to warn you that it's going to erase any files from the backup diskette, so it simply starts backing up the files and displaying their names:

```
*** Backing up files to drive A: ***
Diskette Number: 01

\MKT\BUDGET\BGT1.PLN
\MKT\BUDGET\BGT2.PLN
\MKT\BUDGET\BGT3.PLN
```

If your backup procedure involves periodically backing up a few files from several different directories, you can use the /A option to put all the backup files on one diskette.

A word of caution about this technique: If a file you add to a backup diskette has the same name and extension as a file already on the diskette, DOS changes the extension of the added file to @01, regardless of what it was before.

To see this, back up \MKT\WP\DATE.DOC again, this time using the /A option to add it. Type the following:

```
C>backup date.doc a: /a

*** Backing up files to drive A: ***
Diskette Number: 01

\MKT\WP\DATE.DOC
```

Now check the directory of the backup diskette:

```
C>dir a:

 Volume in drive A has no label
 Directory of  A:\

BACKUPID @@@       128    1-01-90   3:56p
DATE     DOC       168    1-01-90   3:55p
BGT1     PLN       152   10-16-85   8:17a
BGT2     PLN       152   10-16-85   8:17a
BGT3     PLN       152   10-16-85   8:17a
DATE     @01       168    1-01-90   3:55p
         6 File(s)     356352 bytes free
```

If you back up the file again, DOS changes the extension of the new backup to @02, and so on. To restore a file with such an altered extension, you must delete or rename the earlier version, change the altered extension back to its original form, and then restore the file. This is the only situation in which you should change anything on a backup diskette. In other instances, erasing or renaming files on a backup diskette can keep DOS from being able to restore the files.

Also, if files in different directories have the same name and extension, you should back them up to separate diskettes instead of combining them on the same backup diskette.

RESTORING FILES
TO THE FIXED DISK

**restore <drive>
<path><filename>
/S /P**

     It's easy to restore a file from a backup diskette to the fixed disk. Simply put the backup diskette in the diskette drive and type the Restore command, specifying the name of the file to be restored. The Restore command needs the path and file-name information added to files by the Backup command, so you can only restore files that were backed up with the Backup command.

     The Restore command has five parameters:

restore <drive> <path><filename> /S /P

     <drive> is the letter, followed by a colon, of the drive that contains the backup diskette (such as A:). You must include <drive>.

     <path> is the path name of the directory to which the file is to be restored. If you omit <path>, the file is restored to the current directory.

     <filename> is the name of the file to be restored. If you don't specify <filename>, all files backed up from the directory indicated by <path> are restored. You can use wildcard characters to restore a set of files. You must specify either <path> or <filename>.

     /S restores files to all subdirectories.

     /P tells DOS to prompt you for confirmation before restoring files that have changed since they were last backed up.

     If you're using a network or other multi-user DOS system and the Restore command responds *Not able to restore at this time,* someone else is using the current version of the file you're trying to restore. Try again later.

Warning: If you are using Version 3.1 of DOS, you have two new commands, Join and Substitute (Subst). Briefly, Join allows you to join directories on different drives and Substitute allows you to substitute a drive letter for a path to a subdirectory. If you use either of these commands, do not try to back up or restore files while Join or Substitute is in effect. The files you are working with, as well as others on the disk, might be damaged or lost. (For more information on Join and Substitute, refer to the section "Commands for Occasional Use" in Chapter 17.)

Preparing for the Restore Command Examples

The Restore command examples assume that you just completed the Backup command examples. Type the following to change the date, back up all the files in \MKT\WP, then erase all the files in \MKT\WP:

```
C>date
Current date is Mon 1-01-1990
Enter new date: 10-16-85

C>backup \mkt\wp a:

Insert backup diskette 01 in drive A:

Warning! Files in the target drive
A:\ root directory will be erased
Strike any key when ready

*** Backing up files to drive A: ***
Diskette Number: 01

\MKT\WP\LET1.DOC
\MKT\WP\LET2.DOC
\MKT\WP\LET3.DOC
\MKT\WP\RPT1.DOC
\MKT\WP\RPT2.DOC
\MKT\WP\RPT3.DOC
\MKT\WP\LET1.STY
\MKT\WP\LET2.STY
\MKT\WP\LET3.STY
\MKT\WP\NEW.DOC
\MKT\WP\DATE.DOC

C>erase \mkt\wp\*.*
Are you sure (Y/N)? y
```

This completes the preparation.

Restoring One File

Inadvertently erasing or changing a file is probably the most common reason for restoring a file. You restore a file by including its file name with the Restore command.

For example, to restore \MKT\WP\LET.STY, type:

```
C>restore a: let1.sty
```

DOS prompts you for the backup diskette:

```
Insert backup diskette 01 in drive A:
Strike any key when ready
```

The correct diskette is in the drive, so press any key. DOS displays the name of the restored file:

```
*** Files were backed up 10/16/1985 ***

*** Restoring files from drive A: ***
Diskette: 01

\MKT\WP\LET1.STY
```

You can display the directory to verify that it's back.

Restoring a Set of Files

You can use wildcard characters to restore a set of files. To restore all the files with an extension of DOC backed up from the current directory (\MKT\WP), type the following:

```
C>restore a: *.doc
```

When DOS prompts you for the backup diskette, press any key. DOS displays the names of the files it restores. Again, you can display the directory to verify that the files were restored.

Restoring All the Files in a Directory

If you enter the Restore command with a path name but no file name, DOS restores all files on the backup diskette belonging in that directory. For example, to restore all the files you backed up from MKT\WP, type:

```
C>restore a: \mkt\wp\*.*
```

Again, when DOS prompts for this diskette, press any key. DOS restores all the files you backed up earlier from \MKT\WP, not just those with an extension of DOC.

Restoring All Subdirectories

Just as the /S option of the Backup command backs up the files in a directory and all its subdirectories, the /S option of the Restore command restores the files in a directory and all its subdirectories. To restore the files in \MKT and all its subdirectories, you would type *restore a: \mkt /s.*

Selecting Files to Be Restored

A file you restore replaces a file with the same name on the fixed disk. You may not want to do this, especially if you have changed the file on the fixed disk since the backup diskette was made. You can protect yourself against unwanted changes by using the /P (*Prompt*) option of the Restore command, which tells DOS to prompt for confirmation if the file on the fixed disk has changed since the backup copy was made.

Warning: If you're restoring files that were backed up with a previous version of DOS, be sure to use the /P parameter. If DOS asks whether to restore files named either IBMBIO.COM or IBMDOS.COM, reply n (no). Otherwise, you could replace parts of your DOS program with an earlier version.

To see how the /P parameter works, change LET3.DOC and LET1.STY. First, copy from the console to create a new version of LET3.DOC:

```
C>copy con let3.doc
The new version of let3.doc.
^Z
        1 File(s) copied
```

Copy this file to LET1.STY, making it a new file, too:

```
C>copy let3.doc let1.sty
```

Now restore the entire directory with the /P option:

```
C>restore a: \mkt\wp /p
```

DOS asks for the diskette and begins restoring files in the usual
way, until it finds a file on the fixed disk that has changed since its
backup copy was made.

```
*** Files were backed up 10/16/1985 ***

*** Restoring files from drive A: ***
Diskette: 01

\MKT\WP\LET1.DOC
\MKT\WP\LET2.DOC

Warning! File \MKT\WP\LET3.DOC
was changed after it was backed up
Replace the file (Y/N)?_
```

This message gives you a chance to decide whether you want
to restore the file. Suppose, here, that you don't want to restore it;
type *n* and press Enter. DOS resumes displaying the files it restores,
starting with the one that follows LET3.DOC:

```
\MKT\WP\RPT1.DOC
\MKT\WP\RPT2.DOC
\MKT\WP\RPT3.DOC

Warning! File \MKT\WP\LET1.STY
was changed after it was backed up
Replace the file (Y/N)?_
```

Now suppose you do want to replace the version on the fixed
disk with the backup version; type *y* and press Enter. DOS resumes
displaying the files it restores, starting with LET1.STY:

```
\MKT\WP\LET1.STY
\MKT\WP\LET2.STY
\MKT\WP\LET3.STY
\MKT\WP\NEW.DOC
\MKT\WP\DATE.DOC
```

This completes the examples for backing up and restoring files.
The following section gives the commands to delete the subdirectories and files you created.

DELETING THE SAMPLE FILES
AND DIRECTORIES

You don't need the files and subdirectories you created for these examples. The following commands erase the files and remove the directories. Be sure to enter the Erase commands exactly as shown, to avoid erasing other files.

The comment to the right of each command explains its purpose; don't enter the comment:

```
C>cd \mkt              Change current directory to \MKT
C>erase account        Erase the file ACCOUNT in \MKT
C>erase wp\*.*          Erase the files in \MKT\WP
Are you sure (Y/N)? y
C>rd wp                Remove \MK\WP
C>erase budget\*.pln    Erase the files in \MKT\BUDGET
C>rd budget            Remove \MKT\BUDGET
C>cd \                 Change current directory to root
C>rd mkt               Remove \MKT
```

The fixed disk now contains just the directories and files it had when you started the chapter.

CHAPTER SUMMARY

If you organize your file structure to match your work and develop a backup procedure that protects only those files whose loss would cost you time or data, backing up the fixed disk takes just a little time and a few diskettes. This relatively small investment will be returned many times over, the first time an error—by the system or by you—causes the loss of a valuable file.

You can also create your own commands to back up the fixed disk. Use the techniques described in Chapters 13, 15, and 16, and backing up the fixed disk can become a routine part of using the computer—simplifying the job and guaranteeing consistency no matter who backs up the files on the fixed disk.

CHAPTER
11
CREATING AND EDITING
FILES OF TEXT

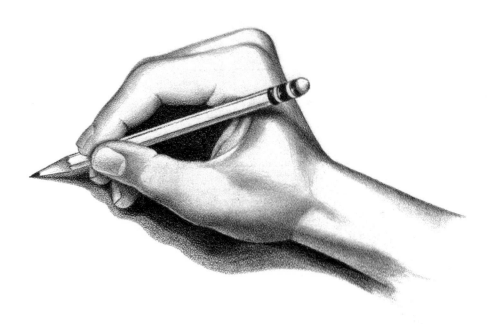

W hen you need to write a note or other short document, it's not always convenient to find a typewriter or to schedule the work with your word-processing people. You could use a word-processing program, but finding the program diskette, loading the program, writing the document, and printing the results might be more trouble than a short document is worth.

What you need is a small, fast program that's easy to use. Edlin, the DOS text editor, is just such a program. After practicing the example in this chapter, you'll be able to use Edlin for those reminder lists, short notes and memos, and batch files.

The example in this chapter presents a situation that could occur in any office. You're a project leader; your team has completed several spreadsheets, a 10-page proposal, and a cover letter. You have copied these files to a diskette and want the team to review the results one last time before the presentation next Monday. You're going to send a copy of the diskette to each team member, and you need a short memo to tell them what's on it.

Note: Edlin is a unique part of DOS. As the example shows, it has its own prompt and its own commands. It is, in fact, a simple word processor. Because of this, the example in this and the following chapter shows you the evolution of a short text file named MEMO.TXT. To disrupt the example as little as possible, the descriptions of Edlin commands are included in the narrative portion of the text. The command formats and allowable parameters are printed, for ease of reference, in the margins, but are not elaborated on as in the preceding chapters. Full descriptions of all Edlin commands and parameters are in the alphabetical reference section in Part 3 of this book.

PREPARING FOR THE EXAMPLE

The example in this chapter requires one formatted diskette. If you have two diskette drives, put the diskette in drive B. If you are using a fixed disk, put the diskette in the diskette drive.

Now change the current drive to drive B; type:

```
A>b:
```

If you have a fixed disk, DOS will prompt you to insert a diskette. The diskette is in the drive, so press any key.

Edlin is an external command file. Whenever you use Edlin, DOS must be able to find the command program on disk.

If you are using two diskette drives, tell DOS to look for commands on the system disk in drive A by typing:

```
B>path a:\
```

If you are using a fixed disk, tell DOS to look in drive C by typing:

```
B>path c:\
```

This completes the preparation for the example.

CREATING A NEW TEXT FILE

edlin
<drive><filename>

When you type *edlin,* followed by the name of a file, in response to the system prompt, DOS copies the Edlin program into memory and starts the program running. Edlin checks to see if the file you named exists. If the file does exist, Edlin copies the file into memory and waits for you to enter any of several commands that say, in effect, "Edlin, do *this* to my file." If the file doesn't exist, Edlin assumes that you want to create one and waits for you to enter the command.

To begin the example for this chapter, type the following to create a file called MEMO.TXT in drive B. Like DOS, Edlin accepts commands in either uppercase or lowercase letters:

```
B>edlin memo.txt
```

Edlin tells you that MEMO.TXT is a new file and waits for a command:

```
New file
*_
```

The asterisk (*) is the Edlin command prompt; it tells you that Edlin is ready for you to type an Edlin command, just as the DOS A> prompt tells you that DOS is ready to accept a command.

All you can do with a new file is insert lines. Most Edlin commands are single letters, so all you need type here is *i* (for *Insert*):

```
*i
```

Edlin responds with:

```
1:*_
```

When you use Edlin, you work with a file line-by-line. To help you keep track of where you are, Edlin displays a line number at the beginning of each line. These line numbers are important, because many of the editing commands can be preceded by a line number or by starting and ending line numbers that define a *range* of lines you wish to work with.

The asterisk following the line number isn't part of the line; it shows you the *current line*, and it is no more a part of your document than the A> prompt or the cursor. Just as DOS remembers the current disk and uses it unless you specify otherwise, Edlin remembers the current line and uses it unless you specify otherwise.

In response to your Insert command, Edlin displays the number it will assign to the first line you enter, followed by the command prompt and the cursor. Because this is a new file, the first line number is 1.

After you enter the Insert command, Edlin accepts each line you type and adds it to the file. You tell Edlin when to end each line by pressing Enter. Each time you press Enter, Edlin moves to the beginning of the next line and displays the new line number, the asterisk, and the cursor. When you want to stop adding lines, press Ctrl-Break (or Ctrl-C).

ENTERING LINES

It's time to enter the first few lines of the sample memo. If you make a typing error, you can backspace and correct it before pressing Enter. But don't worry if you enter a line with errors; as you'll learn, it's easy to correct them.

Type the following lines, but not the line numbers; remember, they're automatically displayed by Edlin. <Ctrl-Break> means

hold down the Ctrl key and press the Break key; <Enter> means
press the Enter key without typing anything:

```
 1:*This diskette has 5 files on it:
 2:*FORECAST.PLN
 3:*OPTION1.PLN
 4:*OPTION2.PLN
 5:*LETTER.DOC
 6:*PROPOSAL.DOC
 7:*<Enter>
 8:*Please check the spreadsheets and print the
 9:*documents to make sure they agree with our
10:*assumptions.
11:*<Enter>
12:*Let's do this quickly, it's due Monday.
13:*<Ctrl-Break>
*_
```

Ctrl-Break shows on your screen as ^C and tells Edlin you
don't wish to insert any more lines, so Edlin moves the cursor to
the next line and displays its prompt, *, telling you it's waiting for
another command.

DISPLAYING LINES

<range>l

There are several reasons you might want to display your files:

• To see if you have included everything you meant to include.

• To check what you have done.

• To edit your file.

The List command (l) displays one line or a range of lines. If you
type a line number followed by l, Edlin displays up to 23 lines (one
screenful), starting with the line you specify. To see the example
you just inserted, use the List command to display the document,
starting at line 1. Type:

```
*1 l
```

Edlin responds with:

```
 1: This diskette has 5 files on it:
 2: FORECAST.PLN
 3: OPTION1.PLN
 4: OPTION2.PLN
 5: LETTER.DOC
 6: PROPOSAL.DOC
 7:
 8: Please check the spreadsheets and print the
 9: documents to make sure they agree with our
10: assumptions.
11:
12: Let's do this quickly, it's due Monday.
*_
```

You can display a range of lines by preceding the l with the first and last line numbers you wish to see, separated by a comma. For example, to display only lines 2 through 6, type:

```
*2,61
```

Edlin shows you:

```
 2: FORECAST.PLN
 3: OPTION1.PLN
 4: OPTION2.PLN
 5: LETTER.DOC
 6: PROPOSAL.DOC
*_
```

ADDING LINES TO A FILE

<line>i

You can insert lines anywhere in an existing file by preceding the Insert command with a line number. Edlin inserts the new line or lines *before* the line you specify, and it automatically renumbers the lines following the insertion.

For example, to insert a blank line before the list of file names in the example, type:

```
*2i
 2:*<Enter>
 3:*<Ctrl-Break>

*_
```

To insert lines at the end of a document, use the Insert command and either specify a line number larger than the last line number or use the symbol #, which means "the line after the last line." To use # to add a signature line to your example, type:

```
*#i
        14:*<Enter>
        15:*Tom
        16:*<Ctrl-Break>

*_
```

Now suppose you decide to add a title to your memo. The beginning is line 1, so specify line 1 with the Insert command:

```
*1i
        1:*Final Project Review -- 10/16/85
        2:*<Enter>
        3:*To: Project team
        4:*<Enter>
        5:*<Ctrl-Break>

*_
```

Display the file now to see the insertions. Type:

```
*1l
```

Edlin shows you:

```
        1: Final Project Review -- 10/16/85
        2:
        3: To: Project team
        4:
        5:*This diskette has 5 files on it:
        6:
        7: FORECAST.PLN
        8: OPTION1.PLN
        9: OPTION2.PLN
       10: LETTER.DOC
       11: PROPOSAL.DOC
       12:
       13: Please check the spreadsheets and print the
       14: documents to make sure they agree with our
       15: assumptions.
       16:
```

```
              17: Let's do this quickly, it's due Monday.
              18:
              19: Tom
      *_
```

Note that Edlin has renumbered all the lines.

ENDING AN EDITING SESSION

When you end an editing session with e (the End Edit command), Edlin stores your edited file on disk and returns you to DOS. After the file has been stored, DOS displays the system prompt (A>). Type the End Edit command:

```
      *e
```

DOS responds with the system prompt:

```
      B>_
```

PRINTING A FILE

copy
<drive><filename>
<device>

A file stored on diskette is of limited value if you can't print a copy of it, so DOS makes it easy to print a file. First, make sure the printer is turned on. Next, use the DOS Copy command to copy the practice file to the printer. Type the following:

```
      B>copy memo.txt prn
```

DOS prints the file and tells you:

```
      1 File(s) copied
```

Your memo is ready for distribution. For many short jobs, that's all there is to it. Using Edlin, you can create and print a file in only a few minutes.

EDITING AN EXISTING TEXT FILE

There will be times you'll want to change an existing text file, perhaps to add items to a list, delete a sentence or two from a memo, or change some wording.

Use Edlin now to edit your practice file. Type Edlin, followed by the name of the file, MEMO.TXT:

```
B>edlin memo.txt
```

This time it's not a new file, so Edlin tells you that it has read to the end of your input file and copied the file into memory, then displays its prompt:

```
End of input file
*_
```

DELETING LINES

<range>d

You can use Edlin to delete a line by typing the number of the line followed by d (the Delete command). For example, suppose you decide not to include line 10 (LETTER.DOC) in your memo. To delete the line, type:

```
*10d
```

Edlin acknowledges by moving to the next line and displaying the * prompt.

To delete several lines, precede the d with the numbers of the first and last lines to be deleted, separated by a comma (the range of lines). To delete the heading (lines 1 through 4) in your practice memo, type:

```
*1,4d
```

To verify that the lines have been deleted, type:

```
*1l
```

Edlin responds with:

```
 1:*This diskette has 5 files on it:
 2:
 3: FORECAST.PLN
 4: OPTION1.PLN
 5: OPTION2.PLN
 6: PROPOSAL.DOC
 7:
 8: Please check the spreadsheets and print the
 9: documents to make sure they agree with our
10: assumptions.
11:
12: Let's do this quickly, it's due Monday.
13:
14: Tom
*_
```

Again, note that Edlin has renumbered the lines.

CANCELING AN EDITING SESSION

Suppose you change a file, then decide you really don't want
the changes. You can cancel the editing session with q (the Quit
command) and return to DOS. The revised version of your file
won't be stored on disk.

So that you don't inadvertently cancel an editing session and
lose your work, Edlin prompts you to confirm the Quit command.
If you type *y*, Edlin returns you to DOS without storing the revised
file. If you type anything else, Edlin ignores the Quit command.
With this command, you don't have to press Enter after replying
to the prompt.

For example, to cancel your editing session, type:

```
*q
```

When Edlin responds, type *y:*

```
Abort edit (Y/N)? y
B>
```

Edlin returns you to DOS, and DOS displays its system prompt. Edit
the file again:

```
B>edlin memo.txt
End of input file
*_
```

Now, display it to see that the lines you deleted earlier are still in the version stored on disk:

```
*1l
            1:*Final Project Review -- 10/16/85
            2:
            3: To: Project team
            4:
            5: This diskette has 5 files on it:
            6:
            7: FORECAST.PLN
            8: OPTION1.PLN
            9: OPTION2.PLN
           10: LETTER.DOC
           11: PROPOSAL.DOC
           12:
           13: Please check the spreadsheets and print the
           14: documents to make sure they agree with our
           15: assumptions.
           16:
           17: Let's do this quickly, it's due Monday.
           18:
           19: Tom
*_
```

It's the same version you stored with the End Edit command.

SEARCHING FOR A GROUP OF CHARACTERS

<range>?s<string>

As a file gets longer, the List command becomes a less and less efficient way to locate and display a particular line. If your sample memo were 80, 90, or 100 lines long, for example, it would take several List commands to display the whole thing, because the screen can display only 23 lines at a time.

You can locate a line much more quickly by telling Edlin to search for a unique group, or *string,* of characters the line contains. But note the word "unique." You could become very frustrated if you specified a string of commonly occurring letter combinations, such as *the* or *ing.* Remember, Edlin makes no judgments. If you specified the string *the,* Edlin might dutifully show you every the, then, there, hither, and thither in your document.

To search for a string of characters, type the number of the line where Edlin should begin searching, then type *s* (for the Search command) and the string.

Suppose the sample memo was several pages long, the list of file names was on page 3, and you wanted to delete a file name. Instead of displaying several screens to find the right line, you can use the Search command to find the first line containing the string PLN (the extension of the first three file names). Edlin displays the first line it finds that contains PLN.

Even though the sample memo is actually much shorter, perform this search anyway. To start searching at the beginning of the file for PLN (note the capitalization), type:

```
*1sPLN
```

Edlin displays the first line that contains PLN:

```
        7: FORECAST.PLN
    *_
```

The line Edlin finds—or the line you choose—becomes the current line. In the preceding example, the current line is line 7. If no line contains the string you have specified, Edlin responds *Not found*.

Suppose you know that several lines contain the same string. You can amplify the Search command to tell Edlin to display a prompt, after it shows you each line, that asks whether this is the line you want. If you respond *y,* Edlin stops the search; if you reply *n,* Edlin searches for the next line that contains the string.

To tell Edlin you want to be shown this prompt, type a question mark before the s. For example, suppose you know that several lines contain PLN; you want to find OPTION2.PLN; you're not sure which line it's on. To find OPTION2.PLN, type the following:

```
*1?sPLN
```

Edlin responds:

```
        7:*FORECAST.PLN
O.K.? n
        8: OPTION1.PLN
O.K.? n
        9: OPTION2.PLN
O.K.? y
*_
```

As with most Edlin commands, you can specify a range of lines to search. If you know that you only need to find the occurrence of the string in lines 2 through 5, you can limit the search by typing *2,5sPLN*. If you don't specify a starting line, Edlin starts searching from the line that follows the current line. If you don't specify an ending line, Edlin searches to the end of the file.

EDITING A LINE

Up to this point, you have been editing the memo by inserting and deleting entire lines. You can also edit individual lines, to change the wording or to correct typing errors. Edlin gives you two ways to change a line: You can use the Replace command, or you can use the editing keys. The next section discusses the Replace command; the one after discusses the editing keys.

Replacing One String with Another

<range>?r<string1>
<F6 or ^Z><string2>

The Replace command (r), like the Search command, tells Edlin to look for a string of characters. Each time it finds the string, however, Edlin replaces the old string with a new string of characters you have included in the Replace command.

The format for the Replace command is much like the format of the Search command: a range of line numbers, R for Replace, and then the string to search for. Since the Replace command replaces one string with another, the Replace command ends with the string that is to replace the old one. If you don't specify a replacement string of characters, Edlin deletes the string and replaces it with nothing. If you do specify a new string, you must separate the two strings. You do this by pressing F6 or Ctrl-Z.

Note: When you press F6 or Ctrl-Z, Edlin displays it as ^Z. But the symbols ^ and Z aren't actual characters. If you press the left arrow key, you erase both the ^ and the Z, because the pair represents one symbol. When you see ^Z in the following examples, press F6 or Ctrl-Z.

In the sample memo, suppose you remember that the extension of word-processing files is TXT, not DOC. You could change each line that contains DOC, but it's faster to use the Replace command to change all the occurrences of DOC with one command. If you don't specify an ending line, Edlin assumes you mean the entire file. To change DOC to TXT throughout the practice file, type:

```
*1rDOC^ZTXT
```

Edlin displays each line it changes:

```
        10: LETTER.TXT
        11: PROPOSAL.TXT
*_
```

As with the Search command, the last line changed becomes the current line (line 11 in the example). If no line contains the string, Edlin responds *Not found.*

But what if you want to change some, not all, of the occurrences of the first string? Again, as with the Search command, you can tell Edlin to prompt you for confirmation after it displays each line that would change. When Edlin prompts for confirmation, it shows the changed version, but the change isn't permanent yet, so you can decide whether to make the change. If you type *n,* Edlin will scrap the new version and keep the original. You ask for the prompt by typing *?* before the command name (r).

Suppose you want to change PLN to DIF, except in the line that refers to OPTION1.PLN; you want to leave that one unchanged. Because one occurrence of PLN is going to stay the same, you need to tell Edlin to prompt for confirmation. Type the following to make the changes:

```
*1?rPLN^ZDIF
        7: FORECAST.DIF
O.K.? y
        8: OPTION1.DIF
O.K.? n
        9: OPTION2.DIF
O.K.? y
*_
```

To look at the results, type:

```
*1 l
          1: Final Project Review -- 10/16/85
          2:
          3: To: Project team
          4:
          5: This diskette has 5 files on it:
          6:
          7: FORECAST.DIF
          8: OPTION1.PLN
          9:*OPTION2.DIF
         10: LETTER.TXT
         11: PROPOSAL.TXT
         12:
         13: Please check the spreadsheets and print the
         14: documents to make sure they agree with our
         15: assumptions.
         16:
         17: Let's do this quickly, it's due Monday.
         18:
         19: Tom
*_
```

You can change the lines back by typing:

```
*1 rDIF^ZPLN
          7: FORECAST.PLN
          9: OPTION2.PLN
```

and:

```
*1 rTXT^ZDOC
         10: LETTER.DOC
         11: PROPOSAL.DOC
*_
```

The Replace command is one of Edlin's most powerful features, but use it with some care. You could change every occurrence of a string of characters in the entire file with one command—including some changes you didn't intend. (If you want an example, try typing *1rdoc^Ztxt* and listing the file; if you do this, change it back again by typing *1rtxt^Zdoc.*)

Remember, each occurrence of the string in a line is changed, so be sure you want all the changes you make. If you change a range of lines, check to make sure there aren't any occurrences that you don't want to change.

If you don't specify a starting line in the Replace command, Edlin starts with the line that follows the current line. If you don't specify an ending line, Edlin continues to the end of the file. To limit the changes to one line, specify the same line as both the beginning and the end of the range (for example, to change LETTER to MEMO in line 10, the command would be *10,10LETTER^zMEMO*).

Using the Editing Keys

Even when you change a line or lines with the Replace command, you're still probably thinking more in terms of the entire document than you are about individual lines. To make specific changes, you use the editing keys shown in Figure 11-1.

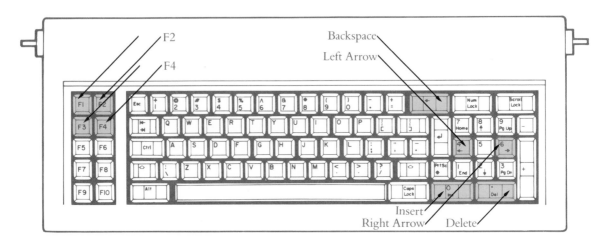

Figure 11-1. Editing keys

Changing a line

To tell Edlin you want to change a line, you type the line number and press Enter. Edlin displays the line, moves to the next line, displays the line number again, then waits for further instructions. You can then use the editing keys to copy the characters you want, skip the characters you don't want, or insert new characters. To help you become familiar with the editing keys, Figure 11-2 summarizes the keys and their functions. You may find it helpful to review this figure before going on to the next practice session.

Now use the editing keys to edit line 3 of the sample memo. To do this, type the line number, 3, and press Enter:

```
*3
```

Edlin responds:

```
3:*To: Project team
3:*_
```

Key	Function
Right arrow	Copies one character.
Left arrow	Erases the last character you copied.
Ins	Causes characters you type to be inserted in the new line. Pressing Ins again stops the insert.
Del	Skips one character in the old line (effectively deleting it from the new line).
Backspace	Same as left arrow.
F1	Same as right arrow.
F2	Copies to a certain character in the old line (type the character after pressing F2).
F3	Copies the remaining characters in the line.
F4	Skips to a certain character in the old line (type the character after pressing F4).

Figure 11-2. Edlin editing key functions

Think of the displayed line as the old line, and the row underneath, with the cursor at the beginning, as the new line. You edit a
line by copying the characters you want to keep from the old line to
the new line, and by inserting any new characters in the new line.
The editing keys tell Edlin which characters to copy.

Now press the right arrow key. The first letter of the old line
appears on the new line:

```
3:*To: Project team
3:*T_
```

You copied one character from the old line to the new line.
Continue pressing the right arrow key. Each time you press it, you
copy another character. When you reach the end of the line, pressing
the right arrow key has no effect, because you have copied all the
characters to the new line:

```
3:*To: Project team
3:*To: Project team_
```

If you pressed Enter now, you would be telling Edlin you had
finished editing line 3. The line would remain unchanged, because
you copied all the characters from the old line to the new without
making any changes.

Press the left arrow key. The cursor moves one column to the
left, erasing the last character you copied to the new line:

```
3:*To: Project team
3:*To: Project tea_
```

Continue pressing the left arrow key. Each time you press it,
you erase another of the characters that you copied to the new line.
When you reach the beginning of the line, you've erased all the
characters you copied to the new line; you're now back where
you started.

```
3:*To: Project team
3:*_
```

If you pressed Enter now, the line would again remain unchanged because you haven't copied any characters and Edlin
assumes you don't want to change the line.

The F(unction) keys

Note: If you are using a computer that does not have these keys, check your documentation for their equivalents.

F3

There are quicker ways to copy characters than using the right arrow key. Press the key labeled F3. Because F3 copies all the original characters from the cursor location to the end of the line, the entire old line is copied to the new line. Hold down the left arrow key until the cursor is back to the beginning of the line.

F2

The F2 key copies all the characters in the original line up to a particular character you specify. F2 is something like a search command that works inside a line; to use it, press F2 and type the character you want the copy to stop at.

For example, suppose you want to change the word *Project* to *Product* in the example. To do this, press F2 to copy all the characters up to the j, type *du* to replace *je,* then copy the rest of the line. Press F2, then *j:*

```
3:*To: Project team
3:*To: Pro_
```

Now type *du:*

```
3:*To: Project team
3:*To: Produ_
```

The characters you type replace the corresponding characters from the old line, so in the new line, *du* has replaced *je.* Press F3 to copy the rest of the old line:

```
3:*To: Project team
3:*To: Product team_
```

Now, use the left arrow key to move the cursor back to the beginning of the line.

As you just saw, characters you type replace the corresponding characters from the old line. If you press the Insert key before typing the characters, however, Edlin inserts the characters into the new line without replacing any characters in the old line.

To insert the word *New* after the word *To:* in line 3, for example, first copy *To:* by pressing the right arrow key four times (once for each character, including the blank after the colon):

```
3:*To: Project team
3:*To: _
```

Notice that line 3 still says *Project*. You didn't press Enter after changing it to *Product,* so the old line remains unchanged.

Now press the Insert key, type *New* (don't forget to add a blank between words), and press F3 to copy the rest of the old line:

```
3:*To: Project team
3:*To: New Project team_
```

Use the left arrow key to move the cursor back to the left margin again.

Now suppose you want to delete one or more characters in your original line. You use the Delete key, which tells Edlin to skip the next character in the old line. Because the character isn't copied from the old line, the character is deleted from the new line.

For example, to delete *To:* from line 3, press the Delete key four times (once for each character, plus the blank). Nothing seems to happen, but when you press F3 to copy the rest of the line, you see:

```
3:*To: Project team
3:*Project team_
```

You didn't copy *To:,* so it's not in the new line. Move the cursor back to the left margin again.

F4

But suppose you want to delete a number of characters. Isn't there a faster way? Yes, just as the F2 key copies to a specified character in the old line, the F4 key skips to a specified character in the old line, deleting the characters it skips, all at once. The form of

using F4 is the same as for F2: press F4, then the letter where you wish to stop. To delete *To: Project* in line 3, for example, you could press the Delete key 12 times, but it's quicker to use F4. Press F4, then *t* to skip *Projec*. Press the Delete key twice to delete the *t* and the blank. Now press F3 to copy the rest of the line:

```
3:*To: Project team
3:*team_
```

Remember, no matter how many changes you make, you can always cancel them by pressing Ctrl–Break before you press Enter. When you press Enter, the line is changed. Press Ctrl–Break to cancel the edit of line 3.

If you wish to end your practice session here, type *e* to End Edit and return to DOS. Because the End Edit command automatically saves your file on diskette, you will be able to use the sample again in the next chapter, which covers other ways to revise an Edlin file.

CHAPTER SUMMARY

This concludes the first session with Edlin. The next chapter shows you how to revise a text file and describes several additional Edlin commands.

If you're not going to continue with the next chapter right away, be sure to save the diskette that contains MEMO.TXT.

CHAPTER
12
USING EDLIN
TO REVISE A FILE

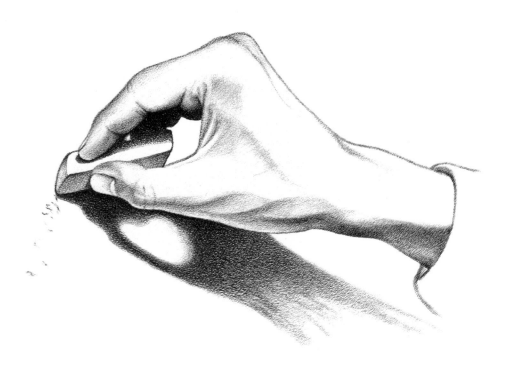

The previous chapter showed you how to create a text file, enter lines in it, and change entire lines. Edlin would be useful even if this were all it could do, but there's more: Edlin includes several ways to revise, or edit, a text file. This chapter shows you how to use these additional capabilities of Edlin, particularly for revising files. Using these features, you can:

- Display the file a screenful at a time with the Page command.

- Enter more than one Edlin command on a line by separating the commands with semicolons.

- Move one or more lines to another place in the file with the Move command.

- Copy one or more lines to another place in the file with the Edlin Copy command.

- Copy another file from a disk to the file you're editing with the Transfer command.

PREPARING FOR THE EXAMPLE

If you are continuing directly from Chapter 11, no preparation is needed. Go on to the heading "Printing Your File."

If you are starting a new session, you'll need the file you created in Chapter 11. Put the diskette that contains MEMO.TXT in drive B and change the current drive from A to B by typing:

```
A>b:
```

On a system with a fixed disk, DOS will prompt for a diskette when you change the current drive. Press any key.

You must again tell DOS where to find the Edlin commands. For a system with two diskette drives, type:

```
B>path a:\
```

For a system with a fixed disk, type:

```
B>path c:\
```

Now type the following to edit MEMO.TXT:

```
B>edlin memo.txt
```

Edlin responds:

```
End of input file
*_
```

This completes the preparation for the example.

PRINTING YOUR FILE

Suppose you have completed your memo, but now decide to make some changes. The practice memo is short enough to change on the screen, but it is sometimes more helpful to print a file and mark the changes on the paper copy before transferring them to a disk file.

If you are working with Edlin, you don't have to return to DOS to print your file. You could press the Shift-PrtSc key combination, but this prints just one screenful (including commands and messages, as well as the file).

You can print the entire file by pressing Ctrl-PrtSc (which prints everything that is displayed) and displaying the file with the List command. Turn your printer on and type the following; remember *1,#l,* means list all lines from 1 to # (the line after the last line):

```
*1,#l<Ctrl-PrtSc><Enter>
```

Your file is printed.

Before you type any other command, remember to press Ctrl-PrtSc again to stop simultaneously printing everything you display.

REVISING YOUR MEMO

Assume you have finished the memo but just realized that the team members don't have to print the documents filed on the diskettes—they can review them on the screen. You decide to add instructions for reviewing the documents, and to make a few other

```
 1: Final Project Review_ 10/16/85
 2:
 3: To: Project team  UPPERCASE
 4:
 5:*This diskette has 5 files on it:
 6:
 7: FORECAST.PLN
 8: OPTION1.PLN  HIGHER SALES
 9: OPTION2.PLN  NO STAFF INCREASE
10: LETTER.DOC
11: PROPOSAL.DOC
12:
13: Please check the spreadsheets and  MAKE  print the
14: documents to make  sure they agree with our
15: assumptions.
16:
17: Let's do this quickly, it's due Monday.
18:
19: Tom   TO BE      {  YOU CAN REVIEW THE DOCUMENTS ON THE SCREEN.
 *_   INSERTED       TO CHECK THE PROPOSAL, TYPE:
       BEFORE        TYPE B: PROPOSAL | MORE
       LINE 16       THIS DISPLAYS ONE SCREEN AT A TIME.
                     PRESS THE SPACE BAR TO DISPLAY THE
                     NEXT SCREEN, OR CTRL-BREAK TO STOP.
```

Figure 12-1. Sample memo marked with changes

changes to the memo as well. Figure 12-1 shows a copy of the file marked with the changes you plan to make; it won't take long to make these changes.

First, to change *Project team* in line 3 to uppercase, type *3* to tell Edlin you want to edit line 3. When Edlin responds with the original line and the new line number, copy the first five characters by pressing the right arrow key five times; then type the uppercase characters to replace the lowercase ones:

```
*3
        3:*To: Project team
        3:*To: PROJECT TEAM
*_
```

Here is a quick way to confirm your change. Type the line number and press Enter. Edlin assumes you want to edit the line again and displays the newly revised line for you. Press Enter again.

The second Enter tells Edlin to save the line without any further changes. Confirm the changes to line 3:

```
*3<Enter>
        3:*To: PROJECT TEAM
        3:* <Enter>
*_
```

Next, the revisions in Figure 12-1 show that you want to add descriptions to the file names in lines 8 and 9. To add text at the end of a line: Type the line number, press Enter, press F3 to copy the entire line, type the added text, and press Enter again. To add three blanks and the words *Higher sales* to line 8, type:

```
*8
        8:*OPTION1.PLN
        8:*OPTION1.PLN    Higher sales
*_
```

When you have finished editing a line, you can press Enter when Edlin displays its next prompt and Edlin will assume you want to edit the next line. You want to add text at the end of line 9, so press Enter, press F3 to copy the entire line, and type three blanks followed by *No staff increase:*

```
*<Enter>
        9:*OPTION2.PLN
        9:*OPTION2.PLN    No staff increase
*_
```

Check your progress by listing the file:

```
*11
         1: Final Project Review -- 10/16/85
         2:
         3: To: PROJECT TEAM
         4:
         5: This diskette has 5 files on it:
         6:
         7: FORECAST.PLN
         8: OPTION1.PLN    Higher sales
         9:*OPTION2.PLN    No staff increase
        10: LETTER.DOC
        11: PROPOSAL.DOC
```

```
12:
13: Please check the spreadsheets and print the
14: documents to make sure they agree with our
15: assumptions.
16:
17: Let's do this quickly, it's due Monday.
18:
19: Tom
*_
```

Now you want to delete the last two words, *print the,* of line 13 and replace them with one word, *make.* Type *13* and press Enter; press F3 to copy the entire line, then use the left arrow key to erase *print the:*

```
*13
13:*Please check the spreadsheets and print the
13:*Please check the spreadsheets and _
```

Type *make* and press Enter:

```
13:*Please check the spreadsheets and print the
13:*Please check the spreadsheets and make
*_
```

You want to delete more words, *documents to make,* at the beginning of the next line; press Enter to edit line 14.

```
*<Enter>
14:*documents to make sure they agree with our
14:*_
```

To make the change, you can either press the Delete key 18 times or skip to the second s (*sure*) in the line. It's faster to skip, so press F4 and type *s*. Nothing happens on the screen, because you haven't copied any characters yet. You want to skip to the second s, so press F4 and type *s* again. Press F3 to copy the rest of the line, but don't press Enter:

```
14:*documents to make sure they agree with our
14:*sure they agree with our_
```

The words at the beginning have been deleted, and now the line is short enough to include the only word in the next line, *assumptions.*

To make your memo look nicer, type *assumptions* (don't forget a blank at the beginning and a period at the end):

```
        14:*documents to make sure they agree with our
        14:*sure they agree with our assumptions.
    *_
```

Line 15 contains only one word, *assumptions,* which you already moved up to the previous line. You've completed all the revisions up to this point; it's also where you want to insert instructions for displaying the files. Edit the line. It's the next line, so just press Enter and, instead of copying any characters, start entering the new text, which will replace the old:

```
*<Enter>
        15:*assumptions.
        15:*You can review the documents on the
    *_
```

Now insert the remaining new lines before line 16. Type:

```
*16i
        16:*screen. To check the proposal, type:
        17:*<Enter>
        18:*TYPE B:PROPOSAL | MORE
        19:*<Enter>
        20:*This displays one screen at a time.
        21:*Press the space bar to display the
        22:*next screen, or Ctrl-Break to stop.
        23:*<Ctrl-Break>

    *_
```

Ctrl–Break in line 23 tells Edlin you have finished inserting lines. You have completed your revisions, so list the entire memo:

```
*1l
        1: Final Project Review -- 10/16/85
        2:
        3: To: PROJECT TEAM
        4:
        5: This diskette has 5 files on it:
        6:
        7: FORECAST.PLN
        8: OPTION1.PLN    Higher sales
        9: OPTION2.PLN    No staff increase
       10: LETTER.DOC
       11: PROPOSAL.DOC
```

```
12:
13: Please check the spreadsheets and make
14: sure they agree with our assumptions.
15: You can review the documents on the
16: screen. To check the proposal, type:
17:
18: TYPE B:PROPOSAL ¦ MORE
19:
20: This displays one screen at a time.
21: Press the space bar to display the
22: next screen, or Ctrl-Break to stop.
23:*
    *_
```

The entire file won't quite fit on one screen. To see the rest, start displaying with the next line, 24:

```
*241
    24: Let's do this quickly, it's due Monday.
    25:
    26: Tom
    *_
```

Your revised memo, complete with instructions, is ready for your team. Just store the memo, print a copy for each member of the project team, tuck one in each diskette envelope, and deliver them.

To save the memo, type:

```
*e
```

Edlin stores the file on disk and returns you to DOS:

```
B>
```

BACKUP FILES

When you edit an existing file, Edlin works with a copy that it has placed in your computer's memory. The original version remains, unchanged, on the diskette. When you end an editing session on the working copy of an existing file, Edlin changes the extension of the unchanged original to BAK (for backup) and stores the revised version on the disk in addition to the BAK version. If there is already a file with the same name and an extension of BAK, Edlin erases the old BAK file before renaming the version it copied

into memory for you to work with. If you need the original version, you can use the BAK file. You'll have to change its extension, however, because Edlin won't edit a file with an extension of BAK. You might, for example, use the Rename command to change MEMO.BAK to MEMO.OLD.

PAGING THROUGH A FILE

<range>p

If you typed *e* to End Edit at the conclusion of the previous session, tell DOS you want to use Edlin to edit MEMO.TXT by typing:

```
B>edlin memo.txt
```

Edlin responds:

```
End of input file
*_
```

Earlier, you displayed the file screen-by-screen with the List command by increasing the line number by 23 (the number of lines per screen) each time. (*1l* for the first screenful, then *24l* for the second screenful, and so on). The Page command (p) simplifies matters by letting you page through a file without keeping track of line numbers. Start with line 1 and page through the practice memo:

```
*1p
         1: Final Project Review -- 10/16/85
         2:
         3: To: PROJECT TEAM
         4:
         5: This diskette has 5 files on it:
         6:
         7: FORECAST.PLN
         8: OPTION1.PLN    Higher sales
         9: OPTION2.PLN    No staff increase
        10: LETTER.DOC
        11: PROPOSAL.DOC
        12:
        13: Please check the spreadsheets and make
        14: sure they agree with our assumptions.
        15: You can review the documents on the
        16: screen. To check the proposal, type:
        17:
```

```
          18: TYPE B:PROPOSAL ¦ MORE
          19:
          20: This displays one screen at a time.
          21: Press the space bar to display the
          22: next screen, or Ctrl-Break to stop.
          23:*
     *_
```

To see the next 23 lines, type:

```
     *p
          24:Let's do this quickly, it's due Monday.
          25:
          26:*Tom
     *_
```

If you don't specify a line number, the Page command displays the current line and the following 22 lines. The Page command changes the current line to the last line displayed, so you can page through a file just by typing *p* for each screenful.

ENTERING MORE THAN ONE COMMAND ON A LINE

If an action requires more than one command, you can put all the commands on the same line, separating the commands with semicolons. Edlin carries out each command as if it had been entered on a separate line. Some of the following examples use this technique.

MOVING LINES

<range>,<line>m

You can move a paragraph or other block of lines from one place to another in the file with the Move (m) command. First, you specify the starting and ending line numbers of the block to be moved, then you specify the number of the line before which the block should be placed, separating the numbers with commas.

For example, suppose you want to move lines 5 through 12 from where they are to just before the last sentence (line 24). To move the

lines and to verify the move, type the following, separating the commands with a semicolon:

```
*5,12,24m;1p
```

You see:

```
 1: Final Project Review -- 10/16/85
 2:
 3: To: PROJECT TEAM
 4:
 5: Please check the spreadsheets and make
 6: sure they agree with our assumptions.
 7: You can review the documents on the
 8: screen. To check the proposal, type:
 9:
10: TYPE B:PROPOSAL | MORE
11:
12: This displays one screen at a time.
13: Press the space bar to display the
14: next screen, or Ctrl-Break to stop.
15:
16: This diskette has 5 files on it:
17:
18: FORECAST.PLN
19: OPTION1.PLN    Higher sales
20: OPTION2.PLN    No staff increase
21: LETTER.DOC
22: PROPOSAL.DOC
23:*
*_
```

Note that Edlin renumbers the lines, just as when you insert or delete lines.

If you omit either the starting or ending line number, Edlin assumes you mean the current line. To move one line that is not the current line, specify it as both the beginning and end of the block (for example, to move line 26 to just before line 5, the command would be *26,26,5m*). After the lines are moved, the first line that was moved becomes the current line.

COPYING LINES

**\<range\>,\<line\>,
\<number\>c**

You can copy a block of lines to another place in the file with the Copy (c) command. To do so, specify the beginning and ending line numbers of the block and the number of the line before which the block is to be copied, just as you did with the Move command. Copy differs from Move in that the block you specify remains in its original location and is repeated in the new location.

For example, suppose you want to copy the line that begins with *This diskette has,* plus the list of files (lines 16 through 22), to the end of the document so you can use these lines as a label. Type the following Copy and Page commands to copy the lines and to verify the copy (remember that # means the line that follows the last line of the file):

```
*16,22,#c;16p
```

You see:

```
16: This diskette has 5 files on it:
17:
18: FORECAST.PLN
19: OPTION1.PLN    Higher sales
20: OPTION2.PLN    No staff increase
21: LETTER.DOC
22: PROPOSAL.DOC
23:
24: Let's do this quickly, it's due Monday.
25:
26: Tom
27: This diskette has 5 files on it:
28:
29: FORECAST.PLN
30: OPTION1.PLN    Higher sales
31: OPTION2.PLN    No staff increase
32: LETTER.DOC
33:*PROPOSAL.DOC
*_
```

You can make several copies of a block of lines with one Copy command by adding a comma and the number of copies just before the c. For example, to make five more copies of the same block of lines, type the following:

```
*16,22,#,5c;27p;p
```

If you omit the starting or ending line number, Edlin assumes the omitted line number is the current line. To copy one line other than the current line, specify it as both the start and end of the block. After the lines are copied, the first line that was moved becomes the current line.

<line>t<filename>

COPYING ANOTHER FILE

You can copy another file into the file you're editing. Suppose you have a file that contains the name and address of each member of the project team. If you want to include the address list in this memo, you don't have to type it again; you can merge the two files with the Transfer (t) command.

To see how this works, quit the edit of this file, use Edlin to create a small file named ADDRESS on the diskette in drive B, then return to editing MEMO.TXT again. To do this, type:

```
*q
Abort edit (Y/N)? y
B>edlin address
New file
*i
        1:*XXX ADDRESS LIST XXX
        2:*<Enter>
        3:*<Ctrl-Break>

*1,1,2,3c;1p
        1: XXX ADDRESS LIST XXX
        2: XXX ADDRESS LIST XXX
        3: XXX ADDRESS LIST XXX
        4: XXX ADDRESS LIST XXX
        5:*
*e

B>edlin memo.txt
End of input file
*p
```

The first 23 lines of MEMO.TXT are on the screen.

To copy another file with the Transfer command, you specify the line before which the file is to be placed, then type *t* and the name of the file. Do not use commas in this case.

To copy the file named ADDRESS to just before line 3 and then to see the result, type:

```
*3taddress;1p
        1: Final Project Review -- 10/16/85
        2:
        3: XXX ADDRESS LIST XXX
```

```
 4: XXX ADDRESS LIST XXX
 5: XXX ADDRESS LIST XXX
 6: XXX ADDRESS LIST XXX
 7:
 8: To: PROJECT TEAM
 9:
10: This diskette has 5 files on it:
11:
12: FORECAST.PLN
13: OPTION1.PLN    Higher sales
14: OPTION2.PLN    No staff increase
15: LETTER.DOC
16: PROPOSAL.DOC
17:
18: Please check the spreadsheets and make
19: sure they agree with our assumptions.
20: You can review the documents on the
21: screen. To check the proposal, type:
22:
23:*TYPE B:PROPOSAL ¦ MORE
*_
```

If you don't specify the line number, Edlin copies the file to just above the current line, and the first line of the copied file becomes the current line.

EDITING FILES TOO LARGE TO FIT INTO MEMORY

<number>w

<number>a

Although you'll probably find Edlin handy mostly for short documents, you can also use Edlin to edit very large files— even those that are larger than the amount of memory your computer has available for your data (this is not the same as your computer's amount of memory, since part of memory must also be used to hold Edlin itself, manage the display, and so forth).

When you edit a very large file, Edlin starts loading the file into memory, stopping when it has filled 75 percent of the available memory; this leaves room for you to add to the file. If you insert enough additional text to fill the remaining 25 percent of available memory, or if you want to work with the part of the file that was not loaded, you can move the part of the file in memory onto disk to make room for loading the next part of the file.

Two Edlin commands control this process: Write Lines (w), which stores (writes) the part of the file in memory (<number> of lines) onto disk; and Append Lines (a), which loads the next part of the file (<number> of lines) from disk into memory. The practice file is not large enough to demonstrate these commands, so simply bear them in mind for your own later use.

CHAPTER SUMMARY

Although Edlin is a simple text editor and lacks many of the features required of a word processor, its speed and simplicity make it an excellent tool for creating and revising short text files. The examples in Chapters 11 and 12 showed you how you can use Edlin to write a short memo. The remaining chapters of this book describe some of the advanced features of DOS, many of which require short files of text; you'll find that Edlin is admirably suited to taking advantage of these features.

CHAPTER

13

CREATING YOUR
OWN COMMANDS

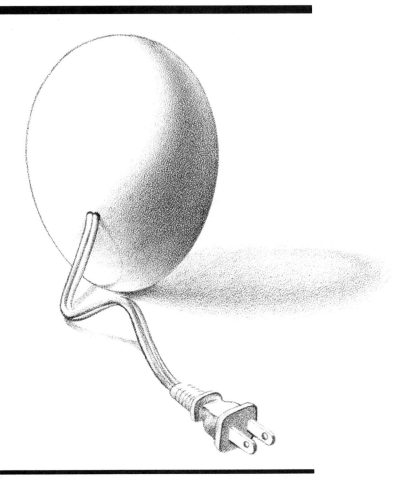

A s the preceding chapters show, DOS gives you a great deal of control over your computer system. But DOS is necessarily general purpose, because many people use it for many different purposes. So that you can adapt the computer to your work, DOS lets you create your own special-purpose commands by combining existing DOS commands.

The technique is simple: To make your own command, you create a text file that contains DOS commands. You can give such a file—called a *batch file*—any valid name except the name of an existing command; the extension of the file must be BAT. To use your command, simply type the name of the batch file; DOS carries out the commands the file contains as if you had typed each of them separately. Commands you create this way are called *batch commands*.

This chapter describes how to create batch files and carry out batch commands. It also describes the Remark command, which is intended for batch files, and shows you how to modify the DOS start-up procedure if there are certain commands you always carry out when you start your system.

A BATCH OF WHAT?

The term *batch* has its origins in the early days of large computers, when most work was done by submitting a deck of punched cards to the data-processing department. The punched cards had to contain all the instructions required for the program to run correctly. There was no chance of interaction with the system. The data-processing personnel ran these jobs in batches and delivered the output.

In effect, you do the same thing when you use a batch command, because the batch file contains all the instructions needed to carry out a job. Batch, then, is used to describe a computer job that runs without interruption, as opposed to an *interactive* job—such as word processing—that consists of an exchange of instructions and responses between you and the computer.

You can use batch files to automate frequently used command sequences, and to make the system more accessible to colleagues who use application programs but who may not know DOS as well as you do.

HOW DOS SEARCHES FOR A COMMAND

If you type something when DOS is displaying the system prompt, DOS assumes you have typed a command name. It then follows a particular sequence in trying to carry out the command:

1. It checks to see if you typed the name of a built-in command, such as *dir* or *copy.* If you did, DOS runs the program that carries out that command.

2. If what you typed isn't a built-in command, DOS checks to see if you typed the name of a file with an extension of COM or EXE (a command file). If you did, DOS loads the program contained in the file and runs it.

3. If what you typed isn't the name of a command file, DOS checks to see if you typed the name of a file with an extension of BAT (a batch file). If you did, DOS carries out the commands in the batch file.

The sequence is important, because it explains why a command file with the same name as a built-in command won't be carried out, or why a batch file with the same name as a built-in command or command file won't be carried out.

PREPARING FOR THE EXAMPLES

You need one formatted diskette and some sample files for the examples in this chapter. If you're not using a fixed disk, leave your system diskette in drive A and put a formatted disk in drive B. If you're using a fixed disk, put the formatted diskette in the diskette drive. Type the following to change the current drive to B (if you're using a fixed disk, the initial system prompt will be C>, not A>):

```
A>b:
B>_
```

Creating the Sample Files

You will use the following sample files in this chapter:

LETR1.DOC
LETR2.DOC
LETR3.DOC

Note: If you're using a fixed disk, DOS displays the message Insert diskette for drive B: and strike any key when ready *after you type the first Copy command in the following procedure. You have already put the diskette in the drive, so when you see the message, press any key to continue.*

Type the following to create the sample files (press F6, or Ctrl-Z, and Enter where you see ^Z):

```
B>copy con letr1.doc
This is the sample file.
^Z
        1 File(s) copied

B>copy letr1.doc letr2.*
        1 File(s) copied

B>copy letr1.doc letr3.*
        1 File(s) copied

B>_
```

CREATING A BATCH FILE

A batch file is simply a text file, with an extension of BAT, that contains DOS commands. It's a simple matter to create a batch file. You can create one just as you create any other text file: Copy from the console to a text file; use Edlin, or use a word processor if it can store files without inserting its own format codes.

The examples in this chapter have you copy from the console to create short batch files. The only drawback to this technique is that you can't go back to correct an error after you have entered a line. If you make a typing error while entering an example, either press Ctrl-Break and then re-enter the line or use Edlin to correct the error in the file.

Suppose you use a word-processing program and name the files that contain letters LETR1.DOC, LETR2.DOC, LETR3.DOC, and so forth. You use the Directory command fairly often to display the names of those particular files. Instead of typing *dir letr*.doc* each time, you could put the Directory command in a batch file named DIRLET.BAT. Type the following to create the batch file:

```
B>copy con dirlet.bat
dir letr*.doc
^Z
        1 File(s) copied

B>_
```

The first line you typed names the batch file; the second line contains the command DOS carries out. Test your batch command by typing its name:

```
B>dirlet

B>dir letr*.doc

 Volume in drive B has no label
 Directory of  B:\

LETR1    DOC       26 10-16-85  12:03p
LETR2    DOC       26 10-16-85  12:04p
LETR3    DOC       26 10-16-85  12:05p
        3 File(s)     357376 bytes free

B>_
```

The first line displayed after you enter your batch command is the Directory command, because DOS displays the commands in a batch file as they are carried out. It's as if you typed the command itself.

You could make the batch command even easier to type by naming the batch file just LDIR.BAT. It might prove simpler in the long run, however, to make the name long enough to give a hint of what the command does, especially if you create several.

Displaying Messages from a Batch File

The Remark (rem) command doesn't cause DOS to do anything, but it is a valid command. You can include a message with the Remark command. The command form is:

rem <message>

Although this command doesn't seem to be especially useful at the command level, it lets you display a message by using a batch command. To see how the Remark command works, create another version of DIRLET.BAT that displays a descriptive message; type the following:

```
B>copy con dirlet.bat
rem DIRECTORY OF LETTERS
dir letr*.doc
^Z
        1 File(s) copied

B>_
```

The new version of DIRLET.BAT replaces the first version you created a few minutes ago.

Test this new version by typing:

```
B>dirlet
```

The Remark command causes DOS to display the message before it displays the directory:

```
B>rem DIRECTORY OF LETTERS

B>dir letr*.doc

 Volume in drive B has no label
 Directory of  B:\

LETR1     DOC       26  10-16-85  12:03p
LETR2     DOC       26  10-16-85  12:04p
LETR3     DOC       26  10-16-85  12:05p
        3 File(s)       357376 bytes free

B>_
```

Carrying Out the Same Batch Command With Different Data

You have seen that most DOS commands include one or more parameters you use to make your instructions more specific. When you enter a Directory command, for example, you can specify a file name, to display some portion of the files on a disk, and the /W option, to display the wide form of the directory. The Copy command is another example; it requires two parameters: the name of the file to be copied, and the name to be given to the new copy.

Parameters let you use the same DOS command with different data. You can give your batch files the same capability with a feature called *replaceable parameters.*

A replaceable parameter is a special symbol you put in a batch file. When you use the batch file, DOS replaces the symbol with a parameter you include when you type the batch command. The symbol consists of a percent sign followed by a one-digit number, such as %1. You can use the numbers 0 to 9 in replaceable parameters, and you can include more than one replaceable parameter in a batch file.

The number of the symbol identifies which parameter replaces the symbol. If a batch command takes two parameters, for example, DOS replaces %1 wherever it occurs in the batch file with the first parameter you type, and it replaces %2 with the second parameter you type. Replaceable parameters can be used anywhere in a batch command.

For example, suppose you wanted a batch command that would print a file by copying it to the printer. (You've already got a DOS Print command, but go through the example anyway; it illustrates the use of replaceable parameters.) All the batch file needs is a Copy command and one replaceable parameter that identifies the file to be printed. The command is called *Prnt* to avoid confusion with the Print command. Type the following:

```
B>copy con prnt.bat
copy %1 prn
^Z
        1 File(s) copied

B>_
```

To test your Prnt batch command, make sure the printer is turned on and type the following:

```
B>prnt letr1.doc
```

DOS displays the command after replacing %1 with the batch-command parameter, LETR1.DOC, and prints the file:

```
B>copy letr1.doc prn
        1 File(s) copied

B>_
```

Figure 13-1 shows several versions of PRNT.BAT that you might create for printing other documents. Each version contains at least one replaceable parameter; the last version contains two. To the left of each version is an example of how the batch command would be typed, and to the right are the corresponding commands that would be carried out after DOS replaced the replaceable parameters. The batch-command parameters, the replaceable parameters in each version of the batch file, and the result after DOS replaces them with the batch command parameters, are in *italics*.

Batch command you would type	Contents of PRNT.BAT	Commands that would be carried out
A>prnt *memo.doc*	copy *%1* prn	A>copy *memo.doc* prn
A>prnt *memo*	copy *%1*.doc prn	A>copy *memo*.doc prn
A>prnt *memo rept*	copy *%1*.doc prn	A>copy *memo*.doc prn
	copy *%2*.doc prn	A>copy *rept*.doc prn

Figure 13-1. Replaceable parameters in a batch file

Replaceable parameters make batch files much more flexible. Your batch commands needn't be limited to handling the same files or devices all the time—they can be used just like DOS commands to operate with any file or device.

Canceling a Batch Command

Just as with other DOS commands, you press Ctrl-Break to cancel a batch command. But when you cancel a batch command, DOS prompts you to confirm. To see this, create a short batch file named DIRS.BAT that displays the directory of the diskettes in drive A and in the current drive. Type:

```
B>copy con dirs.bat
dir a:
dir
^Z
        1 File(s) copied

B>_
```

The system diskette is in drive A, so the Directory display is long enough to give you time to press Ctrl-Break. Enter the Dirs batch command, then press Ctrl-Break as soon as it starts displaying the file names:

```
B>dirs

B>dir a:

 Volume in drive A has no label
 Directory of   A:\

ANSI     SYS      1651   3-07-85   1:43p
ASSIGN   COM      1509   3-07-85   1:43p
ATTRIB   EXE     15091   3-07-85   1:43p
BACKUP   COM      5577   3-07-85   1:43p
BASIC    COM     17792   3-07-^C

Terminate batch job (Y/N)? _
```

If you respond no, the command being carried out is canceled, but DOS continues with the next command in the batch file. Type *n;*

DOS carries out the next command, which displays the directory of the disk in the current drive:

```
B>dir

  Volume in drive B has no label
  Directory of  B:\

  DIRLET    BAT        41   10-16-85   12:13p
  PRNT      BAT        13   10-16-85   12:22p
  DIRS      BAT        13   10-16-85   12:31p
  LETR1     DOC        26   10-16-85   12:03p
  LETR2     DOC        26   10-16-85   12:04p
  LETR3     DOC        26   10-16-85   12:05p
          6 File(s)         356352 bytes free
  B>_
```

If you respond yes to the terminate question, DOS cancels the entire batch command and displays the system prompt. Type the Dirs batch command again, but this time respond *y:*

```
B>dirs

B>dir a:

  Volume in drive A has no label
  Directory of  A:\

  ANSI     SYS       1651   3-07-85   1:43p
  ASSIGN   COM       1509   3-07-85   1:43p
  ATTRIB   EXE      15091   3-07-85   1:43p
  BACKUP   COM       5577   3-07-85   1:43p
  BASIC    C^C

Terminate batch job (Y/N)? y
B>_
```

DOS returns to the command level without completing the batch command.

Creating Your Own Start-up Procedure

Each time you start or restart the system, DOS prompts for the date and time; this is its start-up procedure. It's really just carrying out a Date and a Time command. You can substitute your own

start-up procedure by creating a special batch file named AUTO-EXEC.BAT that contains commands you always enter when you turn on your system.

Whenever DOS completes its diagnostic tests, it checks to see whether there is a file named AUTOEXEC.BAT on the system disk. If there is not, DOS carries out the Date and Time commands and displays the system prompt; if there is an AUTOEXEC.BAT file, DOS carries out the commands in AUTOEXEC.BAT, skips the Date and Time commands, and displays the system prompt.

It's a good idea to keep the date and time current; you can put Date and Time commands in the AUTOEXEC.BAT file to ensure that you can set the date and time correctly whenever you start or restart the system.

For example, suppose each time you start the system you change the current drive to drive B and display the directory. You can tell DOS to carry out these commands automatically by putting them in AUTOEXEC.BAT. To test this, create an AUTOEXEC.BAT file by copying from the console to the system disk.

If you're not using a fixed disk, type the following:

```
B>copy con a:autoexec.bat
```

If you are using a fixed disk, type the following:

```
B>copy con c:autoexec.bat
```

Now type the commands to be put in AUTOEXEC.BAT:

```
rem NEW START-UP PROCEDURE
date
time
b:
dir
^Z
        1 File(s) copied

B>_
```

You created the file on the system disk, because that's where DOS looks for AUTOEXEC.BAT. To test your start-up procedure, you must restart the system.

*Note: If you're using a fixed disk, open the door latch on the diskette drive
so DOS will restart from the fixed disk. Shortly after you restart the system
you'll see the message* Insert diskette for drive B: and strike any key
when ready. *At this point, close the door latch and press any key to complete
the start-up procedure.*

Now restart the system by pressing Ctrl-Alt-Del. The start-up
screen differs from what you have seen before (if you're using a
fixed disk, the system prompt will be C>, not A>):

```
A>rem NEW START-UP PROCEDURE

A>date
Current date is Tue  1-01-1980
Enter new date (mm-dd-yy): 10-16-85

A>time
Current time is  0:00:17.41
Enter new time: 12:50

A>b:

B>dir

 Volume in drive B has no label
 Directory of  B:\

DIRLET   BAT        41  10-16-85  12:13p
PRNT     BAT        13  10-16-85  12:22p
DIRS     BAT        13  10-16-85  12:31p
LETR1    DOC        20  10-16-85  12:03p
LETR2    DOC        20  10-16-85  12:04p
LETR3    DOC        20  10-16-85  12:05p
         6 File(s)       356352 bytes free

B>_
```

Now your start-up procedure not only changes the current
drive and displays the directory; it prompts for the date and time
just as DOS normally does.

You can also use AUTOEXEC.BAT to handle special start-up
requirements. If you have added equipment options to your system
that require special set-up instructions with the Mode command,
for example, put the commands in AUTOEXEC.BAT so that you
needn't type them each time you start or restart the system. For
example, some options include an electronic clock and calendar that

set the date and time automatically; if you have such an option, create an AUTOEXEC.BAT file without the Date and Time commands to keep DOS from unnecessarily prompting you to set the date and time.

If other people use the system to run an application program, such as a word processor or a spreadsheet, you can make a copy of the system diskette for them that includes an AUTOEXEC.BAT file with the commands to start the application program automatically.

You can also use AUTOEXEC.BAT as a convenient way to restore the system to its normal state if you have temporarily changed some conditions, such as the setting of the serial-communications port or the characteristics of the color display.

Making a Chain of Batch Files

You can use a batch command in a batch file that defines another batch command. The second batch file could contain another batch command. This is called *chaining*, because each batch file is linked to the next one.

When DOS carries out the last command in a batch file, it returns to the command level and displays the system prompt. Because of this, if you put a chained batch command in another batch file, the chained batch command must be the last command in the preceding file.

If you were to put a chained batch command in the middle of another batch file, DOS would carry out the commands in the first file, up to the chained batch command; then it would jump to the chained batch file, carry out its commands, and return to command level. Any commands that followed the chained batch command in the first batch file would not be carried out, because DOS does not return to a previous batch file.

For example, suppose you decide to create two batch commands:

- Dirprt, which displays the directory entry of a file, then prints the file.

- Disprt, which displays a file and then prints it.

Both batch commands end by printing the file. You have already entered a batch command named Prnt that prints a file; you can use it as a chained batch file to create both the Dirprt and Disprt batch commands. Type the following:

```
B>copy con dirprt.bat
dir %1
prnt %1
^Z
         1 File(s) copied

B>copy con disprt.bat
type %1
prnt %1
^Z
         1 File(s) copied

B>_
```

Make sure the printer is on and use your AUTOEXEC.BAT file as a sample to test the Dirprt batch command. Type:

```
B>dirprt a:autoexec.bat
```

First, DOS substitutes *a:autoexec.bat* for *%1,* displays the Directory command in DIRPRT.BAT, and carries it out:

```
B>dir a:autoexec.bat

 Volume in drive A has no label
 Directory of  A:\

AUTOEXEC BAT        50  10-16-85  12:51p
        1 File(s)      59392 bytes free
```

Next, DOS displays the Prnt batch command after again substituting *a:autoexec.bat* for *%1:*

```
B>prnt a:autoexec.bat
```

Now DOS displays and carries out the Copy command (*copy %1 prn*) from the PRNT.BAT file, again substituting *a:autoexec.bat* for *%1:*

```
B>copy a:autoexec.bat prn
        1 File(s) copied

B>_
```

The file is printed.

Test the Disprt batch command by typing:

```
B>disprt a:autoexec.bat
```

First, DOS displays the Type command in DISPRT.BAT and carries it out by listing the contents of AUTOEXEC.BAT:

```
B>type a:autoexec.bat
rem NEW START-UP PROCEDURE
date
time
b:
dir
```

From here on, the Disprt batch command responds just as the Dirprt batch command did, because both batch files chain to PRNT.BAT:

```
B>prnt a:autoexec.bat

B>copy a:autoexec.bat prn
        1 File(s) copied

B>_
```

Again, the file is printed.

Chaining batch files is a good way to build powerful batch commands, because it lets you use one batch file in several different ways and reduces the chance of your batch files getting long and complicated.

Unless you want DOS to follow the start-up procedure you set up in AUTOEXEC.BAT, you won't need the file any longer, so erase it by typing the following:

```
B>erase a:autoexec.bat
```

SOME USEFUL COMMANDS

This chapter concludes by describing a few batch commands you may find useful; they might also give you some ideas for other commands you could create. Each topic includes a description of what the command does, the contents of the batch file, and one or two examples of its use.

These examples are illustrative, not hands-on exercises, because you may not have the necessary files or devices to use them. But remember that they're here; you'll probably find a situation in which they can be helpful.

Printing a File

Earlier in the chapter you created the Prnt batch command, which prints a file by copying it to the printer. PRNT.BAT contains:

```
copy %1 prn
```

To use the Prnt command, you would type the name of the batch file followed by the name of the file to be printed. For example, to print a file named REPORT.DOC, you would type:

```
B>prnt report.doc
```

DOS would display the Copy command, print the file, and would acknowledge:

```
B>copy report.doc prn
        1 File(s) copied

B>_
```

As the examples in Figure 13-1 showed, you can make batch commands more specific by including common parts of a file name or extension in the batch file. For example, if you frequently print files whose extension is DOC, you could enter the command in the batch file as *copy %1.doc;* to print the file named REPORT.DOC you would only have to type *prnt report*.

Printing a File in Small Type

If your printer is compatible with Epson or IBM printers, you can use the Mode command to change to the smaller type, so that 132 characters can be printed on a line. This type is handy for wide reports or spreadsheets and putting the Mode and Copy commands

in a batch file named SMALL.BAT makes them easy to use.
SMALL.BAT contains:

```
mode lpt1: 132
copy %1 lpt1:
mode lpt1: 80
```

The Small command takes one parameter, the name of the file to
be printed in small type. To use the Small command to print the file
REPORT.DOC, you would type:

```
B>small report.doc
```

DOS would display the Mode and Copy commands and print the file
in small type:

```
B>mode lpt1: 132
LPT1: set for 132

B>copy report.doc lpt1:
        1 File(s) copied

B>mode lpt1: 80
LPT1: set for 80

B>_
```

The second Mode command resets the printer to normal type.

Cleaning Up Disk Storage

Because Edlin and many word processors create a backup file
with an extension of BAK each time you edit a file, your disks can
get crowded with files you may not need. The CLEANUP.BAT batch
file described here would erase all the files whose extension is BAK.
CLEANUP.BAT contains:

```
erase %1*.bak
```

The Cleanup command takes one parameter, the drive letter
of the directory. If you omit the parameter, the command cleans up
the disk in the current drive. For example, to erase all files whose
extension is BAK on the disk in the current drive, you would
type *cleanup*.

To erase all files whose extension is BAK on the disk in drive B, you would type *A>cleanup b:*.

Setting Up a Non–IBM Display

If you're using a non-IBM display (either color or monochrome) with the color/graphics adapter, you may have to use the Mode command to shift the image left or right each time you start the system; this is an ideal situation for an AUTOEXEC.BAT file.

Suppose you use the Mode command to shift your display two columns to the right each time you start the system. To make that procedure part of your start-up, and still set the date and time, you can put the following commands in an AUTOEXEC.BAT file:

```
mode 80,r,t
date
time
```

If you had this AUTOEXEC.BAT file, each time you started or restarted the system DOS would begin by displaying the test pattern of 80 numbers:

```
01234567890...01234567890123456789012 3456789

Do you see the leftmost 0? (Y/N)
_
```

The display is shifted two columns right. To move it two more columns right, you would reply *n;* DOS would shift the image and display the test pattern again. Now you would reply *y*, and DOS would move on to the Date and Time commands:

```
A>date
Current date is Tue  1-01-1980
Enter new date (mm-dd-yy): 10-16-85

A>time
Current time is  0:00:17.41
Enter new time: 12:50

A>_
```

This procedure is considerably easier than typing the Mode command each time.

Batch files let you create your own commands to meet your specific needs. As you use DOS more, you'll probably find many uses for this capability. This chapter just introduces batch files. Chapters 15 and 16 show you how to use several additional commands that make batch commands one of the most powerful features of DOS.

CHAPTER
14

TAKING CONTROL
OF YOUR SYSTEM

U p to now, you have used the DOS commands in their standard form. DOS, however, gives you a great deal of flexibility in controlling the way some commands do their work for you.

This chapter describes where commands get their input and what they do with their output; it shows you how to control some commands, and describes some additional commands that give you the building blocks for your own set of customized commands.

It is easy to visualize what happens with command output, so even though it may seem odd to discuss results before discussing what causes them, the next section, on command output, provides you with a foundation for understanding command input as well.

REDIRECTING COMMAND OUTPUT

The result, or output, of most commands is some action, such as copying a file (with the Copy command) or controlling the operation of a device (with the Mode command). The output of a few commands, however, such as Directory, Check Disk, and Tree, is a report. Up to now, you have used these reports primarily as displays — DOS has sent them to the *standard output* device, the console. (Recall, from Chapter 7, that DOS uses the name CON, or console, for both the keyboard, which is input only, and the display, which is output only.)

As you'll see in this chapter, DOS also lets you send reports and other output to some other device, such as a printer, or to a file. This is called redirecting the output of the command. The technique is simple: To redirect the output of a command that sends its results to standard output (the display), follow the command name with > and the name of the device or file to which the output is to be sent. The > looks something like an arrowhead pointing toward the alternate output device or file.

This technique makes it easy, for example, to print a copy of the directory, as you did in Chapter 4. To repeat that example, but this time with an understanding of what happens, make sure the printer is turned on and type the following (if you're using a fixed disk, the system prompt will be C>):

```
A>dir > prn
```

The > tells DOS to redirect the output of the Directory command, and PRN tells DOS where to send it: to the printer. The directory should be printing now; cancel the printing by pressing Ctrl-Break if you don't want to print the entire directory.

REDIRECTING COMMAND INPUT

You have seen how quickly and easily you can redirect output to a device or a file. You can just as easily redirect input, in effect telling certain DOS commands to get their data from a source other than the one (often called *standard input*) they would normally use.

Together, redirected input and output are known as *I/O-redirection*. Although I/O redirection is based on some fairly esoteric concepts, it is easy to understand, as the examples in this chapter show.

Three DOS commands make particularly effective use of I/O redirection. They are known collectively as *filter commands*.

FILTER COMMANDS

Filter commands take standard input, change it in some way, and send the result to standard output. They are called filter commands because they work much like a filter in a water system, which takes the incoming water, changes it in some way, and sends it along the system.

DOS includes three filter commands that allow you to:

- Arrange lines in ascending or descending order with the Sort command.

- Search for a string of characters with the Find command.

- Temporarily halt the display after each 23 input lines (to give you a chance to read the screen) with the More command.

You can redirect both the input and output of a filter command. The filter commands aren't really intended to be used with keyboard input, but rather with their input redirected to a file or even to the output of another command. This chapter shows you how to use and combine the filter commands to create your own powerful, specialized commands.

PREPARING FOR THE EXAMPLES

I/O redirection and filter commands give you the elements of a simple file-management program. While they won't replace a file manager or a database-manager program, they allow you to use DOS to search and sort simple lists, without spending extra money or time on another program.

The example in this chapter uses a sample file that almost everyone needs: a list of names and telephone numbers. Too often, files of telephone numbers and business cards are out-of-date, incomplete, or in the other office. Questions arise: "Was that number in the telephone index or the business-card file?" Or "Did I file the number under Jones or under Accountants?" This example shows you how to let DOS keep track of your phone list and eliminate these questions. To try it, you need a formatted diskette with room for a small file.

If you have two diskette drives, put the formatted diskette in drive B. Type the following commands to change the current drive to B and to set the command path to the root directory of the system diskette in drive A:

```
A>b:
B>path a:\
```

Go on to the heading "Entering the Sample File."

If you're using a fixed disk, no special preparation is needed, but remember that the system prompt in the example will be C>, not B>.

Entering the Sample File

The sample file is named PH. You'll create the file with Edlin. (You could also use your word processor if, like Microsoft Word, it lets you save a document without inserting its own formatting codes.)

Each line of the file contains six items of data: last name, first name, area code, telephone number, a key word that identifies a category, and a short description. The key words are: CUST for customer, CONS for consultant, and VEND for vendor. You will enter the items in specific columns, so you can sort the list by any item you choose.

To create the file PH, type the following:

```
B>edlin ph
New file
*i
        1:*_
```

Edlin is waiting for you to enter something.

To help you get the items in the correct columns, the following entry shows the first line with each blank replaced by a period. Enter the line as shown, but don't enter the periods; press the space bar once for each period:

```
1:*Jones.....Michele...(747).429-6360..cons.chemist
```

End the line by pressing the <Enter> key.

Now enter the remaining lines in the sample file, which is shown in Figure 14-1. Don't enter the line numbers, and remember, you already entered the first line.

```
 1:  Jones      Michele     (747)  429-6360   cons  chemist
 2:  Smith      John        (747)  926-2945   vend  furniture
 3:  White      Alice       (747)  425-7692   cust  accountant
 4:  Green      Fred        (541)  926-4921   cust  math teach
 5:  Black      John        (747)  426-3385   cons  mech eng pkg
 6:  Smith      Ed          (541)  835-8747   vend  caterer
 7:  Jones      Alison      (747)  429-5584   cons  chem engineer
 8:  IBM        sales       (747)  463-2000   vend  Dave Hill
 9:  Jones      James       (747)  636-3541   cust  architect
10:  Black      Alice       (747)  426-7145   cust  elec eng
```

Figure 14-1. Telephone and business-card list

When you have entered all the lines, type Ctrl-Break to end the Insert command and *e* (End Edit) to save the file. When DOS has stored the file, it displays the system prompt.

Now you're ready to use the file. For example, to see the entry for Alice White, type:

```
B>find "Wh" ph

---------- ph
White     Alice      (747) 425-7692   cust accountant
```

That's fast, but it's just the beginning.

THE SORT FILTER COMMAND

sort /R / +<column>   The Sort filter command arranges, or sorts, lines of input and sends them to standard output (the display, unless you redirect the output—for example, to the printer). If you enter the command with no options, it sorts the lines in ascending order (A to Z, or lowest to highest number), starting in the first column.

The Sort command has two parameters:

sort /R / +<column>

/R *(Reverse)* sorts the lines in reverse order (Z to A instead of A to Z, or highest to lowest number).

/ +<column> where <column> is a column number, sorts the lines starting at the specified column, rather than starting in the first column.

To sort a particular file, you can redirect the input of the Sort command by following the command name with < and the name of the file to be sorted; use a blank both before and after the <. If you don't redirect the input, the Sort command sorts lines that you type at the keyboard (standard input).

Sort Filter-Command Examples

Figure 14-2 shows the column number of each of the six items in the telephone list: last name, first name, area code, telephone number, key word, and description. You'll use these numbers to sort the file in different ways.

```
1          11          21   27            37   42
Jones      Michele     (747) 429-6360     cons chemist
```

Figure 14-2. *Column numbers of items in the telephone list*

The simplest way to sort the file is in ascending order, starting in the first column (in the sample file, this is the last name). Type:

```
B>sort < ph
```

DOS quickly displays the sorted result:

```
Black      Alice       (747) 426-7145     cust elec eng
Black      John        (747) 426-3385     cons mech eng pkg
Green      Fred        (541) 926-4921     cust math teach
IBM        sales       (747) 463-2000     vend Dave Hill
Jones      Alison      (747) 429-5584     cons chem engineer
Jones      James       (747) 636-3541     cust architect
Jones      Michele     (747) 429-6360     cons chemist
Smith      Ed          (541) 835-8747     vend caterer
Smith      John        (747) 926-2945     vend furniture
White      Alice       (747) 425-7692     cust accountant
```

The file itself isn't changed; what you see is simply the result of DOS reading, sorting, and displaying the lines of the file.

Note: If you typed sort ph *instead of* sort < ph, *nothing happened. DOS is waiting for you to type something: You left out the redirection symbol (<) that tells DOS where to find the lines to sort, so DOS is waiting for lines from standard input (the keyboard). You can correct this by pressing Ctrl-Z, then the Enter key, to end standard input. DOS displays the system prompt, and you can enter the Sort command again.*

To sort the file in reverse order, use the /R option:

```
B>sort /r < ph
```

It doesn't take DOS any longer to sort backwards:

```
White     Alice     (747) 425-7692   cust accountant
Smith     John      (747) 926-2945   vend furniture
Smith     Ed        (541) 835-8747   vend caterer
Jones     Michele   (747) 429-6360   cons chemist
Jones     James     (747) 636-3541   cust architect
Jones     Alison    (747) 429-5584   cons chem engineer
IBM       sales     (747) 463-2000   vend Dave Hill
Green     Fred      (541) 926-4921   cust math teach
Black     John      (747) 426-3385   cons mech eng pkg
Black     Alice     (747) 426-7145   cust elec eng
```

Suppose you wanted to arrange the list by the key word—first the consultants, then the customers, then the vendors. The first letter of the key word is in column 37, so use the column option:

```
B>sort /+37 < ph
```

Now it's easy to pick out the different categories:

```
Jones     Alison    (747) 429-5584   cons chem engineer
Jones     Michele   (747) 429-6360   cons chemist
Black     John      (747) 426-3385   cons mech eng pkg
White     Alice     (747) 425-7692   cust accountant
Jones     James     (747) 636-3541   cust architect
Black     Alice     (747) 426-7145   cust elec eng
Green     Fred      (541) 926-4921   cust math teach
IBM       sales     (747) 463-2000   vend Dave Hill
Smith     Ed        (541) 835-8747   vend caterer
Smith     John      (747) 926-2945   vend furniture
```

Sorting is fast, easy, and useful.

THE FIND FILTER COMMAND

**find /V /C /N
<"string" >
<filename>**

The Find filter command searches input lines for a string of characters you specify. If you enter the command with no options, it displays all lines that contain the string.

The Find command has five parameters:

find /V /C /N <"string"> <filename>

/V displays all lines that do not contain the string.

/C *(Count)* displays just the number of lines that are found, not the lines themselves.

/N *(Number)* displays the input line number with each line found.

<"string"> is the string of characters you want to search for. It must be enclosed in quotation marks. The Find command distinguishes between uppercase and lowercase letters, so "cons" and "CONS", for example, are different strings, even though they contain the same letters.

<filename> is the name of the file to be searched. If you omit <filename>, the Find command searches standard input. You can include several different file names in a single Find command simply by separating the file names with blanks. If some of the files are not in the current drive, precede their file names with the letter, followed by a colon, of the drive they are in.

Find Filter-Command Examples

To display the entries for all consultants, type the following:

```
B>find "cons" ph
```

The first line identifies the input file (PH, in this case). Each line that contains the string is displayed immediately after:

```
---------- ph
Jones      Michele    (747) 429-6360   cons chemist
Black      John       (747) 426-3385   cons mech eng pkg
Jones      Alison     (747) 429-5584   cons chem engineer
```

To see how the Find command works with more than one file, type the following to make two duplicate copies of PH:

```
B>copy ph ph1
B>copy ph ph2
```

Now type the Find command you used in the preceding example, but this time include PH1 and PH2:

```
B>find "cons" ph ph1 ph2
```

DOS displays the name of each file as it finds "cons" in PH, PH1, and PH2:

```
---------- ph
Jones     Michelle    (747)  429-6360    cons chemist
Black     John        (747)  426-3385    cons mech eng pkg
Jones     Alison      (747)  429-5584    cons chem engineer

---------- ph1
Jones     Michelle    (747)  429-6360    cons chemist
Black     John        (747)  426-3385    cons mech eng pkg
Jones     Alison      (747)  429-5584    cons chem engineer

---------- ph2
Jones     Michelle    (747)  429-6360    cons chemist
Black     John        (747)  426-3385    cons mech eng pkg
Jones     Alison      (747)  429-5584    cons chem engineer
```

Obviously, using the Find command to search for a character string in several files is more productive when the contents of the files differ, but this example shows the method, if not the full capability of the command.

Return now to the original phone list, PH. If you just want to know how many consultants are in the list, use the /C option:

```
B>find /c "cons" ph
```

This time, the line that identifies the input file also shows the count:

```
---------- ph: 3
```

Three lines in the file contain "cons".

As often happens in a real telephone index, the sample file uses different words or abbreviations to mean the same thing. Both "engineer" and "eng" are used, for example, to describe an engineer. Both words contain "eng", however, so you can find all the engineers by typing the following:

```
B>find "eng" ph

---------- ph
Black     John        (747)  426-3385    cons mech eng pkg
Jones     Alison      (747)  429-5584    cons chem engineer
Black     Alice       (747)  426-7145    cust elec eng
```

Finding lines that *don't* contain the string

To display the entries *not* in the 747 area code, use the /V option:

```
B> find /v "(747" ph

---------- ph
Green      Fred        (541) 926-4921   cust math teach
Smith      Ed          (541) 835-8747   vend caterer
```

Including the left parenthesis with 747 distinguishes between entries with an area code of 747 and entries that might contain 747 in the phone number. Try the example without the left parenthesis:

```
B> find /v "747" ph

---------- ph
Green      Fred        (541) 926-4921   cust math teach
```

Ed Smith's telephone number is 926-8747, so his entry wasn't displayed even though his area code is 541. When you specify the characters to find, be sure to include enough to specify what you're looking for. In the sample file, for example, *"(7"* would be enough to specify the 747 area code; it wouldn't be enough, however, if the file contained another area code beginning with 7. As you saw, you must include the left parenthesis to distinguish an area code from some other sequence of numbers.

Including line numbers with the output

To display the entries for people named Smith and to include the line numbers of the entries, use the /N option:

```
B> find /n "Smith" ph

---------- ph
[2]Smith    John        (747) 926-2945   vend furniture
[6]Smith    Ed          (541) 835-8747   vend caterer
```

The two entries displayed are the second and sixth lines of the sample file.

Combining Find command options

You can combine Find command options. For example, to display the entries not in the 747 area code and to include their line numbers, use both the /V and /N options:

```
B>find /v /n "(7" ph

---------- ph
[4]Green      Fred        (541) 926-4921   cust math teach
[6]Smith      Ed          (541) 835-8747   vend caterer
```

(If you are a Version 2 user, you see a blank line, *[11]*, at the bottom of the preceding display. There are only 10 lines in the file, so what does that *[11]* mean? The last character in the file is the special code that marks the end of the file, the one that DOS displays as ^Z. The Version 2 Find command counts this end-of-file marker as a separate line. Keep this in mind when you combine the /V option with either the /N option, as this example does, or the /C option, which counts that last line.)

MORE ON REDIRECTING

Earlier in this chapter, you redirected the input to the Sort command by specifying the file PH. You can also redirect the output of a filter command. To print the entries for all vendors (redirect output from the display to the printer), type the following:

```
B>find "vend" ph > prn
```

The entries are printed. If your phone list has two or three hundred entries, this technique of using options and redirecting output is a quick way to print a selected group of entries.

Redirecting Both Input and Output

You can redirect both input and output by following the command name with < and the name of the input file or device, then with > and the name of the output file or device. Be sure to include blanks before and after both < and >.

For example, to print the sorted version of PH, type:

```
B>sort < ph > prn
```

The sorted file is printed (type Ctrl-Break if you don't want to wait for it to finish printing).

You could, of course, redirect both the input and output of a command from, and to, the same file. Doing this, however, can make your original file unusable for reasons beyond the technical scope of this book. If you want to sort a file and keep the same file name, redirect the output to a temporary file, delete the original file, then use the DOS Rename command to give the temporary file the original file name.

For example, if you wanted to sort PHSORT in reverse order and have the result still named PHSORT, you would use the following sequence of commands: First, sort the original to a temporary file (*sort /r <phsort> temp*). Then, delete the original file (*erase phsort*). Finally, rename the temporary file (*ren temp phsort*).

Now PHSORT would contain the telephone list sorted in reverse order. Again, you could verify the contents by displaying PHSORT with the Type command.

Adding Redirected Output to a File

When you redirect output to an existing file, the contents are erased and the redirected output replaces what was there. But you can also add redirected output to an existing file by using $>>$, instead of $>$. If the file doesn't exist, it is created, just as when you use $>$.

CONNECTING COMMANDS WITH A PIPE

A powerful way of using a filter command is to redirect the output of some other command to the input of the filter command. In effect, the two commands are connected, with the output of the first command feeding directly into the filter command. Continuing the analogy to a water system, this connection is called a *pipe*.

You tell DOS to pipe the output of one command to the input of another by typing | (the shifted form of the key to the left of the Z) between the names of the two commands; the | provides the connection between the two commands. The More filter command provides a simple example.

The More Filter Command

The More filter command displays 23 lines (one screenful) and a line that says -- *More* --, and then it pauses. When you press any key, it displays the next 23 lines and pauses again, continuing in the same way until all the input has been displayed.

The directory of the system disk is more than one screenful, so use it as an example by typing the following:

```
B>dir | more
```

This command tells DOS to redirect the output of the Directory command to the input of the More command. The More command displays the first 23 lines of the directory and -- *More* -- in the 24th row. Press any key to see the rest of the directory. The More command lets you review a long output sequence or file without having to press Ctrl-Num Lock to start and stop the display.

Combining Filter Commands

You can pipe the output of one Find command to the input of another Find command to make a more specific search. A real list like the sample phone list, for example, might include several dozen customers. Suppose you want to display only the customers in the 747 area code. To do this, pipe the output of a Find command that searches for "cust" to another Find command that searches for "(7". Type the following:

```
B>find "cust" ph | find "(7"

White     Alice     (747) 425-7692   cust accountant
Jones     James     (747) 636-3541   cust architect
Black     Alice     (747) 426-7145   cust elec eng
```

If you check an earlier list of the file, you'll see that Fred Green is a customer, but his area code is 541, so the second Find command eliminated the entry for his name. Notice that the line that identifies the file (---------- *ph*) isn't displayed. The first Find command pipes ---------- *ph* as part of its output to the second Find command, but because the line does not contain the string "(7", it is not included as part of the output of the second Find command.

You can also pipe the output of the Find command to the Sort command. To see all the consultants sorted by last name, type the following:

```
B>find "cons" ph | sort

---------- ph
Black      John        (747) 426-3385   cons mech eng pkg
Jones      Alison      (747) 429-5584   cons chem engineer
Jones      Michele     (747) 429-6360   cons chemist
```

You can combine as many commands as you like. Suppose you want to print a list of all customers in the 747 area code, sorted by telephone number. You can search PH for "cust", pipe that output to a Find command that searches for "(7", pipe that output to a Sort command that sorts at column 27 (the telephone number), and redirect the output to the printer. Type the following:

```
B>find "cust" ph | find "(7" | sort /+27 > prn

White      Alice       (747) 425-7692   cust accountant
Black      Alice       (747) 426-7145   cust elec eng
Jones      James       (747) 636-3541   cust architect
```

If your list included several dozen customers, this could be a handy way to organize a calling campaign.

The Difference Between > and |

Sometimes the distinction between > and | isn't readily apparent, but the difference is easy to demonstrate. Sort is a filter command. To make the output of the Directory command the input to the Sort command, type the following:

```
B>dir | sort
```

As you would expect, DOS displays the directory stored in alphabetic order. If the directory includes two unfamiliar files whose names are something like %PIPE1.$$$ or 072F2321, and whose lengths are 0, don't be alarmed. These are temporary files DOS creates in order to pipe the output of one command to the input of another; DOS deletes the files automatically when the commands are completed.

Now type:

```
B>dir > sort
```

This time you didn't see anything on the screen because you told DOS to redirect the output of the Directory command to a file named SORT. Confirm this by displaying the file with the Type command:

```
B>type sort
```

The file contains the directory, not sorted, and with no temporary files. It's an ordinary directory. You created a file named SORT when you redirected the output of the Directory command.

CHAPTER SUMMARY

As you can see, input and output redirection, filter commands, and pipes let you create powerful, very specific commands. The next two chapters show you how to combine these capabilities with the advanced batch commands, to put the power of the computer at your command.

CHAPTER
15

CREATING
SMART COMMANDS

The previous two chapters showed how batch files, I/O redirection, pipes, and filter commands let you change the way DOS commands work and let you build your own commands. This chapter shows how DOS gives you more control over the way it carries out the commands you build into a batch file, and makes it possible for you to develop powerful commands tailored to your specific needs.

You can make your commands display their own instructions or warning messages; or, you can specify a set of circumstances under which DOS carries out one command—or a different sequence of commands altogether. You can even make the system pause until you tell it to proceed.

This chapter shows you how to develop a batch file that uses most of these capabilities. The next chapter extends the example, describes two additional batch commands, and shows several useful commands you can create. When you complete these two chapters, you'll be ready to apply the full power of DOS to your needs.

PREPARING FOR THE EXAMPLES

For these examples, you'll need one or two formatted diskettes and some sample files. If you completed the examples in Chapter 14, "Taking Control of Your System," use the diskette on which you stored the phone list file. If you are not using a fixed disk, you also have to copy some command files onto one of your practice diskettes. Follow the instructions under the heading that describes your system.

If You Are Not Using a Fixed Disk

If you're not using a fixed disk, you need two formatted diskettes. Put the diskette with the phone list into drive B. You're going to take the system diskette out of drive A in a moment, so

enter the following commands to copy the Find, Sort, and More commands to the practice diskette:

```
A>copy find.exe b:
        1 File(s) copied

A>copy sort.exe b:
        1 File(s) copied

A>copy more.com b:
        1 File(s) copied
```

The examples in this chapter have you modify a batch file several times. You use Edlin commands to make the changes, so copy the Edlin program to drive B by typing the following:

```
A>copy edlin.com b:
        1 File(s) copied
```

Now remove the system diskette from drive A and replace it with the second formatted diskette. Change the current drive to B by typing:

```
A>b:

B>_
```

If You Are Using a Fixed Disk

If you're using a fixed disk, you need only one formatted diskette; put it in drive A. All the commands you need are on the fixed disk, so you can use the examples as shown, except that the system prompt will be C>, not B>.

Creating the Sample Files

You will use six sample files in the next two chapters:

P.DOC	Q.DOC
P.BAK	Q.BAK
P.OLD	Q.OLD

Type the following to create the sample files (press F6 and Enter where you see ^Z):

```
B>copy con p.doc
This is a sample file.
^Z
        1 File(s) copied

B>copy p.doc p.bak
        1 File(s) copied

B>copy p.doc p.old
        1 File(s) copied

B>copy p.* q.*
P.DOC
P.BAK
P.OLD
        3 File(s) copied
```

If you're creating these files on a diskette, you'll need this diskette in the next chapter, so label it BATCH COMMANDS (if it's already labeled for the phone list file, just add the new words). This completes the preparation for the examples.

CREATING AN ARCHIVE COMMAND

Disk files proliferate as you use your computer. You'll probably archive files from time to time, erasing them from your working disks and copying them to long-term storage diskettes, just as you occasionally remove documents from your paper files and put them in long-term storage.

This chapter shows you how to use the DOS batch commands with a series of examples that develop an Archive command. Starting with just a Copy command, you expand the batch file to display instructions, provide a safeguard against inadvertently erasing a previously archived file, and erase the file after it is archived.

The diskette in drive A represents the archive diskette, the one you store in a safe place. The diskette in drive B—or the fixed disk, if you're using one—represents the working disk that contains files you want to archive.

Your Archive command will be a file named ARCHIVE.BAT. The initial version contains only a Copy command. To create the file, type the following:

```
B>copy con archive.bat
copy %1 a:%1
^Z
        1 File(s) copied
```

This file is the starting point for your Archive command. It requires only one parameter, the name of the file to be archived. The Copy command copies this file (%1 in the Copy command) to the diskette in drive A, giving it the same name (a:%1) as the original. To see how the batch file works, make sure the archive diskette is in drive A; archive P.DOC by typing:

```
B>archive p.doc
```

DOS responds by displaying and carrying out the Copy command in the batch file:

```
B>copy p.doc a:p.doc
        1 File(s) copied
```

This isn't much, but then it's only a starting point. You'll add significantly to this simple command as you go through the examples in this chapter.

MODIFYING THE SAMPLE BATCH FILE

This chapter describes four batch commands: Echo, Pause, If, and Goto. Each command description explains the purpose of the command, then adds it to ARCHIVE.BAT. The modified version of the batch file is shown with the changed or added lines shaded, then instructions are given for making the changes with Edlin.

CONTROLLING SYSTEM MESSAGES

echo on off
<message>

The Echo command controls whether commands in a batch file are displayed, and it lets you display your own messages. It has three parameters:

echo on off <message>

on causes commands to be displayed as they are carried out (this is called "turning echo on"). Echo is on unless you turn it off with the off parameter.

off causes commands not to be displayed as they are carried out (this is called "turning echo off"). Eliminating the commands from the display can make a batch file easier to use by reducing clutter on the screen.

<message> is a string of characters, such as a reminder or warning, to be displayed. <message> is displayed whether echo is turned on or off.

You can include only one parameter with an Echo command. If you omit all parameters (just type *echo*), DOS displays the status of echo (either *ECHO is on* or *ECHO is off*).

The first change you'll make to your Archive command is to add an Echo command at the beginning to turn echo off and another Echo command to display a title message.

Here is the modified version of ARCHIVE.BAT (the Edlin line numbers are displayed for reference):

```
1: echo off
2: echo Archive Procedure
3: copy %1 a:%1
```

Using Edlin, type these commands to make the change:

```
B>edlin archive.bat
End of input file
*i
        1:*echo off
        2:*echo Archive Procedure
        3:*<Ctrl-Break>

*e
```

To archive P.DOC with your new Archive command, type the name of the batch file and the name of the file to be archived:

```
B>archive p.doc
```

Because a batch command always starts with echo on, DOS displays the first Echo command, which turns echo off. Then it carries out the second Echo command, which displays the title of your command, and the Copy command, from the original ARCHIVE.BAT file, which copies the file:

```
B>echo off
Archive Procedure
          1 File(s) copied
```

Messages produced by a command itself (such as *1 File(s) copied* in the preceding example) are always displayed, whether echo is on or off.

Your Archive command is starting to take shape. It's time to add some instructions.

MAKING THE SYSTEM PAUSE

pause <message>

Some DOS commands, such as Format and Diskcopy, display a message and wait for you to respond, giving you a chance to confirm your intention or complete preparation by inserting a diskette or turning on the printer. You can have your batch files do the same; use the Pause command, which displays its own built-in message, *Strike a key when ready . . .* and makes the system wait until you press any key.

The Pause command has one parameter:

pause <message>

<message> is a string of characters, such as a reminder or warning, to be displayed by the Pause command. <message> is displayed only if echo is on.

You'll add a Pause command to ARCHIVE.BAT now. You'll also add a message reminding you to make sure the archive diskette is in drive A before copying the file. But: Any message you include as a parameter with the Pause command is displayed only if echo is on and you have turned echo off in line 1 of ARCHIVE.BAT.

You can still use the Pause command, however. Instead of using the message capability of the Pause command, just use an Echo command to display the reminder, then add a Pause command without a message. This way of doing things is a bit more work than just adding a message after the Pause command, but the result is a command that is easier to use because the display is uncluttered by all the commands that would be displayed if you were to turn echo on.

The modified version of ARCHIVE.BAT is:

```
1: echo off
2: echo Archive Procedure
3: echo Make sure archive diskette is in drive A
4: pause
5: copy %1 a:%1
```

The Edlin commands to make this change are as follows. (*Note:* Even though line 3 is shown on two lines in the text, you should type everything from *echo* to *A* as one line when you enter it):

```
B> edlin archive.bat
End of input file
* 3i
        3:* echo Make sure archive diskette is in drive A
        4:* pause
        5:* <Ctrl-Break>

* e
```

Test this version by typing:

```
B> archive p.doc

B> echo off
Archive Procedure
Make sure archive diskette is in drive A
Strike a key when ready . . . _
```

The Echo command displays the reminder, then the Pause command displays its message telling you to strike a key, and the system waits. Complete the command by pressing any key. DOS copies the file and acknowledges:

```
    1 File(s) copied
```

CONTROLLING WHICH COMMANDS ARE CARRIED OUT

**if not <condition>
<command>**

Besides carrying out DOS commands as though you had typed them individually, batch files let you specify that a command should be carried out only if some condition (such as whether a file exists) is true. This capability makes your batch files more flexible, letting you adapt them to a variety of situations.

The If command specifies the condition to be checked and the DOS command to be carried out. It has three parameters:

if not <condition> <command>

not qualifies the statement so that <command> is carried out only if <condition> is not true.

<condition> is the condition to check. It has two commonly used forms:

exist<filename> checks whether the named file exists. You can specify a path name, if necessary. If <filename> exists, the condition is true.

<string1>= =<string2> compares the two character strings. If they are identical, the condition is true. Note that there are two equal signs.

<command> is any DOS command.

You'll add an If command to ARCHIVE.BAT to control when a warning message is displayed.

Adding Protection to Your Archive Command

When you copy a file with the Copy command, you tell DOS the name of the original and the name to be given to the new copy. DOS checks to see if there is already a file with the same name as the copy on the disk; if there is, DOS erases the existing file and replaces it with the copy. What if you didn't realize that a file with the same name existed on the disk? You might inadvertently lose a valuable file.

To protect yourself against such an oversight you will include two more commands in ARCHIVE.BAT. First, you will add an If command that checks to see whether the file to be archived already exists on the archive diskette in drive A. If it does, an Echo command in the second part of the If command displays a warning message telling you that you can cancel the command by pressing Ctrl-Break.

Then you'll add a Pause command to give you time to read the warning message and, if necessary, cancel the Archive command by pressing Ctrl-Break. Here is the modified version of ARCHIVE.BAT:

```
1: echo off
2: echo Archive Procedure
3: echo Make sure archive diskette is in drive A
4: pause
5: if exist a:%1 echo a:%1 exists. Press
   CTRL-BREAK to cancel, or
6: pause
7: copy %1 a:%1
```

Here are the Edlin commands to make this change. As before, type line 5 on one line, even though it is shown on two in the text.

```
B>edlin archive.bat
End of input file
*5i
        5:*if exist a:%1 echo a:%1 exists. Press
           CTRL-BREAK to cancel, or
        6:*pause
        7:*<Ctrl-Break>

    *e
```

Test this version of your Archive command by typing:

```
B>archive p.doc

B>echo off
Archive Procedure
Make sure archive diskette is in drive A
Strike a key when ready . . . _
```

Press any key to continue the command:

```
a:p.doc exists. Press CTRL-BREAK to cancel, or
Strike a key when ready . . . _
```

Don't press any key yet.

You might not want to replace the copy of the file in drive A. Press Ctrl-Break to cancel the command. DOS asks whether you really mean it:

```
Terminate batch job (Y/N)? _
```

Type *y* to confirm. DOS cancels the rest of your Archive command and displays the system prompt without copying the file. If you had not pressed Ctrl-Break, the file would have been copied as before, erasing the previously archived version of P.DOC.

Smoothing a Rough Edge

Your Archive command is getting more useful; you've protected yourself from inadvertently erasing an existing file. But there's a problem now. See what happens if the name of the file to be archived isn't the name of a file already on the diskette in drive A. Erase P.DOC from drive A and archive it again:

```
B>erase a:p.doc

B>archive p.doc

B>echo off
Archive Procedure
Make sure archive diskette is in drive A
Strike a key when ready . . . _
```

Fine so far. Press the space bar to continue:

```
Strike a key when ready . . . _
```

That's not so good. The system comes right back and pauses again, even though everything is OK, because the Pause command that follows the If command is always carried out. Press the space bar again:

```
1 File(s) copied
```

DOS copies the file as it should. Your Archive command is working properly, but the two pauses could be confusing, especially if someone else uses your batch command. How can this be fixed?

You could delete the first Pause command; but, if you did, you wouldn't have a chance to make sure the correct diskette was in drive A. That's not a very good solution.

Or, you could delete the second Pause command and change the If command, making the "file exists" warning a Pause message instead of an Echo message, as it is now. But then, recall that you would have to delete the command *echo off* at the beginning of the batch file so that the message following the new Pause command would be displayed. And that would mean all your commands in the file would be displayed. This solution would make the response to your Archive command somewhat cluttered and confusing, so it isn't too good, either.

There is, however, a way to change your Archive command so that the second Pause command is carried out only if the file to be archived is on the diskette in drive A. This solution requires using another command for batch files, the Goto command.

CHANGING THE SEQUENCE OF COMMANDS

goto <label>

The batch files you have created up to now carry out the DOS commands they contain in the order in which the commands appear. Your batch commands would be more flexible if you could control the order in which the commands are carried out. The Goto command gives you this control by telling DOS to go to a specific line in the command file, rather than to the next command in the sequence.

You tell DOS where to go in the batch file by specifying a label. A label identifies a line in a batch file; it consists of a colon (:) immediately followed by a string of characters (such as :START). A label is not a command. It merely identifies a location in a batch file. When DOS goes to a label, it carries out whatever commands follow the label.

The Goto command has one parameter:

goto <label>

<label> is the label that identifies the line in the batch file where DOS is to go.

The Goto command is often used as part of an If command. For example, the If command checks some condition. If the condition is not true, DOS carries out the next command; if the condition is true, DOS carries out the Goto command and moves to some other part of the batch file.

Remember the problem with your Archive command? If the file to be archived is already on the diskette in drive A, you want to display a warning message and pause; otherwise, you just want to copy the file. This situation is tailor-made for an If command that includes a Goto command.

The modified version of ARCHIVE.BAT is:

```
1: echo off
2: echo Archive Procedure
3: echo Make sure archive diskette is in drive A
4: pause
5: if not exist a:%1 goto safe
6: echo a:%1 exists. Press CTRL-BREAK to cancel, or
7: pause
8: :safe
9: copy %1 a:%1
```

These changes warrant a bit more explanation:

- The If command still checks to see whether the name of the file to be archived exists on the diskette in drive A. Now, however, the command includes the parameter *not*, which means that the command in the second part of the If command is carried out only if the condition is not true (that is, if the file does not exist on the diskette in drive A).

- The second part of the If command—the command to be carried out if the condition is true—is changed to a Goto command that tells DOS to skip to a label called :SAFE.

- If the file to be archived doesn't exist on the diskette in drive A, the Goto command is carried out and DOS jumps to the label :SAFE, skipping the intervening Echo and Pause commands. The Copy command following :SAFE copies the file.

• If the file to be archived does exist on the diskette in drive A, the Goto command is not carried out and DOS continues on to the Echo and Pause commands. If you don't cancel by pressing Ctrl-Break, DOS carries out the Copy command. In this instance, DOS ignores the line that contains the label :SAFE because the only purpose of the label is to identify a location in a batch file for a Goto command.

Use the following Edlin commands to make these changes. The symbol <Ins> means press the Insert key; <F2> means press the F2 function key; <F4> means press the F4 function key:

```
B>edlin archive.bat
End of input file
*5,5,6c
*5
        5:*if exist a:%1 echo a:%1 exists .Press
            CTRL-BREAK to cancel, or
        5:*→→→<Ins>not <F2>egoto safe
*6
        6:*if exist a:%1 echo a:%1 exists. Press
            CTRL-BREAK to cancel, or
        6:* <F4>e<F4>e<F3>
*8i

        8:*:safe
        9:* <Ctrl-Break>

*e
```

P.DOC is on the diskette in drive A (you archived it a bit earlier), so first see if this version of your Archive command warns you that the file exists. Type the following:

```
B>archive p.doc

B>echo off
Archive Procedure
Make sure archive diskette is in drive A
Strike a key when ready . . . _
```

Press any key to continue the command:

```
a:p.doc exists. Press CTRL-BREAK to cancel, or
Strike a key when ready . . . _
```

There's the warning. Press any key to complete the command:

```
1 File(s) copied
```

But the problem came up when the file wasn't on the archive diskette: You got the second pause anyway. Test your revised Archive command in this situation by archiving P.BAK:

```
B>archive p.bak

B>echo off
Archive Procedure
Make sure archive diskette is in drive A
Strike a key when ready . . . _
```

Press any key to continue:

```
    1 File(s) copied
```

Problem solved. Because P.BAK wasn't on the archive diskette in drive A, the Goto command was carried out; it caused DOS to skip over the intervening Echo and Pause commands and to copy the file.

Your Archive command works properly. You had to do a little more work to avoid the double pause, but now the command is less confusing and easier to use. You'll probably encounter this kind of circumstance fairly often as you create commands. Just remember: It takes a little more time to make a command easy to use, but the investment is usually worthwhile, especially if someone other than you will use the command.

Using Wildcard Characters with a Batch File

You can use wildcard characters to archive a series of files with your Archive command. Type the following command to archive all the files named P:

```
B>archive p.*

B>echo off
Archive Procedure
Make sure archive diskette is in drive A
Strike a key when ready . . . _
```

Press any key:

```
a:p.* exists. Press CTRL-BREAK to cancel, or
Strike a key when ready . . . _
```

You archived P.DOC and P.BAK in earlier examples, so they're on the archive diskette. The Archive command doesn't identify the specific file that exists, but it does give you a chance to cancel if there's a possibility you don't want to erase the file.

Press Ctrl-Break to cancel the rest of the command, and respond to the DOS prompt for confirmation with *y:*

```
Terminate batch job (Y/N)? y
```

If you had pressed any key other than Ctrl-Break, all the files named P would have been copied to the diskette in drive A, replacing any versions that might already have been there.

Erasing the Original of an Archived File

Archiving involves not only copying a file to an archive diskette; it also means deleting the original. Your Archive command only copies; now it's time to make it delete, too. But just as it's prudent to check whether the file exists on the archive diskette before you make the copy, it's also prudent to check again before erasing the original, just to be sure the file was copied to the archive diskette.

You need only one additional If command to check whether the file to be archived is on the archive diskette and, if it is, to erase the original from the working disk. Here is this modified version of ARCHIVE.BAT:

```
 1: echo off
 2: echo Archive Procedure
 3: echo Make sure archive diskette is in drive A
 4: pause
 5: if not exist a:%1 goto safe
 6: echo a:%1 exists. Press CTRL-BREAK to cancel, or
 7: pause
 8: :safe
 9: copy %1 a:%1
10: if exist a:%1 erase %1
```

The Edlin commands to make this change are:

```
B>edlin archive.bat
End of input file
*10i
        10:*if exist a:%1 erase %1
        11:*<Ctrl-Break>

*e
```

The screen responses of this version of your Archive command are the same as in the previous version, but the new command erases the original file after copying it. Test it by archiving P.DOC again:

```
B>archive p.doc

B>echo off
Archive Procedure
Make sure archive diskette is in drive A
Strike a key when ready . . . _
```

Press any key to continue:

```
a:p.doc exists. Press CTRL-BREAK to cancel, or
Strike a key when ready . . . _
```

You want to copy the file to the archive diskette, so press any key:

```
   1 File(s) copied
```

See if the original version of P.DOC is still on your working diskette by typing:

```
B>dir p.doc

 Volume in drive B has no label
 Directory of  B:\

File not found
```

The original is gone. Your Archive command does copy the specified file to the archive diskette and then delete the original. Functionally, the command is complete.

DRESSING UP YOUR
ARCHIVE COMMAND

The value of your batch files depends not only on what they do, but also on how easy they are to use correctly. This ease of use is particularly important if you use a batch file only occasionally, or if someone else uses it, and it's vital if the batch file erases other files, as your Archive command does.

That's why, for example, your Archive command starts by turning echo off: An uncluttered screen helps to make the responses less confusing. You can also do some other things to make a batch file easy to use:

* Clear the screen.

* Use the Echo command to display messages that report progress or results.

* Use blanks or insert tabs so you can position messages displayed by the Echo command where they are noticeable.

* Use the Echo command to display blank lines where they improve the readability of the screen.

You can also use the Remark command to put notes to yourself in the batch file. As long as echo is off, these remarks aren't displayed. Remarks can help you remember how a batch file works, if you have to change it or if you want to create a similar command, using the same technique; remarks are especially useful if the batch file is long or you haven't looked at it for a while.

The following changes don't add any capability to your Archive command, but they do make it easier for someone to understand what's happening. The changes are described in more detail in a moment. Here is the modified version of ARCHIVE.BAT:

```
1: echo off
2: cls
3: REM THREE TABS IN FOLLOWING ECHO COMMAND
4: echo                              ***ARCHIVE PROCEDURE***
5: echo ^@
6: echo Make sure archive diskette is in drive A
7: pause
8: REM BRANCH AROUND WARNING IF FILE NOT ARCHIVED
```

```
 9: if not exist a:%1 goto safe
10: echo ^@
11: REM CTRL-G SOUNDS A BEEP
12: echo ^Ga:%1 exists. Press CTRL-BREAK to cancel, or
13: pause
14: :safe
15: copy %1 a:%1
16: if exist a:%1 erase %1
17: echo ^@
18: echo %1 archived.
```

The purpose of each change is as follows:

- In line 2, the Clear Screen command starts your Archive command off with a blank screen, giving you complete control over the display.

- In line 3, the Remark command reminds you that the space at the beginning of the Echo command in line 4 is created by three tabs.

- In line 4, the title (*** ARCHIVE PROCEDURE ***) is made more prominent and is displayed in the center of the screen by the insertion of three tabs after the Echo command.

- In line 5, an Echo command displays a blank line below the title. The ^@ represents the function key labeled F7, which causes the Echo command to display a blank line. (If you are using Version 3.1, you may see the symbols in reverse order— @^ — if you edit or list the file.)

- In line 8, the Remark command explains the purpose of the Goto command in line 9.

- In line 10, another Echo command displays a blank line to make the warning message in line 12 more visible.

- In line 11, the Remark command explains how the beep is sounded by the Echo command in line 12.

- In line 12, the ^G (again, sometimes reversed in Version 3.1 of DOS) in the message displayed by the Echo command represents a character called Ctrl-G, which causes the system to beep and calls attention to the warning. To type Ctrl-G, hold down the Ctrl key and press G.

- In line 17, the Echo command displays another blank line, to make the message in line 18 more visible.

- In line 18, the Echo command displays a message that tells which file was archived.

Here are the Edlin commands to make these changes (type line 4 as a single line):

```
B>edlin archive.bat
End of input file
*2i
        2:*cls
        3:REM THREE TABS IN FOLLOWING ECHO COMMAND
        4:*<Ctrl-Break>

*4
        4:*echo Archive Procedure
        4:*→→→→<Spacebar><Tab><Tab><Tab>***ARCHIVE
            PROCEDURE***
*5i
        5:*echo<Spacebar><F7>
        6:*<Ctrl-Break>

*8i
        8:*REM BRANCH AROUND WARNING IF FILE NOT ARCHIVED
        9:*<Ctrl-Break>

*10i
        10:*echo<Spacebar><F7>
        11:*REM CTRL-G SOUNDS A BEEP
        12:*<Ctrl-Break>

*12
        12:*echo a:%1 exists. Press CTRL-BREAK to cancel, or
        12:*→→→→→<Ins><Ctrl-G><F3>
*#i
        17:*echo<Spacebar><F7>
        18:*echo %1 archived
        19:*<Ctrl-Break>

*1l
```

The final command displays the entire file. Compare it to the modified form of ARCHIVE.BAT on pages 286-287. If there are any differences, correct them before saving the revised version. (If you have trouble with any of the special keys used in line 12, just type the entire new line). When the file is correct, save it by typing *e*.

Although you haven't changed anything your Archive command does, its screen responses are quite different now. Test the new version by archiving P.OLD (which isn't on the archive diskette):

```
B>archive p.old
```

Because ARCHIVE.BAT now starts by clearing the screen, everything you see from this point on is displayed by your Archive command. When the command prompts you to check the diskette in drive A, press any key to continue. The screen looks like this:

```
                         ***ARCHIVE PROCEDURE***

Make sure archive diskette is in drive A
Strike a key when ready . . .
        1 File(s) copied

p.old archived
```

Test ARCHIVE.BAT again to see how it responds when the file already exists on the archive diskette. P.DOC and P.OLD are no longer on the diskette in drive B (you archived them after making the change that erases the file), so archive P.BAK. Type the following, pressing any key to continue the command after each pause:

```
B>archive p.bak
```

The screen looks like this:

```
                         ***ARCHIVE PROCEDURE***

Make sure archive diskette is in drive A
Strike a key when ready . . .

a:p.bak exists. Press CTRL-BREAK to cancel, or
Strike a key when ready . . .
        1 File(s) copied

p.bak archived
```

ARCHIVE.BAT is quite a bit longer than when you began, but your Archive command doesn't look much like a homemade command any more. Although you needn't always go to such length when you create a command, it's nice to know that a little extra effort can make your work look professional. If others will use the batch files you create, the investment of your effort can quickly pay off in shorter training time, more efficient use of the system, and fewer mistakes.

CHAPTER SUMMARY

This chapter covered a lot of ground. Experimenting is the best way to put what you learned here into practice. Just be sure to use disks that don't contain files you need until you're sure your batch commands are working properly.

The next chapter describes two additional batch commands that let you create even more flexible batch files, and it shows you several useful batch commands you can use to start your personal collection. You need the archive diskette in drive A. Remove this diskette and label it ARCHIVED FILES.

CHAPTER
16

CREATING MORE
SMART COMMANDS

The previous chapter showed you how to use the advanced capability of batch files. Knowing how to create batch files is only half the job, however; the other half is finding uses for them. This chapter shows you how to create some commands to search through the phone list file you created in Chapter 14; it also describes two advanced batch commands and shows several useful batch files to give you some ideas for your own use.

PREPARING FOR THE EXAMPLES

For the first examples in this chapter, you need the phone list file (PH) that you created in Chapter 14, "Taking Control of Your System." If you haven't gone through the examples in Chapters 14 and 15, you should do so before proceeding with this chapter.

If you're using diskettes, put the diskette that contains the PH file in drive B and change the system prompt to B>.

If you're using a fixed disk, PH should already be in the root directory. You needn't make any preparation but, as in Chapter 15, note that the system prompt will be C>, not B>.

COMMANDS TO SEARCH THROUGH A FILE

In Chapter 14, you created a file of names, addresses, and telephone numbers, and you used the Find and Sort commands to display entries. You can also put the Find and Sort commands in batch files to create your own search commands and achieve some of the capabilities of a simple record-management program.

For example, the simplest search uses the Find command to display all records that contain a particular string. Create a batch file named SHOW.BAT by typing the following:

```
B>copy con show.bat
echo off
find "%1" ph
^Z
        1 File(s) copied
```

This batch file gives you a Show command that displays all records from PH that contain a string you specify as the parameter to your Show command. To search the phone list, type *show*

followed by the string. For example, to display all consultants (entries that contain the string "cons"), type:

```
B> show cons
```

DOS displays all entries for consultants:

```
B>echo off

---------- ph
Jones      Michele    (747) 429-6360   cons chemist
Black      John       (747) 426-3385   cons mech eng pkg
Jones      Alison     (747) 429-5584   cons chem engineer
```

This procedure is easier than typing *find "cons" ph*. Read on; you'll find that you can use batch files to make more powerful searches just as easily.

Compound Searches

As the examples in "Taking Control of Your System" showed, you can combine Find commands to search for records that contain various combinations of character strings, such as all consultants named Jones or all entries outside the 747 area code. Putting these Find commands in a batch file saves even more typing than the Show command you just created.

For example, suppose you want to create a command to show all entries that contain both one string and another. As you saw in Chapter 14, this requires two Find commands, with the output of the first piped to the second. You could call such a command Showand; create a file named SHOWAND.BAT by typing:

```
B>copy con showand.bat
echo off
find "%1" ph | find "%2"
^Z
        1 File(s) copied
```

This batch command takes two parameters: the two strings the Find command searches for. Now you can search the phone list for entries that contain two strings as easily as you can search it for entries containing one string; just type *showand* followed by the two strings. For example, to display all consultants named Jones, type:

```
B> showand cons Jones
```

DOS displays the records that contain both strings:

```
B>echo off

Jones     Michele    (747) 429-6360   cons chemist
Jones     Alison     (747) 429-5584   cons chem engineer
```

This is definitely easier than typing *find "cons" ph | find "Jones"*.

What if you want to create a command that shows all entries except those that contain a particular string? Use a Find command with the /V parameter. You could call this command Showxcpt; create SHOWXCPT.BAT by typing the following:

```
B>copy con showxcpt.bat
echo off
find /v "%1" ph
^Z
        1 File(s) copied
```

This batch command requires one parameter, the string you don't want to see. For example, to display all entries not in the 747 area code, type the following:

```
B>showxcpt (7
```

DOS displays all lines from PH that don't contain (7:

```
B>echo off

---------- ph
Green     Fred    (541) 926-4921   cust math teach
Smith     Ed      (541) 835-8747   vend caterer
```

These three batch files—SHOW, SHOWAND, and SHOWXCPT— let you search a file quickly in several ways. You can combine all three searches into a single command just by changing SHOW.BAT.

Chaining Batch Files To Create Powerful Commands

As Chapter 13, "Creating Your Own Commands," described, you can chain batch files, using the name of one batch file as a command in another batch file. When you do this, DOS carries out the commands in the second batch file as if you had typed its name; if

the second batch file contains the name of a third batch file, DOS carries out its commands, and so forth.

You can modify SHOW.BAT to cover all three types of searches you just performed by chaining it to either SHOWAND.BAT or SHOWXCPT.BAT. When you do this, the parameters you type with the revised SHOW command must specify the type of search as well as the string or strings to search for.

You're creating your own Show command with the following parameters:

show xcpt and <string1> <string2>

xcpt searches for entries that don't contain a string.
and searches for entries that contain two strings.
<string1> and <string2> are the strings to search for. If you include *and,* you must include both <string1> and <string2>; otherwise just include <string1>.

If you don't specify either *xcpt* or *and,* your Show command searches for all entries that contain <string1>.

This more powerful version of SHOW.BAT is still fairly short; type the following:

```
B>copy con show.bat
echo off
if %1==xcpt showxcpt %2
if %1==and showand %2 %3
find "%1" ph
^Z
            1 File(s) copied
```

The first If command checks whether the first parameter (%1) typed with the Show command is *xcpt* (recall the == compares two strings to see if they are identical). If %1 is the same as *xcpt,* SHOWXCPT.BAT is carried out; the second parameter you type with the Show command (%2) is the string to search for; it is specified as the single parameter that SHOWXCPT.BAT requires.

The second If command checks whether the first parameter typed with the Show command is *and.* If it is, SHOWAND.BAT is carried out; the second and third parameters typed with the Show command (%2 and %3) are the two strings to search for; they are specified as the two parameters that SHOWAND.BAT requires.

If the first parameter (%1) typed with the Show command is neither *xcpt* nor *and,* the Find command is carried out to perform a simple search.

Except for the Echo command, only one of the commands in SHOW.BAT is carried out in any particular search. Figure 16-1 shows the contents of SHOW.BAT and an example of each type of search you can make. For each example, the figure lists the Show command as you would type it, and substitutes values for the replaceable parameters in SHOW.BAT. The command in SHOW.BAT that is carried out isn't shaded. An arrow to the right represents chaining to SHOW-XCPT or SHOWAND; the contents of each chained batch file, with values substituted for its replaceable parameters, are shown below the chained batch file.

Now, you can make any of the three types of searches with the Show command. The simple search works as it did in the earlier Show command. For example, to display all entries that contain Jones, type:

```
B>show Jones

B>echo off

---------- ph
Jones      Michele     (747) 429-6360   cons chemist
Jones      Alison      (747) 429-5584   cons chem engineer
Jones      James       (747) 636-3541   cust architect
```

Or, to display all entries that don't contain a particular string, type *xcpt* as the first parameter. For example, to display all entries outside the 747 area code, type:

```
B>show xcpt (7

B>echo off

---------- ph
Green      Fred        (541) 926-4921   cust math teach
Smith      Ed          (541) 835-8747   vend caterer
```

Or, to search for two strings, type *and* as the first parameter. For example, to display all entries that contain both Jones and eng, type:

```
B>show and Jones eng

B>echo off
Jones      Alison      (747) 429-5584   cons chem engineer
```

If you put your telephone numbers and business cards in a text file like this, these three batch files put the contents of the file at your

Contents of SHOW.BAT:

```
echo off
if %1==xcpt showxcpt %2
if %1==and showand %2 %3
find "%1" ph
```

```
B>show cust
```

```
echo off
if cust==xcpt showxcpt
if cust==and showand
find "cust" ph
```

```
B>show xcpt cust
```

```
echo off
```

```
if xcpt==xcpt showxcpt cust    -----> showxcpt cust
if xcpt==and showand cust
find "xcpt" ph                         echo off
                                       find /v "cust" ph
```

```
B>show and cust Jones
```

```
echo off
```

```
if and==xcpt showxcpt cust
if and==and showand cust Jones  --> showand cust Jones
find "and" ph
                                    echo off
                                    find "cust" ph | find "Jones"
```

Figure 16-1. Chaining batch files

fingertips. Not only can you search for an entry quickly, you can easily display groups of related entries.

You can use this same technique with other data files that may not justify a full database program, but whose contents are a constant part of your work; some more examples are shown in Chapter 17, "Tailoring Your System." This application, like the use of Edlin, is another example of DOS making your computer more valuable without using any additional software.

SOME USEFUL BATCH FILES

To give you some ideas about the sort of batch commands that might help you from day to day, several useful batch files are shown here. These are not step-by-step examples; each description gives the purpose of the batch file, shows its contents, explains how it works, and describes how you would use it.

An effective way to become familiar with batch commands is to experiment. You could enter the following batch files, for example, then play with them, making changes and seeing the effects of the changes. Just be sure to use disks that don't contain irreplaceable copies of files you need.

You can create the batch files by copying from the console to a file or by using Edlin. Where line numbers are shown in the listings, they're just for reference; don't enter them. Most of the batch files include one or more Echo commands to add a blank line to the display (for readability); they appear as echo ˆ@, but to make them work properly, you must press the space bar and the F7 key before you press Enter. (F7 is displayed as ˆ@, but recall from Chapter 15 that you may sometimes see it displayed as @ˆ.)

Cleaning Up Disk Storage

Because Edlin and many word processors create a backup file with the extension BAK each time you edit a file, your disks can get crowded with backup files you may not need. The CLEANUP.BAT batch file described here displays the directory entries of all files with an extension of BAK, then it pauses. At that point, you can cancel the command by pressing Ctrl-Break; if you press any key to proceed, the command erases the files.

CLEANUP.BAT contains:

```
1: echo off
2: cls
3: echo ***Will erase the following files:***
4: dir %1*.bak
5: echo ^@
6: echo ^GPress CTRL-BREAK to cancel, or
7: pause
8: erase %1*.bak
```

Notice that there is no blank between %1 and *.bak in lines 4 and 8; this lets you specify a drive letter or path name as a parameter with the file name (for example, type *a:report* or *mkt**report*).

The ^@ in line 5 represents the F7 function key. The ^G (or G^) in line 6 is Ctrl-G, which sounds a beep. To enter it, hold down the Control key and press G.

To erase all BAK files from the current directory on the current drive, type *cleanup* and press any key when the Pause command prompts you.

To erase all BAK files from another directory or drive, type the drive letter, followed by a colon, or the path name as a parameter (for example, *cleanup a:* or *cleanup* *mkt**wp*).

Directory of Subdirectories

The Directory command displays *<DIR>* instead of the file size to identify a subdirectory. If a directory contains many files, it can be a bit difficult to pick out the subdirectories. The DIRSUB batch file described here displays only the entries for subdirectories.

DIRSUB.BAT contains:

```
1: echo off
2: echo ***Subdirectories in %1***
3: echo ^@
4: dir %1 | find "<"
```

In this file, the output of the Directory command is piped to a Find command that displays all directory lines that contain <.

You can type one parameter (%1) with the Dirsub command to specify the directory whose entries are to be displayed. The parameter can include any of the following: a drive letter, path name, or file name. If you don't type a parameter, this Dirsub command displays the subdirectories in the current directory.

To see the subdirectories in the current directory, you would type *dirsub*. To see the subdirectories in the root directory of the disk in drive B, you would type *dirsub b:*. To see the subdirectories in the directory \MKT\WP, you would type *dirsub* *mkt**wp*.

The special entries . and .. are in all directories except the root. You can modify DIRSUB.BAT so that it doesn't display these entries, by changing line 4 of the batch file to read:

```
dir %1 | find "<" | find /v "."
```

Now the output of the Find command is piped to a second Find command that uses the /V parameter to eliminate all lines that contain a period. You would use this version of the Dirsub command just as you would use the earlier version.

Moving Files from
One Directory to Another

In a tree-structured file system, sometimes you'll want to move files from one directory to another. You can do this by copying the file to the new directory with the Copy command, then erasing the original with the Erase command. MOVE.BAT combines these into one command.

MOVE.BAT contains:

```
 1: echo off
 2: copy %1 %2
 3: cls
 4: echo Files in target directory:
 5: echo ^@
 6: dir %2
 7: echo ^@
 8: echo If files to be moved are not in directory,
 9: echo press Ctrl-Break to cancel. Otherwise
10: pause
11: erase %1
```

Here is how the batch file works, line by line:

- In line 1, the Echo command turns echo off.

- In line 2, the Copy command copies the files to the target directory.

- In line 3, the Clear Screen command clears the screen.

- In lines 4 and 5, Echo commands display a message and a blank line. (In line 5, remember to press the space bar and the F7 key before pressing Enter.)

- In line 6, the Directory command displays the contents of the target directory.

- In lines 7 through 9, Echo commands display a blank line and a warning message.

- In line 10, the Pause command makes the system pause to let you cancel the Erase command in line 11 if the files you moved are not displayed in the listing of the target directory.

You have created a command with two parameters:

move <source> <target>

<source> is the name of the file to be moved (copied and deleted). You can include a drive letter and path name. If you use wildcard characters in the file name, DOS displays the name of each file it copies.

<target> is the name of the directory to which the <source> files are to be copied. If you omit <target>, the files are copied to the current directory.

For example, assume that the current directory is \MKT\WP. To move the file REPORT.DOC to the directory \ENG\WP, you would type *move report.doc \eng\wp*. To move the file BUDGET.JAN from \ENG\WP to \MKT\WP, you type *move \eng\wp\budget.jan*. To move all files from \MKT\WP to \WORD\MKT, you would type *move *.* \word\mkt*.

TWO ADVANCED BATCH COMMANDS

Note: The batch commands you have worked with up to this point are sufficient for you to create useful batch files tailored to your own needs, to create powerful batch files like the search commands for the phone list file. Rather than continue with the rest of this chapter right now, you might want to put the book aside for awhile and experiment, then return to learn the last two batch commands this book discusses.

The two remaining batch commands, Shift and For, give you even more control over how your batch files work. They're somewhat more complicated than the other batch commands, but the examples should make their use clear.

Preparing for the Advanced Examples

The remaining examples in the chapter require the P files you archived in Chapter 15. Put the diskette you labeled ARCHIVED FILES in drive A.

Shifting the List of Parameters

The Shift command moves the list of parameters you type with a batch command one position to the left. For example, if you type three parameters, after a Shift command what was %3 becomes %2 and what was %2 becomes %1; what was %1 is gone. After a second Shift command, what started out as %3 is %1; what started as %2 and %1 are both gone.

This command lets a short batch file handle any number of parameters; the following sample batch file illustrates the technique. ARCH1.BAT archives any number of files. Here are its contents (remember, the line numbers are just for reference):

```
1: echo off
2: :start
3: if .%1==. goto done
4: echo ***Archiving %1***
5: if not exist a:%1 copy %1 a:
6: shift
7: goto start
8: :done
```

Here's a line-by-line description of how it works:

- As usual, the first line is an Echo command to turn echo off.

- In line 2, the label :START marks the beginning of the commands that will be repeated for each parameter.

- In line 3, the If command checks to see whether a parameter was entered for %1. It does this by comparing .%1 (that's a period immediately followed by %1) to just a period. When DOS finds the .%1, it combines a period with whatever was entered for the current parameter. If *myfile* was entered, for example, the result would be *.myfile*; if there is no parameter for %1 (sometimes called a null parameter), the result would be just a period, satisfying the comparison. When the If command finds a null parameter, meaning there are no more parameters, the Goto command sends DOS to the label :DONE.

- In line 4, the Echo command displays the name of the file that is being archived.

- In line 5, the If command checks whether the file to be archived exists on drive A; if it doesn't, the Copy command copies the file from the current drive to drive A. (The example assumes drive B or drive C is the current drive.)

- In line 6, the Shift command moves the list of parameters one position to the left.

- In line 7, the Goto command sends DOS back to the label :START.

- In line 8, the label :DONE marks the end of the command file.

To use this batch file you type *arch1,* then the names of the files to be archived. The command will stop when . %1 equals .—in other words, when there are no more file names to be substituted for %1.

Before testing the command, copy the file named P.OLD, which you archived in Chapter 15, from the diskette in drive A to the current drive by typing:

```
B>copy a:p.old
```

Now archive P.OLD, Q.DOC, and Q.OLD by typing:

```
B>arch1 p.old q.doc q.old

B>echo off
***Archiving p.old***
***Archiving q.doc***
        1 File(s) copied

***Archiving q.old***
        1 File(s) copied
```

The confirming messages show that DOS did not copy the file that was already on the diskette in drive A (P.OLD), but that it did copy the files that weren't (both Q.DOC and Q.OLD).

This short Archive command doesn't display instructions or warnings like the batch file you created in Chapter 15 did, but it does show how you can use the Shift command to write a batch file that handles any number of parameters. The technique is simple: Do something with %1, shift the parameters, then use a Goto command to send DOS back to the beginning, to do it all over again. Just make sure you define a way to stop the process, or DOS will carry out the command forever.

Carrying Out a Command
More than Once

**for %%p in (\<set>)
do \<command>**

Sometimes you may want DOS to carry out a command more than once in a batch file: for instance, once for each file that matches a file name with wildcard characters. The For command does just that. Like the If command, the For command has two parts: The first part defines how often a command is to be carried out, and the second part is the command to be carried out.

The For command is somewhat more complicated than the other batch commands. If you don't fully understand the description of its parameters, read on and try the examples. As with many other aspects of using a computer, it's easier to use the For command than it is to read about it.

The For command has three parameters:

for %%p in (\<set>) do \<command>

in and *do* are required in the command; they are not parameters.

%%p is a replaceable parameter that is used inside the For command. It is assigned, in turn, each value included in (\<set>).

(\<set>) is the list of possible values that can be given to %%p. You separate the values with blanks, and the entire list must be enclosed in parentheses, such as (1 2 3). You can also specify a set of values with a file name that includes wildcard characters, such as b:*.DOC.

\<command> is any DOS command other than another For command. You can use both batch-command parameters (such as %1) and the For command replaceable parameter (%%p) in \<command>.

It's all less complicated than it sounds. When DOS carries out a For command, it assigns to %%p, in turn, each value you specify in (\<set>), then carries out \<command>. Each time it carries out \<command>, it first substitutes the current value taken from the (\<set>) for %%p.

A brief example shows how the For command works. The following batch command carries out an Echo command three

times, displaying each of the three words enclosed in parentheses. Create FOR1.BAT by typing:

```
B>copy con for1.bat
for %%p in (able baker charlie) do echo %%p
^Z
        1 File(s) copied
```

In this For command, (able baker charlie) is (<set>) and echo%%p is <command>. The For command tells DOS to carry out the Echo command once for each word in parentheses, substituting, in turn, able, baker, and charlie for %%p. Test it by typing:

```
B>for1
```

For a change, this batch file doesn't begin by turning echo off; so, DOS displays each command it carries out, starting with the For command:

```
B>for %p in (able baker charlie) do echo %p
```

DOS then displays and carries out the Echo command once for each value in the set, each time substituting the next value from the set for the replaceable parameter in the Echo command:

```
B>echo able
able

B>echo baker
baker

B>echo charlie
charlie
```

Instead of specifying actual values in the set, you can use replaceable parameters, such as %1. This technique works just like any other batch command, but can be confusing because now you can have %1 and %%p in the same command. Here's the difference: %1 refers to the first parameter typed with the batch command, %2 refers to the second parameter typed with the batch command, and so forth; %%p refers to the value selected from the set enclosed in parentheses within the For command.

The next example shows you the difference. Here, you type the words to be displayed as parameters of the batch command, instead of typing them as part of the For command. Create FOR2.BAT by typing:

```
B>copy con for2.bat
for %%p in (%1 %2 %3) do echo %%p
^Z
        1 File(s) copied
```

This For command tells DOS to carry out the Echo command (echo %%p) once for each value in parentheses, substituting for %%p, in turn, the first, second, and third parameters you type with the For2 command. Test it by typing:

```
B>for2 dog easy fox
```

DOS displays each command it carries out. First it displays the For command:

```
B>for %p in (dog easy fox) do echo %p
```

Note that DOS has substituted values for all replaceable parameters. The set in parentheses is now (dog easy fox), because those are the three parameters you typed; they have replaced (%1 %2 %3). As you may have noticed in the preceding display, DOS has also dropped one of the percent signs from %%p. DOS removes the first percent sign when it substitutes, for %1, %2, and so forth, the parameters you type with the command. It does, however, leave one percent sign to show that a value must still be substituted for %p.

DOS then displays and carries out three Echo commands, each time substituting one value from the set in parentheses for %p:

```
B>echo dog
dog

B>echo easy
easy

B>echo fox
fox
```

If you wish, you can specify the set in a For command with a file name and wildcard characters. DOS assigns to %%p, in turn, each file name that matches the wildcard characters. You can use this technique to create a simple Archive batch file using only a For command. The following command doesn't display instructions and warnings, but it does show you how much can be done with a single batch command.

Create a batch file named ARCH2.BAT by typing the following:

```
B>copy con arch2.bat
for %%p in (%1) do if not exist a:%%p copy %%p a:
^Z
        1 File(s) copied
```

Q.DOC and Q.OLD are on the diskette in drive A (you copied them in the example of the Shift command). Use them to test ARCH2.BAT by archiving all files named Q:

```
B>arch2 q.*
```

DOS displays each command it carries out, starting with the For command (remember, you have not turned echo off):

```
B>for %p in (q.*) do if not exist a:%p copy %p a:
```

DOS then displays and carries out three If commands, each time substituting a file name that matches the set in parentheses for the replaceable parameter in the If command:

```
B>if not exist a:Q.DOC copy Q.DOC a:

B>if not exist a:Q.BAK copy Q.BAK a:
        1 File(s) copied

B>if not exist a:Q.OLD copy Q.OLD a:
```

The messages displayed by the Copy command confirm that DOS didn't copy Q.DOC or Q.OLD because they were already on the archive diskette, but that it did copy Q.BAK.

The For command gives you a quick way to carry out a DOS command several times. As shown in some of the sample batch files that conclude this chapter, the For command makes it possible to create powerful batch commands.

SOME MORE USEFUL BATCH FILES

The following batch files use the advanced batch commands. Again, they aren't step-by-step examples; they are working samples to give you an idea of what can be done with the full set of batch commands. You can enter the batch files by copying from the console or by using Edlin. The line numbers shown are for reference only.

Displaying a Series of Small Text Files

If you work with many small text files, such as batch files or boilerplate paragraphs for a word processor, it's handy to be able to review several files with one command, rather than to print or display them one at a time. The batch file shown here, REVIEW.BAT, uses the Shift, Type, and Pause commands to display any number of files, one at a time. As before, recall that ^@ represents the F7 key. REVIEW.BAT contains:

```
 1: echo off
 2: :start
 3: if .%1==. goto done
 4: cls
 5: echo<Spacebar><Tab><Tab>***FILENAME: %1***
 6: echo ^@
 7: type %1
 8: echo ^@
 9: echo ^@
10: pause
11: shift
12: goto start
13: :done
```

This batch file uses the same technique as the earlier examples of the Shift command. The Echo command in line 5 displays the file name (moved toward the center of the screen with two tabs), so that you'll know what is displayed. Notice that lines 8 and 9 display two blank lines to separate the contents of the file from the Pause command message.

With this Review command, you type the names of the files as parameters. To display several files with the extension DOC, for example, you type *review 1.doc 2.doc 3.doc*. DOS clears the screen and displays the first file, then displays the Pause command message and waits for you to press any key before clearing the screen and

displaying the next file. When the If command in line 3 finds the first null parameter, DOS returns to command level.

Searching Files for a String of Characters

Have you ever searched through your paper files to find a specific letter or reference? Have you ever wondered how many letters you wrote about a particular subject or how often you use a particular word? The three short batch files described here give you several ways to scan a file or set of files for all lines that contain a string of characters.

Displaying all lines that contain a string

To help you find all lines that contain a particular string, SCAN.BAT lets you specify the file to be searched and one string to search for. It displays each line in the file that contains the string. You can also use wildcard characters to search a set of files. Here are the contents of SCAN.BAT:

```
1:  echo off
2:  cls
3:  echo<Spacebar><Tab><Tab>***LINES IN %1 THAT
    CONTAIN %2***
4:  echo ^@
5:  for %%p in (%1) do find "%2" %%p
```

All the work here is done in the last line of the batch file. The earlier lines clear the screen and display a title. The For command in line 5 actually carries out the Find command for each file name that matches the first parameter you type with the Scan command; the Find command is the one that searches for the string that you type as the second parameter.

To display each line that contained the word *sales* in all files with an extension of DOC, you would type *scan *.doc sales*. DOS would clear the screen and display each line containing the word *sales*.

Displaying the number of lines containing the string

COUNT.BAT is a slightly modified version of SCAN.BAT that displays the number of lines in the file that contain the word, but doesn't display the lines themselves.

Here are the contents of COUNT.BAT (changes from SCAN.BAT are shaded):

```
1: echo off
2: cls
3: echo<Spacebar><Tab><Tab>***NUMBER OF LINES
   IN %1 THAT CONTAIN %2***
4: echo ^@
5: for %%p in (%1) do find /c "%2" %%p
```

The only two changes are in the title displayed by the Echo command (line 3) and the addition of the /C parameter to the Find command (line 5).

As an example, to see how many lines in all files with an extension of DOC contained the word *night*, you would type *count * .doc night*. The Count command would clear the screen and display the number of lines in each file that contained the word *night*.

Searching for several strings

Another batch file, SCANALL.BAT, again gives a count of lines, but it uses a different approach. The file or set of files to be searched is named in the batch file, but you can type as many strings as you want as parameters to search for. This approach is particularly useful if you frequently search the same set of files, such as your word-processing files. SCANALL.BAT contains:

```
 1: echo off
 2: :start
 3: if .%1==. goto done
 4: cls
 5: echo ***LINES IN *.DOC THAT CONTAIN %1***
 6: echo ^@
 7: for %%p in (*.doc) do find /c "%1" %%p
 8: echo ^@
 9: pause
10: shift
11: goto start
12: :done
```

This batch file uses both the For and Shift commands to search several files for several strings. A line-by-line description is in order:

• Line 1 turns echo off.

- The label :START identifies the beginning of the commands to be repeated (it is the destination of the Goto command in line 11).

- The If command checks to see whether the parameter is null. If it is, the Goto command sends DOS to the end of the batch file (line 12).

- Line 4 clears the screen.

- The Echo commands in lines 5 and 6 display a title and a blank line.

- The For command searches each file with an extension of DOC and displays the number of lines that contain the string ("%1") specified in the first parameter you type when you use the Scanall command.

- Like line 6, line 8 displays a blank line.

- The Pause command displays its usual message and waits for any key to be pressed.

- Line 10 shifts the parameters one position to the left.

- The Goto command sends DOS to the label :START.

- The label :DONE identifies the end of the batch file (the destination of the Goto command in line 3).

To use the Scanall command, type the words to be searched for as parameters. Remember, the Find command distinguishes between upper- and lowercase letters.

If, for example, you wanted to search for the words *sales, January,* and *region,* you would type *scanall sales January region.*

The Scanall command would clear the screen, search all the files whose extension is DOC for the word *sales,* display the number of lines, and then pause. When you pressed any key, it would scan all the files for the word *January,* again display the results, and so forth for each word you specified. Try it with your own words and several dozen word-processing files; you'll be surprised at how quickly this command searches all the files, particularly if you're using a fixed disk.

If you wanted to display the lines containing the strings, rather than just the count, you could simply omit the /C parameter from the Find command in the batch file. This command could produce a lot of output. To print a record of it, you could press Ctrl-PrtSc after you entered the command but before you pressed the Enter key, to start simultaneously printing and displaying the results.

Displaying a Sorted Directory

In Chapter 4 you displayed the directory sorted by file name. Because the items in a directory entry always begin in the same column, you can sort the directory entries five ways; all but one use the column parameter (/ + <number>) of the Sort command to sort starting at the column where the information begins:

- Name—starts in column 1, so does not require the column parameter.

- Extension—starts in column 10.

- Size—starts in column 16.

- Date—starts in column 25.

- Time—starts in column 34.

If you need to delete some files to make space on a disk, or are just interested in the relative size of files, sorting by size is useful. If you can't remember the name of a file, but can remember the approximate date you last worked with it, sorting by date can be handy. You can create a command to display a directory sorted any of these ways with six short batch files: Five actually sort and display the directory, and one (the command that you type) chains to the correct one of the other five.

First, copy from the console, as you have done before, to create the following one-line batch files; their names tell how they sort the directory:

DIRNAME.BAT:

```
dir %1 ¦ sort ¦ more
```

DIREXT.BAT:

```
1ir %1 ¦ sort /+10 ¦ more
```

DIRSIZE.BAT

```
d1r %1 ¦ sort /+16 ¦  more
```

DIRDATE.BAT

```
dir %1 ¦ sort /+25 ¦ more
```

DIRTIME.BAT

```
dir %1 ¦ sort /+34 ¦ more
```

Each of these batch files sorts and displays the directory specified in the parameter %1 and pipes the output of the Sort command
to the More command, to handle directories more than one screen
long. If no parameter is specified, it sorts and displays the current
directory. The only difference among the batch files is the column
in which sorting begins.

You now need the batch file that chains to the correct one of the
previous five; name the file DIRSORT.BAT. DIRSORT.BAT contains:

```
1: echo off
2: for %%p in (name ext size date time) do
   if %1==%%p dir%%p %2
3: echo First parameter must be NAME, EXT, SIZE,
   DATE, or TIME
```

As before, type each numbered line as one continuous line. Be
sure not to put a blank between dir and %%p when you create the
Dirsort file, or the result won't be a valid file name for any of the
chained batch files.

In the DIRSORT batch file, the For command sets %%p to each
of the words, in turn, in the set in parentheses, and it carries out the
If command, which compares %%p to the first parameter typed
with the Dirsort command. If there is a match, the If command
adds the value of %%p to DIR to produce the name of one of the five
sort batch files, and chains to that batch file (for example, DIR +
NAME would become DIRNAME. The second parameter (%2), if
any, typed with the Dirsort command, is the %1 parameter (the
directory name) for the chained batch file.

If the first parameter you type with the Dirsort command isn't one of the five words in the set in parentheses, the condition in the If command is not true. Then, the Echo command in the next line is carried out, displaying a message that lists the correct parameters, and the Dirsort batch command ends without chaining to one of the files that displays a sorted directory.

To display a sorted directory, you would type the Dirsort command with one or two parameters: The first, which is required, would specify how to sort and could only be: name, ext, size, date, or time; the second parameter, which is optional, would be the drive letter, path, or file name whose directory was to be displayed. If you didn't include the second parameter, the command would display the directory of the disk in the current drive.

For example, to display the current directory, sorted by size, of the disk in the current drive, you would type *dirsort size.* To display the root directory, sorted by name, of the disk in drive B, you would type *dirsort name b:.*

CHAPTER SUMMARY

These batch files should give you a good start on a collection of special-purpose commands, as well as some ideas for creating more of your own. This is where the flexibility of DOS really becomes apparent: The wide range of DOS commands and capabilities is only the starting point for putting DOS to work. With I/O redirection, filter commands, and batch files, you can combine all the other DOS commands into a set of custom-tailored commands, to make your personal computer truly personal.

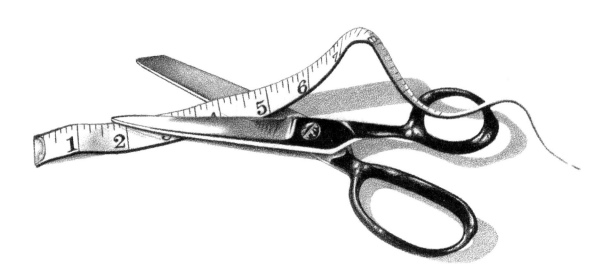

If you have followed the examples in the book, you have used all the major features of DOS. Although it may seem that DOS sometimes offers more options than you need, those options give you flexibility in tailoring DOS; they let you adapt the computer to yourself rather than adapt yourself to the computer.

This chapter shows several ways in which to tailor DOS to your needs or preferences. Not only does this tailoring make DOS fit your work needs better, some of the techniques described here can also make your system immediately useful without your having to buy application programs. Some of these techniques can also make the system more accessible to people who may need to use the computer but who don't have your experience with DOS. And tailoring can also make it easier to achieve consistency in such procedures as backing up a fixed disk, if several people will be using the computer.

This chapter describes:

- Different ways to set up a filing system that matches the way the computer is used.

- Batch commands that simplify using a multi-level filing system.

- Batch commands that automate backing up a fixed disk.

- Several simple record-management schemes similar to the telephone index described in Chapters 14 and 16.

- Commands that help you tailor your system hardware with the DOS CONFIG.SYS file.

- A few of the less frequently used DOS commands.

Examples are included, but they are not step-by-step exercises. The intent of this chapter is to give you some ideas about how to tailor DOS by applying what you have learned in previous chapters.

SETTING UP A FILING SYSTEM

The multi-level file system described in Chapter 9, "A Tree of Files," lets you organize your files to match your work. A file structure is affected by such factors as the application programs

that are used, how many people use the computer, and how many departments are involved. This section shows several different file structures, each organized to focus on a different approach to using the computer. Because every real-life situation is different, these are guides, not exact models.

It doesn't take long to set up a file system—all you need are a few Make Directory commands—but it can be time-consuming to change a file structure after dozens or hundreds of files have been created. A few minutes' thinking ahead of time can result in a file structure that suits the way the computer is used.

In the following examples, the root directory is assumed to contain the DOS command files, general-purpose batch files, and any other files that are needed by anyone using the system regardless of the current directory.

An Application-Based File System

If a computer is used for several applications—as it would be by an independent professional or a small business—a natural way to organize the file structure is by application program. Figure 17-1

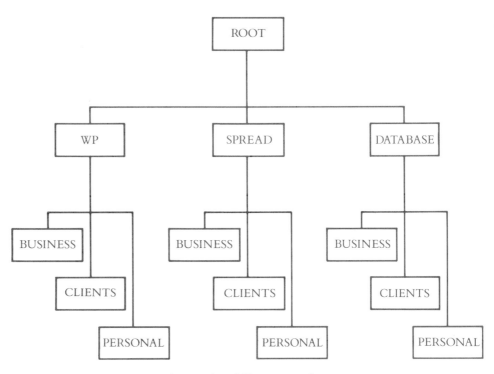

Figure 17-1. Application-based file structure for an independent professional

shows how a file system might be set up by an independent professional who uses the machine for word processing, with a spreadsheet program, and for database management.

The first level of directories (WP, SPREAD, and DATABASE) contains the application programs. The next level (BUSINESS, CLIENTS,
PERSONAL) holds the data files for the applications.

With this file structure, when someone does some word processing, for example, the current directory is set to the directory
that contains the document files (such as \WP\BUSINESS or
\WP\PERSONAL). The Path command is used to set the command
search path to the root directory (for DOS commands and general-
purpose batch files) and to \WP (for the word-processing program).

On the other hand, the file system for a computer used in a
small business might define the second and subsequent directory
levels to correspond to the departments that use the applications,
rather than to the data files for the applications. Figure 17-2 shows
how such a file system might be set up.

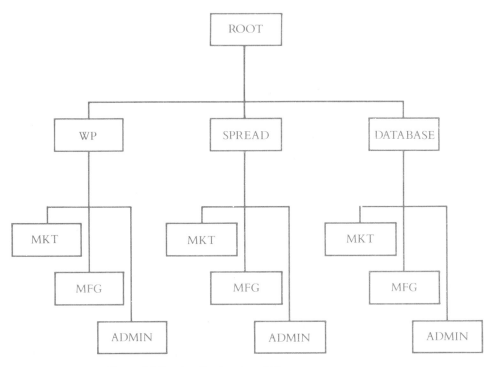

*Figure 17-2. Application-based file structure
for a small business*

A Department-Based File System

Rather than beginning with the application program, as the preceding examples do, files can also be organized to emphasize the departments that use the machine. Figure 17-3 shows a file system for a machine used by the Marketing, Manufacturing, and Administration departments of a company. The application programs are the same as in the previous examples and are used jointly by all three departments. Because each program is in a subdirectory of its own, any department can use any application just by setting the command search path to the appropriate program.

As much as anything else, the choice of how to organize files depends on how the people who use the computer view their work. If they think primarily in terms of what they're doing ("I do word processing"), the application-based structure might be more comfortable. If they think in terms of who they do it for ("I'm the

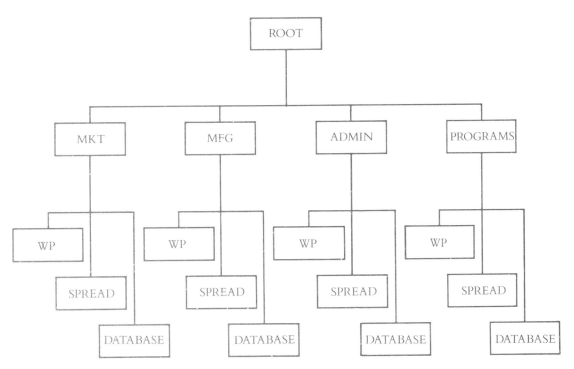

Figure 17-3. Department-based file structure

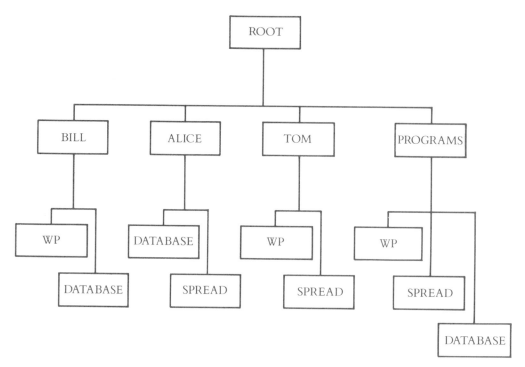

Figure 17-4. User-based file structure

Marketing Administrative Assistant"), the department-based structure might be more appropriate. Neither structure is more efficient
than the other; each simply reflects a different way of looking at
the file system.

A User–Based File System

If several people use the computer, a file structure that empha-
sizes the users might be most appropriate, especially if the people
use the machine for different applications. Figure 17-4 shows a
directory structure for a system used by three people.

Again, directories are defined for the same application programs
used in the other sample file structures. If the computer is used by
people with varying degrees of familiarity with DOS, and if not all
users need each application, this type of file structure can make the
system seem more natural, especially if you create some batch commands that simplify using the directories.

Batch Files to Use Directories

Batch files designed for using directories can be simple or elaborate, depending on who will use them and how much time you want to invest in creating them. Creating separate directories for the people who use the system, for departments, and application programs simplifies the appearance of the system and makes it easier to keep track of files. Separate directories can, however, also mean that you have to change directories more often. You can automate the use of directories with batch files; this technique makes it simple for all users to work with a structured filing system, even if they are not familiar with DOS. If you put the batch files in the root directory and make sure the command search path always includes the root, the batch files for using directories can be accessible from any directory or subdirectory. Switching from one directory and application program to another is always just a matter of typing a single command.

In its simplest form, a batch file to use a directory changes the current directory and sets the command search path. For example, suppose you have the file structure shown in Figure 17-3, and you want a batch file called WORDMKT.BAT in the root directory to help manage word processing for the Marketing department. WORDMKT.BAT could look like the following example (line numbers here and throughout the chapter are for reference only):

```
1: echo off
2: cd \mkt\wp
3: path \;\programs\wp
```

The Change Directory command sets the current directory to \MKT\WP, which contains the Marketing word-processing files; the Path command sets the command path to the root directory (for DOS command files and general-purpose batch files) and \PROGRAMS\WP (for the word-processing program). To use your word-processing program with the Marketing data files, you would just type *wordmkt*.

You could create a similar batch file for each directory that contains data files, and then use any directory just by typing the

Directory that Contains Data Files	Directory that Contains Program	Name of Batch File
\MKT\WP	\PROGRAMS\WP	WORDMKT.BAT
\MKT\SPREAD	\PROGRAMS\SPREAD	SPMKT.BAT
\MKT\DATABASE	\PROGRAMS\DATABASE	DBMKT.BAT
\MFG\WP	\PROGRAMS\WP	WORDMFG.BAT
\MFG\SPREAD	\PROGRAMS\SPREAD	SPMFG.BAT
\MFG\DATABASE	\PROGRAMS\DATABASE	DBMFG.BAT
\ADMIN\WP	\PROGRAMS\WP	WORDADM.BAT
\ADMIN\SPREAD	\PROGRAMS\SPREAD	SPADM.BAT
\ADMIN\DATABASE	\PROGRAMS\DATABASE	DBADM.BAT

*Figure 17-5. Directories and batch files for a
department-based file structure*

name of the appropriate batch file. Figure 17-5 shows the directories
in Figure 17-3 that contain data files and indicates how the corresponding batch files might be named.

To produce the other batch files, you simply change the Change
Directory and Path commands to point to the corresponding directories that contain the data files and application programs. For example, the batch command (SPMFG.BAT) to do spreadsheets for the
Manufacturing department could contain:

```
1: echo off
2: cd \mfg\spread
3: path \;\programs\spread
```

With these batch files in the root directory, you could then type
wordmkt and edit a few Marketing documents, type *spadm* and work
on some spreadsheets for the Administration department, then type

dbmfg and update the Manufacturing inventory data base, all without worrying about—or even knowing about—the correct directory. A set of batch files like these makes the multi-level filing system not only more flexible, but also easier to use.

Improving the appearance of the batch files

To dress up the appearance of your batch files for using directories, you could clear the screen and display the directory. The Change Directory and Path commands would be unchanged; this modified version of WORDMKT.BAT would look like the following:

```
1: echo off
2: cd \mkt\wp
3: path \;\programs\wp
4: cls
5: dir /w
```

The /W parameter of the Directory command is used here, in case the directory contains more than one screenful of files.

Creating your own menu system

If someone unfamiliar with DOS will be using the system, you can use batch files to create a menu system that quickly moves the less experienced user to the correct directory. For example, suppose you have the file structure shown in Figure 17-3; the batch files described here let someone turn on the system and, by typing *mkt,* see the following display:

```
                           *** MARKETING ***

Applications: Word processing
              Spreadsheet
              Data base

Enter W, S, or D
  _
```

If the user types *w,* the following type of directory format screen is displayed (the entries are hypothetical):

```
                    *** MARKETING--WORD PROCESSING ***
Document files:

 Volume in drive C has no label
 Directory of  C:\mkt\wp

TAXMEMO DOC     THP0315 DOC...BUDGET   DOC
INVEN01 DOC     SLSLTR  DOC...THP0311 DOC
CONFNOT DOC     LETR04  DOC...SLSMEMO DOC
LETR07  DOC     INVEN04 DOC...INVEN02 DOC
SVCREC  DOC     LETR06  DOC...
        23 File(s)   7162384 bytes free

C>_
```

Displays of this kind would require four batch files for each department: For the Marketing department, there would be one (MKT.BAT) in the root directory and three (W.BAT, S.BAT, and D.BAT) in \MKT. First, here are the contents of MKT.BAT:

```
 1: echo off
 2: cd \mkt
 3: cls
 4: REM THREE TABS AT BEGINNING OF FOLLOWING ECHO
    COMMAND
 5: echo <Tab><Tab><Tab>*** MARKETING ***
 6: echo ^@
 7: echo Applications: Word processing
 8: echo                 Spreadsheet
 9: echo                 Data base
10: echo ^@
11: echo Enter W, S, or D
12: prompt $a
```

As you can see, most of the commands are Echo commands. The batch file is straightforward: It turns off echo, changes the directory to \MKT, clears the screen, and displays the menu and choices. Then the Prompt command (described later in this chapter) makes the system prompt (C>) invisible, so the user sees only the cursor, and the system returns to command level: Exit MKT.BAT even though, as the sample screen display showed, this batch file appears to be waiting for a reply to the prompt *Enter W, S, or D.*

If the user types *w* (for word processing), DOS carries out the batch file W.BAT in \MKT. Its contents are:

```
1: echo off
2: cls
3: cd wp
4: path \;\programs\wp
5: REM TWO TABS IN FOLLOWING ECHO COMMAND
6: echo <Tab><Tab>*** MARKETING--WORD PROCESSING ***
7: echo Document files:
8: prompt
9: dir *.doc /w
```

This batch file produces the second sample screen display (the response to the menu selection). It, too, is straightforward. It turns echo off, clears the screen, changes the directory to \MKT\WP, sets the command search path to the root and to \PROGRAMS\WP, displays the titles, resets the system prompt to its normal form, and then displays in the wide format the directory entries of all files with an extension of DOC.

To complete the menu system in \MKT, you need two batch files similar to W.BAT, one for your spreadsheet and one for your database program. The contents of S.BAT for the spreadsheet are:

```
1: echo off
2: cls
3: cd spread
4: path \;\programs\spread
5: REM TWO TABS IN FOLLOWING ECHO COMMAND
6: echo <Tab><Tab>*** MARKETING--SPREADSHEET ***
7: echo Spreadsheet files:
8: prompt
9: dir *.pln /w
```

In the preceding and following lists, the changes from W.BAT are shaded. You can see that the format is the same. In this example, spreadsheet files are given the extension PLN. To complete the menu system, here are the contents of D.BAT:

```
1: echo off
2: cls
3: cd database
4: path \;\programs\database
5: REM TWO TABS IN FOLLOWING ECHO COMMAND
6: echo <Tab><Tab>*** MARKETING--DATA BASE ***
7: echo Database files:
8: prompt
9: dir*.dat /w
```

By clearing the screen, displaying your own titles, displaying directory entries, and otherwise controlling the appearance of the system, you can use batch files like these to make the system appear custom-tailored for your own company or department, or even for an individual user. One person who understands how to use the flexibility and power of DOS can make the system easier to use and more productive for everyone else. Batch commands are the key.

AUTOMATING BACKUP OF A FIXED DISK

Chapter 10, "Managing Your Fixed Disk," described how to decide which files need backing up, and when, in order to reduce the number of backup diskettes you need. You can also reduce the amount of time required to back up files.

Suppose you have the file structure shown in Figure 17-3. You decide that each month you should back up all the Marketing and Manufacturing files (all files in \MKT and \MFG and their subdirectories), and each week you should back up all Marketing word-processing documents (files with an extension of DOC) and Manufacturing spreadsheets (files with an extension of PLN), that have changed since the previous week. You can create two batch files—MNTHBKUP.BAT and WEEKBKUP.BAT—that contain the required Backup commands.

The contents of MNTHBKUP.BAT are:

```
1: echo off
2: cls
3: echo *** MONTHLY FILE BACKUP ***
4: echo ^@
5: echo Put a formatted diskette in drive A
6: pause
7: backup \mkt a: /s
8: backup \mfg a: /s /a
9: echo LABEL DISKETTE "BACKUP FOR <month>"
```

The batch file starts by clearing the screen, displaying a title, and instructing the user to put the backup diskette in drive A. The first Backup command backs up all files from \MKT and all its subdirectories. Any previously existing files on the backup diskette are erased. The second Backup command backs up all files from \MFG and all its subdirectories, adding them to the files backed up from \MKT.

The form of WEEKBKUP.BAT is similar:

```
1: echo off
2: cls
3: echo ***WEEKLY DOCUMENT BACKUP***
4: echo ^@
5: echo Put a formatted diskette in drive A
6: pause
7: backup \mkt\wp\*.doc a: /m
8: backup \mfg\spread\*.pln a: /m /a
9: echo LABEL DISKETTE "BACKUP FOR WEEK OF <date>"
```

Like MNTHBKUP.BAT, WEEKBKUP.BAT starts by clearing the screen, displaying a title, and making sure the correct diskette goes in drive A. The first Backup command backs up all files with the extension DOC from \MKT\WP that have been modified since the last backup. Any previously existing files on the backup diskette are erased. The second Backup command backs up all files with the extension PLN from \MFG\SPREAD.

Unless your system is heavily used, only one backup diskette per week is required to back up the changed files of both departments. Because the monthly backup backs up all files, you can re-use the weekly backup diskettes in the following month.

With batch files like these, anyone who uses the system can back up files without knowing how to use the Backup command. All they have to do is type *weekbkup* once a week and *mnthbkup* once a month and follow the instructions. If you put both batch files in the root directory and set the command search path to the root directory with the Path command, you or anyone else can use these batch files no matter what the current directory is.

RENAMING THE FORMAT COMMAND

If you're using a fixed disk, it's possible to erase all files on the fixed disk by inadvertently formatting it. The scenario goes like this: The fixed disk (drive C) is the current drive; you want to format a diskette, so you put it in drive A and type *format* but forget to add *a:* to the command. You have told DOS to format the disk in the current drive (the fixed disk). DOS displays its message warning you that formatting the disk erases all files. Believing that the disk to be formatted is the diskette in drive A, you press the Enter key. DOS dutifully formats the fixed disk, removing everything stored on it.

Although it's not likely you would make both these errors (forget to type *a:* and tell DOS to go ahead without checking), and even though newer versions of DOS give an explicit warning if the disk to be formatted is a fixed disk, the consequences are severe enough that you should consider protecting yourself against the possibility. The technique is fairly simple: Rename the Format command file, and create a batch file named FORMAT that always formats the diskette in drive A. The following commands do it (assuming the current directory is the root directory on the fixed disk):

```
C>rename format.com xformat.com
C>copy con format.bat
xformat a: %1 %2 %3
^Z
          1 File(s) copied
```

To format a diskette in drive A with this batch file, you just type *format;* there's no chance of formatting the disk in the current drive. To use any parameters of the Format command other than the drive letter, include them with your new Format command. To format a single-sided system diskette in drive A, for example, you would type *format /s /1.*

If you should want to format a diskette in a drive other than A, just enter the Format command with the usual parameters, but remember to type the command as *xformat,* because you renamed the command file.

USING DOS AS A RECORD-MANAGEMENT PROGRAM

Chapters 14 and 16 showed you how to use filter commands and batch files to search a telephone list. This procedure can also be used to keep track of any small- to medium-sized file—say, from 50 to 200 entries. This technique doesn't replace a record- or file-management program, but it's simple and quick, and the price is right: You don't need anything except DOS.

The following topics describe other types of information you can keep track of in the same way. Using the same sort of batch files you created in Chapter 16, you can quickly locate any entry or group of entries in your record files.

The descriptions here don't include examples; they simply describe the information included in each line and the columns in which the items of information begin (so you can sort them). As with any batch files, the best way to get comfortable with this technique and apply it to your own needs is to experiment. These examples give you a starting point.

Keeping Track of Your Computer Files

As you use the computer, your collection of computer files will grow and grow. If you use a word processor, for example, keeping track of all the letters and other documents you create can be a problem. Although using wildcard characters with the Directory command makes a particular file easier to find, you still may have to do some searching to answer such questions as, "How many letters did I write in October to the regional sales office?" or "When did we respond to that request from the National Science Foundation?"

You can solve this problem by creating an index file that describes all your word-processing files. You could use the same technique to keep track of any large collection of files.

Figure 17-6 shows the items of information, and the columns in which they begin, to give you the format for an index file that keeps track of word-processing files.

Columns 1 through 3 contain the initials of the originator of the document (THP).

Columns 5 through 12 contain the file name (MFGLET31). All files are assumed to have the same extension.

Columns 14 through 21 contain the date the document was created (10/16/85).

Columns 23 through 79 contain a brief description of the document.

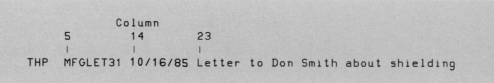

```
                  Column
        5          14        23
        |          |         |
THP   MFGLET31 10/16/85 Letter to Don Smith about shielding
```

Figure 17-6. Word-processing index file

Keep this index file up to date as you create word-processing files, and you can quickly find files and answer questions with batch files like SHOW.BAT, SHOWAND.BAT and SHOWXCPT.BAT, which you created in Chapter 16.

To answer:	Type:
When did we respond to that request from the National Science Foundation?	`show NSF`
What letters did I write to the regional sales office in October?	`show and sales 10/`

Want a list of all the documents about the new inventory system, or a list of all letters sent in March? If you keep your index up to date, the answers are just a command away.

Simple Bibliographic Index

If your work requires a lot of reading, you're probably frustrated at times by how easy it is to forget where you saw something. If research is important to your job, but it is not significant enough to justify purchasing and learning to use a data-base or bibliographic retrieval program, this simple technique might be the answer.

Again, the answer is to create an index file and search it with batch commands. Figure 17-7 shows the the items of information, and the columns in which they begin, to give you the format for an index file that keeps track of magazine articles, books, and other sources of reference material.

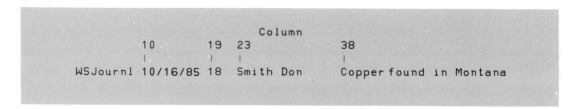

```
                        Column
        10        19 23              38
         |         |  |               |
WSJournl 10/16/85 18  Smith Don       Copper found in Montana
```

Figure 17-7. Bibliographic index file

Columns 1 through 8 contain the abbreviated title of the journal, book, or other source.

Columns 10 through 17 contain the date of the reference.

Columns 19 through 21 contain the page number.

Columns 23 through 36 contain the author's name.

Columns 38 through 79 contain the title or description of the reference.

Again, with batch files like the ones you created in Chapter 16, you can find bibliographic references with one command:

To answer:	Type:
Where did I see that article on kinesthesia?	`show kine`
I remember an article last June about laser surgery.	`show and 6/ laser`

The time it takes to keep this index up to date pays off in the ability to find valuable information much more quickly.

Capital Inventory

If you're an independent professional or you operate a small business, you could easily have a much larger investment in capital goods than you realize. Your accountant and insurance agent probably emphasize the importance of keeping an up-to-date inventory of capital goods, but it's easy to put off this sort of record keeping.

Figure 17-8 shows a simple index file that lets you keep track of your capital goods. It's no substitute for a complete inventory system, but it's a start, and one that lets you quickly search and sort your inventory.

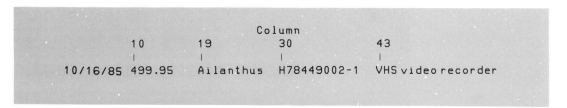

```
                              Column
            10       19       30        43
            |        |        |         |
10/16/85 499.95    Ailanthus  H78449002-1  VHS video recorder
```

Figure 17-8. Capital inventory index file

Columns 1 through 8 contain the date of the acquisition.
Columns 10 through 17 contain the cost of acquisition.
Columns 19 through 28 contain the manufacturer's name.
Columns 30 through 41 contain the serial number.
Columns 43 through 79 contain the description.

Here, too, with batch files like the ones you created in Chapter 16, you can keep track of your inventory with one command:

To answer:	Type:
When did we get the copy machine?	`show copy`
What did we buy before 1985?	`show xcpt /85`

This technique can also be used to keep track of your personal inventory for insurance purposes; with a bit of modification, it could also be used for collections, such as coins, stamps, or first editions.

CHANGING YOUR SYSTEM CONFIGURATION

Unlike the other DOS commands, which tell DOS *what* to do, the configuration commands tell DOS *how* to do something, such as use a device or communicate with a disk drive. These commands are required infrequently, usually only when you add a device to your computer system (thereby changing its *configuration*).

Unlike other DOS commands, you don't type the configuration commands at the keyboard; you put them in a special file called CONFIG.SYS that must be in the root directory of your DOS disk. DOS carries out these commands only when it is started; if you change a command in CONFIG.SYS, you must restart DOS for the command to take effect.

Some application programs or accessory devices require certain commands in CONFIG.SYS. The documentation of the application program or device usually includes step-by-step instructions.

If you need a configuration command and your DOS disk already has a file named CONFIG.SYS in the root directory, use Edlin or some other text editor to add the configuration command to the file. If your DOS disk doesn't have a CONFIG.SYS file in the root

directory, use a text editor to create the file and put the configuration command in it. If you need only one or two configuration commands, however, you can use the Copy command to copy the console to CONFIG.SYS, just as you created the sample files in earlier chapters.

Using the Country Command

country = \<code\>

As described in Chapter 8, the country code is a number that DOS uses to control how the date is displayed. Application programs also have access to this code, and can use it to control other format characteristics, such as currency symbols and what characters (such as commas and decimal points) are used to divide numbers. The Country configuration command lets you set this code.

The Country command has one parameter:

country = \<code\>

\<code\> is the three-digit country code you want to set in DOS. It is usually the same as the country's international long-distance dialing prefix. Figure 17-9 shows the valid country codes. You must include all three digits, including any zeros at the beginning.

Suppose your computer was built for use in the United States, but someone from France also uses it. To tell DOS to follow French conventions for date, currency, and decimals, you could create or modify a DOS system diskette for that person, including the command *country = 033* in CONFIG.SYS. (If there were no CONFIG.SYS file in the root directory, you would create it and put the Country command in it.) Once the CONFIG.SYS file was saved, each time DOS was started from the French disk, it would automatically adopt the French conventions. For example, when DOS displayed the

United States	001	Italy	039	Norway	047
Netherlands	031	Switzerland	041	Germany	049
Belgium	032	United Kingdom	044	Australia	061
France	033	Denmark	045	Finland	358
Spain	034	Sweden	046	Israel	972

Figure 17-9. Country codes

current date and asked for the new date, it would display the date as day-month-year and ask the user to *Enter new date (dd-mm-yy):*.

To change the country code, you would edit CONFIG.SYS again. For the United States, you could either delete the Country command or change *country = 033* to *country = 001* (001 is the code for the United States).

The Device Command and Device Drivers

device = <device>

The Device configuration command specifies a program (a command file with an extension of SYS) that tells DOS how to use a particular <device>. Such a program is called a *device driver.* If you have a Microsoft Mouse, for example, the file named MOUSE.SYS is the device driver that tells DOS how to interpret the mouse movements. To tell DOS to use MOUSE.SYS, CONFIG.SYS should contain a line with the Device command *device = mouse.sys.*

Simulating a Disk Drive in Memory with VDISK.SYS

device = vdisk.sys
<size > <sector>
< directory>/E

DOS reads from and writes to diskettes quickly, and uses a fixed disk even more quickly; both devices are mechanical, however, and quite slow compared to the computer's electronic memory. Starting with version 3.0, DOS lets you set aside a portion of the computer's memory for use as a simulated disk, making it possible for disk operations to be performed at memory speeds. This simulated disk is called a *virtual* disk, because it's virtually the same as having another disk drive. VDISK.SYS is the device driver that defines a virtual disk drive.

A virtual disk behaves like any other disk: It has a drive letter and a directory, and you can specify it in any command that uses a disk. It is much faster than a real disk drive, however, and the difference is especially noticeable when you use commands, such as Copy, that work with disk drives, or when you use application programs that access the disk frequently, as many word processors and data base programs do. To use a virtual disk drive, you copy the files you need to the virtual drive after DOS has started, then copy them back after you have completed the work.

DOS assigns the next available drive letter to the virtual disk drive. On a two-drive system, the next available letter is usually C; on a system with one diskette drive and a fixed disk, the next available letter is usually D.

Although a real disk drive has a fixed capacity, such as 360K or 1.2M, a virtual disk can have whatever capacity you want, within certain limits: It must be at least 64K, and there must be at least 64K of memory remaining for program use after the virtual disk drive is defined. If your computer has enough memory, you can define more than one virtual disk by including more than one Vdisk configuration command in CONFIG.SYS.

This remarkable speedup has some drawbacks, however. The memory used for a virtual disk reduces the amount of memory available to programs, and the contents of a virtual disk are lost each time you turn the computer off. Make sure that your virtual disk leaves enough memory for the programs you use, and be sure to copy the files you want to keep onto a real disk before you turn the computer off. When you work with an application program, you can automate this process by using a batch file to copy your working files to the virtual disk, start the application program, and then copy the revised working files back to the real drive after you leave the application program.

The Device configuration command to define a virtual disk has five parameters:

device = vdisk.sys <size> <sector> <directory> /E

VDISK.SYS is the name of the device-driver program. If it isn't in the root directory of the DOS disk, you must include the drive letter and path name of its directory.

<size> is the size, in kilobytes, of the virtual disk. The minimum is 64, and the maximum is the total available memory on your computer. If you omit <size> or specify an incorrect value, DOS sets <size> to 64.

<sector> is the size, in bytes, of each sector on the virtual disk. You can specify 128, 256, or 512. If you omit <sector> or specify an incorrect value, DOS sets <sector> to 128.

<directory> is the number of directory entries allowed on the virtual disk. You can specify any value from 2 to 512. Each directory takes up 32 bytes of the virtual disk. If you omit <directory> or specify an incorrect value, DOS sets <directory> to 64.

/E can be used only with a computer that has memory extended beyond the normal 640K limit of DOS. It tells DOS to use this extended memory for the virtual disk. Using extended memory for a virtual disk leaves the maximum amount of memory available for programs. Currently, this parameter can be used only with the IBM Personal Computer AT and computers compatible with it.

DOS may adjust some of the numbers you specify. If the <size> you specify doesn't leave at least 64K of memory available, DOS reduces <size> so that 64K of memory is available for programs. If the number of directory entries you specify, times 32 bytes per entry, leaves a partial sector remaining, DOS adjusts the number of directory entries upward to fill that final sector completely.

If there isn't enough memory to create the virtual disk as you specify it, DOS doesn't create the virtual disk.

Example of simulating a disk drive in memory

Suppose your computer has two diskette drives and 512K of memory, and your word processor is Microsoft Word. You want to use a virtual disk to speed your word-processing sessions, and you also want to be sure not to forget to copy the edited files back from the virtual disk after you finish your work. You decide that you can afford to use 180K of memory for the virtual disk, that each sector should be 512 bytes, and that you need only 32 directory entries.

First, using Edlin or another text editor, you would put the following Device configuration command in CONFIG.SYS:

```
device=vdisk.sys 180 512 32
```

Because the system has two real drives, the virtual drive would be drive C. (If the system had one diskette drive and a fixed disk whose drive letter was C, the virtual drive would be D.)

Then you would create the following batch file named WP.BAT in the root directory of your system disk:

```
1: cd \wp
2: copy %1 c:
3: c:
4: word
5: a:
6: copy c:%1 b:
7: delete c:%1
8: cd \
```

Now suppose you start your system and want to edit a file named REPORT.DOC. You type:

```
A>wp report.doc
```

The batch file does the following:

* In line 1, it changes the current directory to the word processing directory.

* In line 2, it copies REPORT.DOC to the virtual disk drive.

* In line 3, it changes the current drive to the virtual drive.

* In line 4, it starts the word-processing program.

* In line 5, after you quit the word-processing program, it changes the current drive back to drive A.

* In line 6, it copies REPORT.DOC (which you edited and saved in the word-processing program) to a data disk in drive B.

* In line 7, it deletes REPORT.DOC from the virtual disk.

* In line 8, it changes the directory back to the root directory of the disk in drive A, leaving you just where you were when you entered the batch command.

You could use this same batch file to edit a set of files with similar file names or extensions by using a wildcard character. For example, to work with all the files whose file name starts with LET and whose extension is DOC, you would type:

```
A>wp let*.doc
```

Notice, however, that this would copy all the files that match the file name (*let*.doc) to the virtual disk and then back to the real disk drive, whether or not you changed them.

You could also copy program files to a virtual disk to reduce the time required to load and start executing a program. This is usually helpful only if you use a very large program that must periodically return to the program disk to load additional portions, or if you routinely use several different programs and switch back and forth.

How you use a virtual disk depends to a great extent on how much memory your computer has and what sort of work you do with it. As with many other DOS commands, you may need to do a bit of experimenting before you find the most useful way for you.

Controlling the Display with ANSI.SYS

DOS includes one device driver, called ANSI.SYS. *ANSI* is an acronym for American National Standards Institute. ANSI.SYS defines a standard set of methods for managing a display, including how to display and erase characters, move the cursor, and select colors. Some programs require your system disk to have a CONFIG.SYS file that contains the command *device = ansi.sys*.

Some Other Configuration Commands

Several other configuration commands control internal operating characteristics and usually deal with how DOS reads from and writes to a disk. Some application programs or devices may include detailed instructions for adding or changing these and some advanced configuration commands (described in Appendix B).

Buffers

buffers = <number>

The Buffers configuration command defines the number of work areas in memory (*buffers*) that DOS uses to handle reading from and writing to a disk. Unless otherwise instructed, DOS uses two buffers. The effect of this configuration command on system performance depends on the type of disk drive you use and the types of programs that you use.

Files

files = <number>

The Files configuration command tells DOS how many files it can use at one time. Unless otherwise instructed, DOS can use a maximum of eight files at a time.

Lastdrive

lastdrive = <letter>

The Lastdrive configuration command specifies the highest drive letter that DOS recognizes as valid. If CONFIG.SYS doesn't contain a Lastdrive command, the highest drive letter DOS recognizes is E. This command is usually used to specify a higher letter (up to Z) if more than five drive letters are needed because the computer is part of a network or uses many simulated disk drives.

COMMANDS FOR OCCASIONAL USE

This book has described all the commands you routinely use to operate DOS. There are a few remaining commands you might occasionally need, and there are several commands that you won't need unless you plan to do some programming or to use some of the advanced capabilities of DOS. The less commonly used commands are described here; the advanced commands are briefly described in Appendix B.

Displaying the DOS Version Number

ver

The Version command displays the number of the version of DOS you're using. If you use more than one version, or if you are using someone else's machine, this gives you a quick way to check the version.

The Version command has no parameters:

ver

If you're using Version 3.1 with an IBM Personal Computer, for example, DOS replies *IBM Personal Computer DOS Version 3.10* in response to the command.

Changing the System Prompt

prompt <string>

As shown in examples in Chapters 3 and 9, you can change the system prompt with the Prompt command to display much more than just the current drive letter. The change takes effect as soon as you enter the command.

The Prompt command has one parameter:

prompt <string>

<string> is a string of characters that defines the new system prompt. You can use any characters you wish. You can also cause the new prompt to include one or more items of useful information by including a dollar sign followed by one of the following characters, to specify what you want the prompt to contain:

Character	Produces
d	The current date
p	The current directory
n	The current drive
t	The current time
v	The DOS version number
g	A greater-than sign (>)
l	A less-than sign (<)
b	A vertical bar (|)
q	An equal sign (=)
e	An Escape character
h	A backspace
$	A dollar sign ($)
—	A signal to end the current line and start a new one (the character is an underscore, not a hyphen)

You can include as many combinations of $, followed by a character, as you wish. DOS ignores any combination of $ followed by a character not in the preceding list. You saw an example of this earlier in this chapter: In the batch file MKT.BAT, the system prompt was set to nothing (made invisible) with the command *prompt $a*.

If you enter the Prompt command with no parameter (just type *prompt*), DOS restores the prompt to its usual form: The letter of the current drive followed by a greater-than sign (for example, A>).

The Prompt command takes effect immediately, so it's easy to experiment. You saw how to change the system prompt to a courteous request (*May I help you?*) in Chapter 3 and you changed it to a two-line description of the current directory in Chapter 9. Don't be

afraid to experiment, because all you need do to restore the system prompt to its standard form is type *prompt*.

Several examples follow. Notice how the system prompt changes each time to show the effect of the previous Prompt command. Press the Space bar before pressing the Enter key to end each command, to leave a blank space between the end of the system prompt and the beginning of the command that you type next.

To define the system prompt as the current directory (including the current drive), type:

```
B>prompt $p

B:\mkt\wp _
```

The example assumes that the current drive is B and that the directory is \MKT\WP. To define the system prompt as two lines that show the date and time, type:

```
B:\mkt\wp prompt $d$_$t

Wed 10-16-1985
14:57:10.11 _
```

The time and date will vary, depending on how you have set the time and date in your system. Press the Enter key several times; you can see that DOS keeps the time current.

Finally, combining several of the options shows just how much you can include in a prompt (it's shown as two lines here, but type the entire Prompt command as a single line):

```
Wed 10-16-1985
15:02:10.11 prompt $v$_$d $t$_Current
directory $q $p$_Command:

IBM Personal Computer DOS Version  3.10
Wed 10-16-1985 15:02:57.68
Current directory = B:\MKT\WP
Command: _
```

Each user can easily tailor the system prompt to the preferred balance of brevity and information by putting a Prompt command in a batch file.

Altering the way DOS interprets drive letters

*Warning: The following three commands (Assign, Substitute, and Join)
let you change the way DOS interprets drive letters. These commands restrict
your use of other DOS commands, such as Label and Diskcopy, that deal with
disks and files. Use the next three commands sparingly, and check the descriptions of the other disk and file commands in your DOS manual to make sure you
understand the restrictions.*

Assigning a drive letter to a different drive

**assign <drive1>=
<drive2>**

Some application programs require that you put the diskettes
with your data files in one particular drive. This can be inconvenient
if you're using a fixed disk and prefer to use it for your data files.
The Assign command gives you a solution: It lets you tell DOS to
make a drive letter refer to a different drive (for example, to tell DOS
to use the fixed disk, drive C, whenever DOS receives a request for
drive B).

Because the Assign command affects *all* requests for a drive, you
should use it with some caution—especially if you are using a fixed
disk. Always bear in mind that some DOS commands, such as Erase,
delete existing files from the diskette in the specified drive. If you
use one of these commands after you have used Assign, you could
inadvertently lose valuable programs or data files.

The Assign command has two parameters:

assign <drive1>=<drive2>

<drive1> is the letter to be assigned to a different drive.
<drive2> is the letter of the drive that is to be used in place
of <drive1>.

If you omit both <drive1> and <drive2>, DOS cancels any
assignments in effect.

For example, suppose you have a graphics program that requires
all data files to be on drive B, but you want to use your fixed disk
(drive C) for data files. To tell DOS to assign all requests for drive B
to drive C instead, you would type *assign b = c.*

The assignment affects all requests for the drive, including any
commands you enter. If you assign drive B to drive C as in the previous example, and then type *dir b:,* DOS displays the directory of the

fixed disk. The assignment remains in effect until you restart DOS or cancel the assignment by typing *assign.*

Treating a directory as if it were a disk

subst <drive> <pathname> /D

The Substitute (subst) command lets you treat a directory as a separate disk. If your directory structure includes long path names, or if you use application programs that accept a drive letter but not a path name, you can use the Substitute command to tell DOS to treat all future references to a particular drive as references to a directory on the disk in a different drive.

After naming a drive letter in a Substitute command or in a Join command (described next), you cannot refer to that drive letter in any other command, so you will probably want to use a drive letter that doesn't refer to an existing drive. In order to do this, you must tell DOS to accept more drive letters than there are disk drives. You do this by putting a Lastdrive command in the CONFIG.SYS file in the root directory of your DOS system disk. The Substitute command has two parameters:

> subst <drive> <pathname> /D

<drive is the letter to be used to refer to <pathname>.

<pathname> is the path name of the directory to be referred to by <drive>. /D deletes any substitutions that involve <drive>. If you include /D, you cannot include <pathname>.

If you omit all parameters (just type *subst*), DOS displays a list of any substitutions in effect.

For example, suppose you find yourself frequently referring to a directory whose path name is \MPLAN\SALES\FORECAST and you would like to use a shorter synonym. To substitute d: for the path name, you would type *subst d: c:\mplan\sales\forecast.* The substitution would remain in effect until you restarted DOS or canceled the substitution by typing *subst d: /d.*

Treating a disk as if it were a directory

join <drive> <pathname> /D

The Join command lets you treat a disk drive as a directory on the disk in a different drive. If you use an application program that requires its data-disk space to be on the program disk, you can use the Join command to tell DOS to treat another drive as a directory on the program disk. The Join command has three parameters:

> join <drive> <pathname> /D

<drive> is the letter of the drive to be connected to the directory specified by <pathname>.

<pathname> is the path name of the directory to which <drive> is to be joined.

/D deletes any joins that involve <drive>. If you include /D, you cannot include <pathname>.

If you omit all parameters (just type *join*), DOS displays a list of any joins in effect.

For example, suppose you have an application program that takes up most of a diskette and you need a lot of disk space for data files. If you put the application program diskette in drive A and a blank diskette in drive B, you could tell DOS to treat the blank diskette in drive B as a directory named \DATA on the diskette in drive A by typing *join b: a:\data*. The join would remain in effect until you restarted DOS or canceled the join by typing *join b: /d*.

CHAPTER
18
DOS AND LOCAL AREA NETWORKS

Personal computers have become commonplace in offices and the home, but advances in software and hardware continue to increase their capability and create more uses for them. One of these developments, the local area network, makes it possible to connect many personal computers and let the people who use them share such expensive options as fixed disks and laser printers.

Because they are so effective in allowing computer users to share hardware, software, and even data, local area networks are becoming increasingly common in all types of work situations: small businesses; departments of large businesses; offices of independent professionals, such as architects, doctors, engineers, and lawyers; academic departments; government offices—anywhere, in fact, that several computers are used by persons with common goals.

WHAT IS A LOCAL AREA NETWORK?

A local area network is a group of personal computers located in the same general area—one building, perhaps, or one floor of a large building—connected by a common cable and running the same network program. The network program moves files back and forth among the computers in the network. When you print a file on the network printer, for example, it is the network program that locates the file and, if necessary, sends it to the computer to which the network printer is attached; there, the network program stores the file on disk and prints it when the printer is available.

Several local area networks and network programs are available, each with its own operating characteristics and commands. This chapter describes the way one network program, Microsoft Networks, is used. Microsoft Networks works with MS-DOS, starting with Version 3.1. It uses the same commands used by PC-Network from IBM Corporation, but can be used with a range of non-IBM computers and network hardware. Both network programs allow you to use the majority of the DOS commands described in this book, with little or no change.

WHY USE A NETWORK?

Suppose your company bought personal computers for you and half a dozen of your colleagues. The computers would certainly give you more powerful tools to use in your work, but this arrangement has two potential shortcomings:

- It is expensive to provide such options as separate printers and fixed disk drives for each computer.

- It is awkward for several users to work with the same program and data diskettes.

Although the cost of hardware decreases each year, providing a printer or fixed disk for every machine isn't always practical—especially if different printers (such as dot-matrix, letter-quality, and laser printers) are used for different types of documents (rough drafts, correspondence, and reports, for example). If only one machine is connected to a particular printer, other users must bring to it a diskette that contains the files they want to print, then either interrupt the user of that machine or wait until it's free—not a convenient solution.

Sharing information creates its own problems. If several users work with the same data base, such as customer records or inventory, they must either share a computer or move the data to their own computers. Sharing a computer is obviously inconvenient. Moving a data diskette around is equally inconvenient. Duplicating the data on each machine is more convenient, but could require several expensive fixed disks and creates the potential for even more problems:

- If one user changes the data base, that copy is different, and other users won't have the new data until their copies are changed. In the meantime, they might well change their copies. Now all the copies are different. Who makes all these changes on the master copy, and when, and how can that person be sure all the changes are made?

- If users make note of the changes but the master data base isn't updated, the changes aren't available until the master copy is updated. How is the master copy changed and distributed? How often should this be done?

Because using inaccurate data can be even more damaging than not having timely access to it, these questions can't be ignored. The larger and more complex the data base you are working with, the more important it is to follow strict procedures for updating the data and making it available. Unfortunately, the larger and more complex the data base, the more likely it is that something will go wrong, resulting in inaccurate data.

Enter the network. If the data base is stored on a shared disk in a local area network, all users have access to the same data; if one user changes the data, all other users have immediate access to the new version. No extra fixed disk, no complicated procedures, no chance of mismatched copies of the data.

Microsoft Networks can make a group of computers much more effective, and can make valuable data much easier to protect when many people must use it. Using the network, however, is no more difficult than using DOS. In fact, using your computer with Microsoft Networks is virtually indistinguishable from using your computer by itself.

Some New Terms

Microsoft Networks adds some new terms to your computer vocabulary:

Network resources: The fixed disks and printers shared by the computers in a local area network.

Server: A computer in a local area network that provides network resources to the others. Because of its function and the volume of information it handles, it must have a fixed disk.

Workstation: A network computer that uses network resources.

Network manager: The person who installs (or arranges for installation of) the network, identifies workstations to the network, and manages the operation of the network server.

Network name: The name (chosen by the user of a network computer, and assigned by the network manager) by which each workstation and server in a network is known. The network name enables the network program to match tasks to the appropriate sending and receiving computers. When used in commands, the network name is usually preceded by two backslashes (\ \ ).

Local: A file or device located on the computer you're using in the network.

Remote: A file or device located on a computer other than the one you're using in a network. Remote in this sense does not necessarily mean far away.

WHAT DO YOU NEED FOR A NETWORK?

Networks require additional hardware and software, but setting up a network can cost much less than the computers in the network. Because a network is made up of sophisticated equipment and software, some planning and preparation are required before it's ready to be used. The equipment and its installation can be broken into three categories:

- Hardware.

- Software.

- Testing.

Network Hardware

Each workstation and server requires a *network interface board,* which is similar to a display adapter or a memory expansion board. This board goes inside the computer case, but installing this board is no more complicated than inserting any other accessory board. The Microsoft Networks software can be used with network interface boards from many different manufacturers.

After the network boards have been installed, the computers must be linked by a cable that plugs into the rear of each interface board. The type of cable and the connectors used depend on which network interface boards you choose. Sometimes, as when installing the cable means pulling it through walls, the job is probably better left to a skilled professional.

Network Software

Just hooking some computers together with a cable doesn't make a network: There must be programs to move data back and forth between the server and the workstations, direct traffic through the wires, let computers connect and disconnect from the network. Microsoft Networks is a collection of such programs, as DOS is a collection of housekeeping and file-handling programs.

Each server and workstation in a network must have a system disk that contains both version 3.1 or higher of MS-DOS and the Microsoft Networks programs. Installing the software requires the following steps:

- Create a file on the Microsoft Networks disk that contains the network name of each computer in the network. (Refer to your network manual for the exact procedures.)

- Copy the appropriate Microsoft Networks program and data files to each server and workstation's system disk.

- Add a few lines to the DOS CONFIG.SYS file (or create it if it doesn't exist) on each server and workstation's system disk.

After completing these steps, you have created a network system disk for each server and workstation. This disk can be used to start both MS-DOS and Microsoft Networks.

Testing the Network

To test the network hardware and software, you start each server and workstation with its network system disk, then type *echotest* at each server and workstation. The ECHOTEST program sends a message from each server (if there is more than one) to each workstation; the workstations receive the message and send it back (echo it) to each server.

The ECHOTEST program displays how many times the message is echoed by each computer, and runs until you stop it. After each computer has echoed about 300 times—this takes about a minute— you can assume that the network is ready for operation.

HOW DO YOU USE THE NETWORK?

Using a computer with Microsoft Networks isn't much different from just using a computer. You'll probably spend most of your time using application programs, such as a word processor, and occasionally use DOS commands to manage your files and do other general work. The network requires only a few additional commands, most of which you can put in a batch file to be carried out once at the beginning of a network session.

After you have connected to the network, it doesn't matter whether the files and printers you use are local or remote. You can edit files, print files, and generally treat the shared fixed disks and printers as if they were attached to your computer. You use Microsoft Networks commands to do the following:

- Start your workstation.

- Use the shared directories and printers.

- Temporarily disconnect from the network.

- Print a file on the network printer.

Starting Your Workstation

When the server is running, all you need do to join your workstation to the network is to start DOS in the normal way, then enter the Net Start Redirector (net start rdr) command to tell the network program who you are and that you want to use the network. This command runs a program that reroutes, or redirects, any requests for remote files or printers to the server.

For example, if the network name of your workstation were LISA, you would connect to the network by entering *net start rdr lisa*. If you use the network regularly, you would probably put this command in an AUTOEXEC.BAT file, to automatically join your workstation to the network each time you start DOS.

Using Shared Directories and Printers

After you have joined your workstation to the network, you can use any of the directories or printers that are available to computers on the network. You identify the directory or printer you wish to use by assigning it a drive letter or printer name with the Net Use command. (If the drive letter or printer name already exists on your own computer, the letter or name becomes unavailable to you until you disconnect from the network directory or printer.)

For example, suppose the server's network name is HOME and it has made available a directory named LETTERS. To use this directory, you would assign it the letter of a drive—D, perhaps. To use LETTERS, you would type *net use d:\\home\letters.* You can now treat LETTERS just as if it were another drive attached to your computer: If you type *d:,* DOS changes the system prompt to *D>* and drive D—the shared directory—becomes the current drive.

Similarly, if a server named HOME made available a printer named DOT, you could use the printer by entering *net use lpt1: \\home\dot.* If you already had a printer named LPT1 attached to your computer, however, you could not use it after entering this Net Use command.

You can disconnect from a network directory or printer with the /D option; to disconnect from the directory in the previous example, you would enter *net use d: /d.* If you're not sure which network directories and printer you're using, you can display a list by typing *net use.*

If you use the same network directories and printer in your sessions on the network, you can put the appropriate Net Use commands immediately after the Net Start Redirector command in an AUTOEXEC.BAT file, and completely automate your connection to the network.

Temporarily Disconnecting from the Network

Because you cannot use a local device if you used its name in a Net Use command, there may be times when you will need to temporarily disconnect from a network directory or printer. The Net Pause command temporarily disconnects either your disks or printer from the server; the Net Continue command resumes the connection.

Suppose you have a printer named LPT1 attached to your work-station but, as in the preceding example, you're connected to the network printer using the name LPT1. Now, you want to print a document on your own (local) printer. To do so, temporarily disconnect from the network printer by typing *net pause prdr* (*prdr* is short for *printer redirection*). Print the file on your printer, then reconnect to the network printer by typing *net continue prdr*. You can also temporarily disconnect from network directories in the same way.

Printing a File on the Network Printer

After you have connected to a network printer, you can print a file on it with the Net Print command. To continue the preceding example, if you connected to the network printer named DOT using the name LPT1, you could print a file named SUMMARY.DOC on the network printer by typing *net print summary.doc lpt1*. (The file named SUMMARY.DOC could be on a disk attached to your computer or on a disk attached to the server.)

You can also use the Net Print command to display the list of files waiting to be printed on the network printer (the print queue). To display the contents of the print queue on a server named HOME, for example, you would type *net print \\home*.

Other Commands

Microsoft Networks includes a few other commands for general network use:

- The Append command lets you tell the network where to find a non-command file if it isn't in the current directory; it is similar to the DOS Path command in this respect.

- The Net Name command displays the network name of the workstation.

- The Net Help command displays a description of how to use the other commands.

In practice, however, the only network command you're likely to type whenever you want to use it is Net Print. You'll probably put the commands to join the network and connect to the shared directories and printer in a batch file, to be executed once at the beginning of a session. If you put them in an AUTOEXEC.BAT file, you could just start DOS and would be automatically linked to the network.

A NEW USER: THE NETWORK MANAGER

Because the network involves several computer systems and requires communication and cooperation among the users, one person is usually given the responsibility of coordinating the installation and ongoing use of the network. This person is the network manager.

After installing and testing the network, the network manager is responsible for starting and stopping the server, making the shared directories and printers available, adding and deleting workstations and servers, and responding to requests for help from network users.

The remainder of this chapter is primarily for the network manager. It shows how to use the system manager commands to do the following:

- Start the network.

- Make directories and printers available.

- Check the status of the network.

- Stop and restart the network.

- Manage the network printer.

(The Net Help command can be used to display a description of the network manager's commands as well as the network users' commands.)

Starting the Network

After you have started DOS on the server, start the network with the Net Start server command. For example, if the network name of the server is HOME, you would type *net start server \\home.* You would probably put this command in an AUTOEXEC.BAT file, to start the network automatically each time you start DOS.

Making Directories and Printers Available

Once the network is started, you use the Net Share command to tell Microsoft Networks which directories and printers to make available to the workstations. Each directory or printer to be shared requires a Net Share command; in addition to the path name of the directory, or the device name of the printer, you also specify the network name, which is usually shorter than a path name and can be made more descriptive.

For example, to make available to users the directory named C:\WORD\SALES\CORRESP and give it the network name LETTERS, you would type *net share letters = c:\word\sales\corresp.* To make available the printer named LPT1 and give it the network name DOT, you would enter *net share dot = lpt1:.*

The Net Share command also lets you control access to directories and printers by assigning passwords. In addition, you can use it to control whether the files in a directory are read-only and whether network users can create new files in the directory.

If you make the same directories and printer (or printers) available each session, you can put the Net Share commands in a file and tell Microsoft Networks to carry out the commands in the file when you enter the Net Start Server command. This completely automates starting the network.

Checking the Status of the Network

Several commands let the network manager monitor the network while it is running:

- The Net Status command displays a list of the shared directories and printers, the number of files waiting to be printed by the network printer, and some general information about the network configuration.

• The Net File command displays how many workstations are using each file that is available.

• The Net Error command displays the 15 most recent network errors and tells when they occurred.

Starting and Stopping the Network

You can't just turn off the server computer when you're ready to stop the network. Microsoft Networks must carry out a series of shutdown tasks in an orderly fashion. If you stop the network while workstations are still connected to it, their users could lose work and files could be damaged, so you must make sure no one is using the network when you shut it down.

The Net Stop command stops the network. Before you enter the Net Stop command, however, you should use the Net Status command to make sure no workstations are active. If any are, notify the users at those workstations and wait for them to disconnect. When no workstations are active, type *net stop*. After a few moments, DOS displays the system prompt, the network is stopped, and you can turn the server computer off.

If you just stopped the network temporarily, to add or delete a workstation, you needn't go through the entire start-up procedure again: The Net Restart command starts the network and returns it to the same state as when the Net Stop command was entered.

Managing the Network Printer

So that the network printer can keep up with print requests from all workstations on the network, files to be printed are stored in a separate directory on the server's fixed disk. This is the network's print queue. Microsoft Networks includes several commands for managing this queue:

• The Net Print command displays the name, size, and first few words of each file in the queue. To use the command, you would type *net print*.

- The Net Print Cancel command stops printing the file currently being printed. To use it, you would type *net print cancel.*

- The Net Print Restart command stops printing the file currently being printed, but puts it back in the print queue rather than canceling it completely (as the Net Print Cancel command does). To use it, you would type *net print restart.*

- The Net Print Kill command removes a file from the queue. To remove a file named PQ1001 from the print queue, you would type *net print kill pq1001.*

- The Net Print On/Off command stops and restarts the printer. To stop the printer, you would type *net print off.* To restart it, you would type *net print on.*

- The Net Separator On/Off command controls whether a separate page that identifies a file by its name and workstation is printed at the beginning of each print job. To print the separator page, you would type *net separator on.* To eliminate the separator page, you would type *net separator off.*

FINAL SUMMARY

This chapter concludes the tutorial part of this book. In the course of eighteen chapters, you have progressed from starting DOS to creating your own personalized commands and menus. You have learned that Edlin is available when you need to write a short document or other text file, you have been introduced to a DOS-based networking program, and you have seen that you can use DOS commands to create a simple record-management system.

By no means have you seen everything that DOS can do for you. There is much that this book doesn't cover, and the most valuable features of DOS could prove to be in a command or application you design for your own specific needs, using this book simply as a source of ideas and techniques.

3

QUICK REFERENCE TO DOS COMMANDS

P art 3 contains a description of each DOS and Edlin command. The descriptions are in alphabetic order, with cross-references to the detailed descriptions and examples in Part 2. For ease of use, and to provide a quick visual reference, each command is accompanied by the symbol that identifies the chapter in which it is discussed.

The full form of each command is shown, with a description of each parameter. There are no examples; the material here lets you quickly answer questions about the form of a command, such as "How do I set the printer width?" or "How do I format a system disk?"

CHAPTER

19

DOS COMMAND REFERENCE

The terms shown in angle brackets (< >) in the following list appear in various commands throughout this book. These terms have been defined in the preceding chapters; they are grouped here to provide you with a quick reference when you need to refresh your memory.

<baud> represents the rate at which data is transmitted through a serial communications port.

<command> represents a DOS command.

<condition> represents a test the If command can check (see the If command description for the exact form of the conditions).

<databits> represents the number of bits sent through a communications port for each character; the value must be 7 or 8.

<drive> represents the letter of a drive, followed by a colon (such as A:).

<filename>, <file1>, or <file2> represents the name of a file; can include a drive letter and extension; unless the command description states otherwise, can also include a path name.

<hours:minutes> represents the time in 24-hour form; the hour number must be separated from the minutes number by a colon.

<.hundredths> represents hundredths of a second; can be any number from 0 to 99, preceded by a period.

represents a line in a batch file that consists of a colon (:) followed by a string of characters.

<line> represents a line number.

<message> represents a message (string of characters) that can be displayed.

<method> represents the way information is shown on a display.

<number> represents a number.

<parity> represents a code that specifies the type of error-checking in a communications port; the value must be O (Odd), E (Even), or N (None).

<path> represents the series of directory names that defines the path to a subdirectory.

<port> represents the name of a communications port, followed by a colon (COM1: or COM2:).

<printer> represents the name of a printer, followed by a colon (PRN:, LPT1:, LPT2:, or LPT3:).

<range> represents starting and ending line numbers, separated by a comma. Either can be omitted; if you omit the starting number, precede the ending number with a comma to indicate that you omitted the starting number.

<:seconds> represents seconds of time; can be any number from 0 to 59, preceded by a colon.

<set> represents a list of values (such as strings, file names, or replaceable parameters).

<size> represents the number of files in a print queue.

<source> represents a file name; a series of file names separated by a plus sign; a device name; or a drive letter followed by a colon.

<spacing> represents how many lines per inch are to be printed; the value must be 6 or 8.

<stopbits> represents the number of bits sent through a communications port to mark the end of a character.

<string> represents a series, or string, of characters.

<target> represents a file name; a device name; or a drive letter followed by a colon.

<width> represents the number of characters that can be printed in one row; the value must be 80 or 132.

The following summary lists and defines the DOS commands, command formats, and parameters described in Part 2 of this book.

Append
Page 230

\<number\>a

An Edlin command. Reads the number of lines specified by \<number\> from disk into memory. Used only when editing a file larger than available memory can hold.

Assign
Page 344

assign \<drive1\> = \<drive2\>

Assigns requests for one disk drive to another disk drive. This command is in the versions of MS-DOS that run on the IBM personal computers.

\<drive1\> is the letter of the drive you don't want to use (the one to be reassigned).

\<drive2\> is the letter of the drive you do want to use.

If you omit both \<drive1\> and \<drive2\>, DOS cancels any assignments currently in effect.

Attribute
Page 83

attrib +R −R \<filename\>

Sets or displays the read-only status of a file or set of files.

+R tells DOS to make \<filename\> read-only (not let it be changed or erased).

−R tells DOS to let \<filename\> be changed or erased.

\<filename\> is the name of the file whose read-only status is to be displayed or changed. If you enter the command with just \<filename\>, DOS displays the name of the file and, if the file is read-only, also displays an R in the first column. You can check or change the read-only status of a series of files by using wildcard characters.

Backup
Page 180

backup \<path\> \<filename\> \<drive\> /A /S /M /D:\<date\>

Makes backup copies of files from one disk to another; erases files already on the target disk, unless the /A option is used.

\<path\> is the path name of the directory from which files are to be backed up. If you don't specify \<path\>, DOS backs up files from the current directory.

<filename> is the name of the file to be backed up. You can use wildcard characters to back up a set of files. If you don't specify <filename>, DOS backs up all files.

<drive> is the letter, followed by a colon, of the drive that contains the backup disk (such as A:). You must specify <drive>.

/A adds the backup files to the backup disk (rather than erasing all files on the backup disk before making the backup copies).

/S backs up all subdirectories.

/M backs up only files that have been modified since the last backup.

/D:<date> backs up all files that have changed since <date>. Enter <date> just as you would for the Date command (numbers that represent the month, date, and year, separated by hyphens, such as 10-16-85).

Buffers
Page 340

buffers = **<number>**

A configuration command. Defines the number of work areas in memory that DOS uses to handle reading from and writing to disk.

<number> is the number of buffers you specify. Unless you instruct otherwise, <number> is 2.

Change Directory
Page 163

chdir <drive><path>

Changes the current directory on <drive> to <path>. If you omit <path>, this command displays the current directory. When typed, the command can be abbreviated *cd*.

Check Disk
Page 113

chkdsk <drive><filename> /V/F

Analyzes the directory and storage use of a disk to make sure that all files are recorded properly; also displays a report that shows how disk storage and the computer's memory are being used.

<drive> is the letter, followed by a colon, of the drive that contains the disk to be checked (such as A:). If you omit <drive>, the command checks the disk in the current drive.

<filename> is the name of a file whose storage is to be checked. DOS displays a message if the file is stored in non-contiguous disk sectors. You can use wildcard characters to check a set of files.

/V displays the name of each directory and file on the disk.

/F tells DOS to correct any errors it finds in the directory if you so specify when the error is found.

Clear Screen
Page 124

cls

Clears the screen.

Compare
Page 85

comp <file1> <file2>

Compares two files to see if their contents are the same or different. This command is in the versions of MS-DOS that run on IBM personal computers.

<file1> and <file2> are the file names of the files to be compared. If you omit <file2>, DOS prompts for it. If you omit <file1> and <file2>, DOS prompts for both.

Copy

The next four descriptions cover forms of the Copy command.

Copy from a device
Page 133

copy <source> <target>

Copies the output of a device to a file or another device.

<source> is the name of the device whose output is to be copied.

<target> is the name of the file or device to which <source> is to be copied.

Be sure that both the source and target devices exist; if you try to copy to or from a device that doesn't exist or isn't ready, DOS may stop running and you may have to restart the system.

Copy a file to a file
Page 73

copy <file1> <file2>

Copies a file to another file.

<file1> is the name of the source file and <file2> is the name of the target file. You can use wildcard characters to copy a set of files.

If you specify a drive other than the current drive for <file1> and omit <file2>, the file is copied to the current drive and given the same name as <file1>. If you specify only a drive letter for <file2>, the file is copied to the disk in the drive you specify and given the same name as <file1>.

If <file1> doesn't exist, DOS displays the file name you specified, followed by *File not found* and *0 File(s) copied,* and returns to command level.

If <file2> doesn't exist, DOS creates it. If <file2> does exist, DOS replaces its contents with <file1>. This latter situation is the same as erasing the existing file, so be careful: Don't make a copy of a file and give the copy the same name as an existing file that you want to keep.

Copy a file to a device
Page 77

copy <filename> <device>

Copies a file to a device.

<filename> is the name of the file to be sent to a device. <device> is the name of the device to which <filename> is to be sent. You can use wildcard characters to copy a set of files.

Be sure <device> exists; if you try to send a file to a device that doesn't exist or isn't ready, DOS may stop running and you may have to restart the system.

Combine files
Page 78

copy <source> <target>

Combines two or more files into a new or an existing file name. Except when files are combined into an existing file, the originals remain intact on disk.

<source> represents the files to be combined. You can use wildcard characters to name the files to be combined, or you can specify a list of several file names separated by plus signs (+). If any file in a list separated by plus signs doesn't exist, DOS goes on to the next name without telling you the file doesn't exist.

<target> represents the file that results from combining the <source> files. If you specify <target>, DOS combines the <source> files into <target>. If you omit <target>, DOS combines the <source> files into the first <source> file.

Copy
Page 227

<range>,<line>,<number>c

An Edlin command. Copies one or more lines (<range>) to just before <line>. If you omit the starting line, the copied lines start with the current line. If you omit the ending line, the copied lines end with the current line. If you omit both lines, the current line is copied. If you include <number>, the lines are copied the specified number of times. The first copied line becomes the current line.

Country
Page 335

country = <**code**>

A configuration command. Lets you set a code that tells DOS certain format characteristics for a given country, including date, currency symbols, and decimal separators.

<code> is the three-digit country code number (a complete list is in Figure 17-9). It is usually the same as the country's international long-distance dialing prefix. You must include all three digits, including any zeroes at the beginning.

Date
Pages 14, 22

date <**month**>-<**day**>-<**year**>

Sets the system calendar. If you don't include any parameters (just type *date*), DOS displays the current setting of the system calendar and prompts you to enter a date. If you include parameters to set the date (for example, *date 10-16-85*), DOS doesn't prompt you.

<month> is a number from 1 to 12, <day> is a number from 1 to 31, and <year> is a number from 80 to 99 (for 1980 through 1999). If you use four digits to enter the year, you can enter dates through 12-31-2099.

Delete
Page 203

<**range**>**d**

An Edlin command. Deletes one or more lines (<range>). The starting and ending lines in <range> are separated by a comma. If you omit the starting line, deletes from the current line to the ending line. If you omit the ending line, deletes only the specified line. If you omit both lines, deletes the current line. The line following the last deleted line becomes the current line.

Device
Page 336

device = <**device**>

A configuration command. Specifies a device-driver program (a command file with the extension SYS) that tells DOS how to use a particular device, such as a Microsoft Mouse.

<device> is the name of the device driver program—
MOUSE.SYS, for example, for the Microsoft Mouse. DOS includes
one device-driver program, ANSI.SYS that defines a standard set
of methods for managing a display, including how to display and
erase characters, move the cursor, and select colors.

Directory
Page 70

dir <filename> /W /P

Displays directory entries.
If you include <filename>, the command displays the entry for
just that file. If <filename> includes wildcard characters, the command displays the entries for all files that match. If you include just
a drive letter, the command displays all entries from the disk in the
drive you specify. If you omit <filename>, the command displays
all entries on the disk in the current drive. If you specify a path
name with <filename>, the command displays entries from the
named subdirectory. If you don't include a path name, the command
displays entries from the current directory.
/W *(Wide)* displays file names and extensions only, in several
columns across the screen. This display contains less information,
but it makes a long list of entries more compact.
/P *(Pause)* displays the entries one screenful at a time; a message
at the bottom of the screen tells you to press any key to continue.

Disk Compare
Page 111

diskcomp <drive1> <drive2> /1 /8

Compares two diskettes. This command is in the versions of
MS-DOS that run on the IBM personal computers.
<drive1> and <drive2> are the drive letters, each followed by
a colon, of the diskettes to be compared (such as A: and B:). If you
omit <drive2>, DOS compares the diskette in <drive1> to the
diskette in the current drive (for example, *A>diskcomp b:* compares
the disk in drive B to the disk in drive A). If you omit both
<drive1> and <drive2>, DOS assumes you want to use only the
current drive and prompts you to switch diskettes during the
comparison.
/1 compares only the first sides of double-sided diskettes.
/8 limits the comparison to eight sectors per track, even if
<drive1> contains a 9-sector diskette.

Disk Copy
Page 108

diskcopy \<source> \<target> /1

Makes a duplicate of a diskette.

\<source> is the drive letter, followed by a colon, of the drive that contains the diskette to be copied (such as A:).

\<target> is the drive letter, followed by a colon, of the drive that contains the diskette that is to receive the copy (such as B:). If you omit \<target>, DOS copies from the diskette in \<source> to the diskette in the current drive.

/1 copies only the first side of a diskette in a double-sided drive.

The versions of MS-DOS that run on the IBM personal computers format \<target> before copying; other versions may require formatted diskettes.

DOS gives the diskette in \<target> the same number of sides and sectors per track as the diskette in \<source>. If the diskette in \<source> has nine sectors per track and the diskette in \<target> was formatted with eight sectors per track, DOS formats the diskette in \<target> to nine sectors before copying.

Echo
Page 274

echo on off \<message>

A batch command. Controls whether commands in a batch file are displayed as they are carried out. If you specify echo on, commands are displayed. If you specify echo off, commands are not displayed. If you include \<message>, the \<message> is displayed even if echo is off. If you omit all options, DOS displays a message that tells whether echo is on or off.

Edlin
Page 197

edlin \<drive>\<filename>

Starts the DOS text editor program, Edlin.

\<drive> is the letter, followed by a colon, of the drive that contains, or is to contain, the text file specified by \<filename>.

\<filename> is the name of an existing file on \<drive>, or it is the name of a new file to be created with Edlin.

End Edit
Page 202

e

An Edlin command. Stores the edited file and returns to DOS. Changes the extension of the unmodified file on disk to BAK (deletes a file with the same name and an extension of BAK, if one exists).

Erase
Page 80

erase <filename>

Erases one or more files.
<filename> is the name of the file to be erased. If you use wildcard characters, erases all files that match.

Files
Page 340

files = <number>

A configuration command. Tells DOS how many files it can use at one time.
<number> is the number of files you specify. Unless you instruct otherwise, <number> is 8.

Find
Page 260

find /V/C/N <"string"> <filename>

A filter command. Searches lines from <filename> for the characters specified in <"string">. If you don't specify <filename>, reads lines from standard input (the keyboard). Unless you use one or more options, passes all lines that contain <"string"> to standard output (the display). More than one file name can be specified by separating them with blanks.
/V Passes lines that do not contain <"string">.
/C *(Count)* passes the number of lines that contain <"string">.
/N *(Number)* includes the line number of each line passed.

For
Page 306

for %%p in (<set>) do <command>

A batch command. Carries out <command> for each value in <set>; %%p is assigned, in turn, each value in <set>. You can use %%p as a replaceable parameter in <command>. If you specify a file name with wildcard characters in <set>, %%p is set to each file name found that matches the name you specified with wildcard characters.

Format

The next two descriptions cover forms of the Format command.

Preparing a Diskette
Page 105

format <drive> /V /1 /4 /8

<drive> is the letter, followed by a colon, of the drive that contains the diskette to be formatted (such as B:). If you omit <drive>, DOS formats the diskette in the current drive.

/V tells DOS you want to give the diskette a volume label.

/1 formats only one side of a diskette in a double-sided drive.

/4 formats only nine sectors per track on a double-sided diskette in a high-capacity drive.

/8 formats the diskette with eight sectors per track.

Warning: If you don't specify <drive> and you leave the system diskette in the current drive, DOS tries to format your system diskette. If you haven't covered the write-protect notch, DOS erases everything on the diskette in the current drive. If the current disk is a fixed disk, DOS could erase everything on the fixed disk. After you type a Format command, be sure you know which disk will be formatted before you press the Enter key.

Creating a System Diskette
Page 107

format <drive> /S

To create a system diskette that can be used to start up DOS, format a diskette and include the /S parameter with the Format command. You can also use any of the other Format command parameters described under "Preparing a Diskette."

Goto
Page 280

goto <label>

A batch command. Causes the commands that follow <label> to be carried out next, no matter where they are located in the batch file.

consists of a colon immediately followed by a string of characters (such as :START). It identifies a line in a batch file.

Graftabl
Page 135

graftabl

Enables DOS to display special graphics characters when the color/graphics adapter is in graphics mode. You needn't enter the Graftabl command again until the next time you start DOS.

Graphics
Page 134

graphics <printer> /R /B

Enables DOS to print graphics images on any of several printers. This command is in the versions of MS-DOS that run on the IBM personal computers.

<printer> is an IBM or compatible printer. Options, described in detail in Chapter 7, are: color1, color2, color4, color8, compact, and graphics.

/R tells DOS to print the screen as you see it—light characters on a dark background.

/B tells DOS to print the background color if you have specified color4 or color8.

After you enter the Graphics command and appropriate parameters, pressing Shift-PrtSc prints everything on the screen of the active display, including graphics images. You needn't enter the Graphics command again until the next time you start DOS.

Note: Not all printers can print graphics. Epson printers with the Graftrax option work with the Graphics command.

If
Page 277

if not <condition> <command>

A batch command. Checks whether <condition> is true. If <condition> is true, <command> is carried out unless you include the parameter word *not*, in which case <command> is carried out if <condition> is not true.

<condition> has two commonly used forms:

exist <filename>
   True if <filename> exists in the current directory. You cannot specify a path, only a drive letter, file name, and extension. You can use wildcard characters to check a series of files.
<string1> = = <string2>
   True if the strings are identical. Note the two equal signs.

Insert
Page 200

<line>i

An Edlin command. Inserts new lines before the specified line. If you don't specify a line, inserts before the current line. To stop inserting, press Ctrl–Break. The last line inserted becomes the current line.

Join
Page 345

join <drive> <pathname> /D

Lets you treat a disk drive as a directory on the disk in a different drive.

<drive> is the letter of the drive to be connected to the directory specified by <pathname>.

<pathname> is the path name of the directory to which <drive> is to be joined.

/D deletes any joins that involve <drive>. If you include /D, you cannot include <pathname>.

If you omit all parameters (just type *join*, DOS displays a list of any joins in effect.

Keyboard
Page 140

keybxx

Changes the keyboard layout to match a specific language. All the command names begin with *keyb*; the last two letters identify a country. The keyboard commands have no parameters; the country names at the right of the following list are for information only:

keybuk	United Kingdom
keybgr	Germany
keybfr	France
keybit	Italy
keybsp	Spain

Label
Page 116

label <drive> <label>

Assigns, changes, or deletes the volume label of a diskette or a fixed disk.

<drive> is the letter, followed by a colon, of the drive that contains the disk whose volume label is to be altered (such as B:). If you omit <drive>, DOS assumes you want to work with the disk in the current drive.

is the volume label to be assigned to the disk in the drive specified by <drive>. If you omit <label>, DOS prompts you to enter the new label.

Lastdrive
Page 341

lastdrive = <letter>

A configuration command. Specifies the last drive letter DOS recognizes as valid.

<letter> is a letter up to Z. If a Lastdrive command is not included in a CONFIG.SYS file, the highest drive letter DOS recognizes as valid is E.

List
Page 199

<range>l

An Edlin command. Displays one or more lines (<range>). The starting and ending lines in <range> are separated by a comma. If you omit the starting line, the command starts 11 lines before the current line and displays to the specified line. If you omit the ending line, the command displays 23 lines starting with the specified line. If you omit both starting and ending lines, the command displays 23 lines centered around the current line.

Make Directory
Page 161

mkdir <drive><path>

Creates the subdirectory on <drive>named by <path>. When typed, the command can be abbreviated *md*.

Mode

The following six descriptions cover different forms of the Mode command. The Mode command is used in the versions of MS-DOS that run on the IBM personal computers.

Printer
Page 127

mode <printer> <width>,<spacing>

This form of the Mode command controls the line width and spacing of the printer.

<printer> is the name of the printer (LPT1:, LPT2:, or LPT3:). <width> is either 80 or 132. <spacing> is either 6 or 8, and must be preceded by a comma, whether or not you include <width>.

You must include <printer>. If you omit <spacing>, DOS leaves the current spacing unchanged. If you omit <width>, DOS leaves the current width unchanged; you must still type the comma before <spacing> to tell DOS that you omitted <width>.

Serial port
Page 129

mode \<port\> \<baud\>,\<parity\>,\<databits\>,\<stopbits\>

This form of the Mode command controls the communications parameters of a serial port.

\<port\> is the name of the communications port (COM1: or COM2:). The remaining parameters, separated by commas, are those described in Figure 7-2.

You must specify a value for \<baud\> each time you enter a Mode command. DOS assumes the following values for the other parameters, unless you specifically change them: \<parity\> = Even; \<databits\> = 7; \<stopbits\> = 2, if \<baud\> is 110, or 1, if \<baud\> is any other value. You needn't specify these parameters unless the device or service with which you want to communicate requires values different from those that DOS assumes.

If you omit any parameter from the Mode command, you must still type the comma that precedes it, to show DOS you omitted it.

Serial printer
Page 132

mode \<printer\> = \<port\>

This form of the Mode command redirects to a serial port the output that would normally go to LPT1:, LPT2:, or LPT3:.

\<printer\> is the name of the printer whose output is to be redirected (LPT1:, LPT2:, or LPT3:). \<port\> is the name of the serial communications port (COM1: or COM2:). You must enter both parameters.

Display
Pages 124, 126

mode \<method\>

This form of the Mode command selects the active display, and it controls the number of characters per line and the colors that are used on a display attached to the color/graphics adapter.

\<method\> can be one of the following values:

Value	Meaning
mono	IBM Monochrome Display
40	40 columns, color unchanged
80	80 columns, color unchanged
bw40	color display, 40 columns, color disabled
bw80	color display, 80 columns, color disabled
co40	color display, 40 columns, color enabled
co80	color display, 80 columns, color enabled

Non-IBM display
Page 125

mode <method>, R or L,T

This form of the Mode command lets you center the image on a non-IBM display attached to the color/graphics adapter.

<method> is the same as <method> in the preceding form of the Mode command.

R shifts the image two columns to the right if 80 columns are displayed, or one column to the right if 40 columns are displayed.

L shifts the image two columns to the left if 80 columns are displayed, or one column to the left if 40 columns are displayed.

T displays a test pattern, asks whether you can see all of it, and lets you shift the display until the image is centered. When you respond *y*, the Mode command is completed.

More
Page 266

more

A filter command. Passes 23 lines of input to standard output (the display), then displays a line that says -- *More* -- and waits for a key to be pressed before passing the next 23 lines. Used to review long files or command output on the screen.

Move
Page 226

<range>,<line>m

An Edlin command. Moves one or more lines (<range>) to just before <line>. The starting and ending lines in <range> are separated by a comma. If you omit the starting line, the move starts with the current line. If you omit the ending line, the move ends with the current line.

If you omit both starting and ending lines, the current line is moved. The first line moved becomes the current line. Separate <range> from <line> with a comma.

Page
Page 225

<range>p

An Edlin command. Displays one or more lines (<range>). The starting and ending lines in <range> are separated by a comma. If you omit the starting line, the command starts one line past the current line and displays to the specified line. If you omit the ending line, the command displays 23 lines starting with the specified line.

If you omit both starting and ending lines, the command displays 23 lines starting one line past the current line.

Path
Page 171

path <drive><path> ;

Tells DOS to look for a command file on <drive> in the directory named by <path> if the command file isn't in the current directory. You can enter more than one <path> in one command, separating them with semicolons. If you omit <path>, however, but include a semicolon (just type *path;*), the command removes all paths. If you omit both <path> and the semicolon (just type *path*), the command displays all currently defined paths.

Pause
Page 275

pause <message>

A batch command. Causes DOS to pause, display the line *Strike a key when ready . . . ,* and wait for you to press any key. If you include <message>, the <message> is displayed if echo is on.

Print
Pages 89, 94

print <filename> /P /C /T /D:<printer> /Q:<size>

Prints files at the same time the system is doing something else. Lets you maintain a list, called the print queue, that holds the names of up to 32 files to be printed.

<filename> is the name of the file to be added to or deleted from the print queue. You can specify a list of file names, separating them with blanks.

/P *(Print)* adds <filename> to the print queue. DOS assumes this parameter if all you specify is <filename>.

/C *(Cancel)* removes <filename> from the print queue. If the document is being printed, printing stops and the paper is advanced to the top of the next page.

/T *(Terminate)* stops all printing. If a document is being printed, the paper is advanced to the top of the next page. All files are removed from the print queue.

/D:<printer> tells DOS to use the printer named <printer>. If you omit /D:<printer>, DOS uses the standard printer, PRN:.

/Q:<size> tells DOS the number of files the print queue can hold; the maximum number is 32. If you omit /Q:<size>, the print queue holds 10 files.

If you enter the Print command with no parameters, DOS displays the list of files in the print queue.

Prompt
Page 341

prompt <string>

Changes the system prompt.

<string> is a character string that defines the new system prompt.

Quit
Page 204

q

An Edlin command. Cancels an editing session. Returns to DOS without storing the revised file.

Remark
Page 238

rem <message>

A batch command. Displays <message> if echo is on. If echo is off, you can use the Remark command to insert explanatory notes in your batch files; these notes are not displayed unless you list the contents of the batch files.

Remove Directory
Page 168

rmdir <drive><path>

Removes the subdirectory on <drive> named by <path>. There can be no files in the subdirectory. When typed, the command can be abbreviated *rd*.

Rename
Page 81

rename <oldname> <newname>

Changes the name of a file. The Rename command simply changes the name of a file; it doesn't copy a file to a different disk.

<oldname> is the name of an existing file. If the file doesn't exist, DOS displays *Duplicate file name or File not found* and returns to command level.

<newname> is the new name you want to give the file specified by <oldname>. If a file with this name already exists on the disk, DOS displays *Duplicate file name or File not found* and returns to command level. Two files on the same disk can't have the same name, so DOS would have to erase the existing file to carry out the command.

This safeguard keeps you from inadvertently erasing one file by renaming another.

You can use wildcard characters to rename a set of files. If both <oldname> and <newname> don't refer to the same drive, DOS ignores the drive letter specified in <newname>.

Replace
Page 207

<range>?r<string1><F6 or ˆZ><string2>

An Edlin command. Replaces <string1> with <string2> in one or more lines (<range>). The starting and ending lines in <range> are separated by a comma. If you omit the starting line, the command starts at one line past the current line. If you omit the ending line, the command continues to the last line. If you omit both lines, the command starts at one line past the current line and continues to the last line. If you omit <string2>, the command deletes <string1>. If you include the ?, the command prompts for confirmation of the change.

Restore
Page 188

restore <drive> <path><filename> /S /P

Restores files that were backed up from one disk to another with the Backup command.

<drive> is the letter, followed by a colon, of the drive that contains the backup diskette (such as A:). You must include <drive>.

<path> is the path name of the directory to which the file is to be restored. If you omit <path>, the file is restored to the current directory.

<filename> is the name of the file to be restored. If you don't specify <filename>, all files backed up from the directory are restored. You can use wildcard characters to restore a set of files.

/S restores all files from the directory and its subdirectories.

/P tells DOS to prompt you for confirmation before restoring files that have changed since they were backed up.

Search
Page 205

<range>?s<string>

An Edlin command. Searches one or more lines (<range>) for <string>. The starting and ending lines in <range> are separated by a comma. If you omit the starting line, the command starts at one line past the current line. If you omit the ending line, the command continues to the last line. If you omit both lines, the command starts at one line past the current line and continues to the last line. If you include the ?, the command prompts for confirmation after each occurrence of <string>; if you respond *n* to indicate that the desired occurrence of <string> has not been found, the command continues the search.

Select
Page 145

select <code> <keyboard>

Creates a country- and language-specific system diskette that includes a CONFIG.SYS file with the appropriate Country command and an AUTOEXEC.BAT file with the appropriate Keyboard command.

<code> is the three-digit country code (listed in Figure 17-9) you want set in the new DOS diskette. You must include all three digits of the country code, including any zeroes at the beginning.

<keyboard> is the two-letter abbreviation of the country whose keyboard layout is to be selected for the new DOS diskette (these are the last two letters of the corresponding Keyboard command). You can enter the keyboard code in either uppercase or lowercase letters.

Shift
Page 304

shift

A batch command. Moves (shifts) the list of batch-file parameters one position to the left, erasing the first in the list.

Sort
Page 258

sort /R /+ <column>

A filter command. Reads lines from standard input, arranges them in the order specified, and passes the sorted lines to standard output. If you type *sort* without any parameters, the lines are sorted from A to Z, or lowest to highest number.

/R arranges the lines in reverse order.

/+ <column> starts sorting at the column specified by <column>. This parameter is used to sort lines by the content of columns beyond the first. For example, *sort /+16* means, "Sort all entries, basing the sorting on the contents beginning in column 16."

Substitute
Page 345

subst <drive> <pathname> /D

Lets you treat a directory as a separate disk.

<drive> is the letter to be used to refer to <pathname>.

<pathname> is the path name of the directory to be referred to by <drive>.

/D deletes any substitutions that involve <drive>. If you include /D, you cannot include <pathname>.

If you omit all parameters (just type *subst*), DOS displays a list of any substitutions in effect.

Time
Pages 15, 22

time <hours:minutes><:seconds><.hundredths>

Sets the system clock. If you don't include any parameters (just type *time*), DOS displays the current setting of the system clock and prompts you to enter the time. If you include parameters to set the time, DOS doesn't prompt you.

<hours:minutes> is the time, based on a 24-hour clock; separate the hour from the minutes with a colon. This is all the information you need enter if you want to set the clock.

<:seconds> and <.hundredths> are optional. Note the colon that precedes the seconds, and the period that precedes the hundredths of a second. If you wanted to include <.hundredths>, you would also need to include <:seconds>.

Transfer
Page 229

<line>t<filename>

An Edlin command. Copies another file to just before <line> in the file you're editing. <filename> can include a drive letter, file name, and extension, but not a path. The file must be in the current directory, unless you specified a path when you entered the Edlin command; in that case, the file must be in the same directory as the Edlin command file.

Tree
Page 170

tree <drive> /F

Displays the path of each subdirectory on a disk. This command is in the versions of MS-DOS that run on IBM personal computers.

<drive> is the letter, followed by a colon, of the drive whose directory structure is to be displayed (such as B:). If you omit <drive>, DOS displays the directory structure of the current drive.

/F displays the name of each file in the root directory and each subdirectory. This can be quite a long list, especially if it is for a fixed disk.

Type
Page 73

type <filename>

Displays the contents of a file. <filename> is the name of the file to be displayed. The Type command displays just one file at a time, so you can't use wildcard characters in the file name. If you do use a wildcard character, or if the file you name doesn't exist, DOS displays *Invalid filename or file not found* and returns to command level.

Version
Page 341

ver

Displays the number of the version of DOS being used.

Virtual disk
Page 336

device = vdisk.sys <size> <sector> <directory> /E

A configuration command. Enables you to simulate a disk drive in memory with the VDISK.SYS device-driver program.

vdisk.sys is the name of the program.

<size> is the size, in kilobytes, of the virtual disk. Minimum size is 64, maximum is the total memory of your computer. If you omit <size>, DOS sets it to 64.

<sector> is the size, in bytes, of each sector on the virtual disk. Allowable sizes are 128, 256, and 512. If you omit <sector> or specify an incorrect value, DOS sets it to 128.

<directory> is the number of directory entries on the virtual disk. Allowable values are 2 to 512. Each directory takes 32 bytes of the virtual disk. If you omit <directory> or specify an incorrect value, DOS sets it to 64.

/E tells DOS to use extended memory for the virtual disk. Can only be used with the IBM Personal Computer AT and compatibles.

Volume
Page 117

vol <drive>

    Displays the volume label assigned to the disk in <drive>.
<drive> is the letter, followed by a colon, of the drive that
contains the disk whose volume label is to be displayed (such as B:).
If you omit <drive>, DOS displays the volume label of the disk in
the current drive.

Write
Page 230

<number>w

    An Edlin command. Writes the number of lines specified by
<number> from memory to disk. Used only when editing a file
larger than available memory.

APPENDIX

A

PREPARING
YOUR FIXED DISK

The instructions in this appendix show you how to prepare your fixed disk so that DOS can be started from it and only DOS can use it. These instructions are for the IBM Personal Computer XT or AT. If you have a different computer, or if you want to use the fixed disk in some other way, see the documentation that came with DOS and with your computer.

There are three parts to preparing the fixed disk. You must:

- Identify the fixed disk to DOS with the Fdisk command.

- Format the fixed disk with the Format command.

- Copy the DOS system files from the system diskette to the fixed disk with the Copy command.

IDENTIFYING THE
FIXED DISK TO DOS

1. Put the DOS system diskette in drive A (the left-hand drive) and turn the system on.

DOS responds by prompting you for the correct date and time:

```
Current date is Tue 1-01-1980
Enter new date (mm-dd-yy): _
```

2. Type today's date in numeric form, separating the numbers with hyphens (for example, you would enter October 16, 1985 as *10-16-85*). Press the Enter key after you enter the date.

DOS prompts you for the time:

```
Current time is  0:01:30.00
Enter new time: _
```

The current time DOS displays will differ, depending on how long your system has been on.

3. Type the current time, using a 24-hour clock and separating the hour and minutes with a colon (for example, you would enter 2:30 p.m. as *14:30*). Press the Enter key after you enter the time.

Now DOS displays the system prompt, telling you that it is ready for you to enter a command:

```
A >_
```

4. Type the Fdisk command:

```
A >fdisk
```

DOS fills the screen with a menu of options for the Fdisk command:

```
IBM Personal Computer
Fixed Disk Setup Program Version 3.10
(C)Copyright IBM Corp. 1983,1984

FDISK Options

Choose one of the following:

        1.   Create DOS partition
        2.   Change Active Partition
        3.   Delete DOS Partition
        4.   Display Partition Data

Enter choice: [1]


Press Esc to return to DOS
```

5. Press the Enter key (this selects item 1).
   If the fixed disk has already been prepared by someone else or by your dealer, DOS responds *DOS partition already created* and ends the command. If you see the message, go on to the heading "Formatting the Fixed Disk."
   If the fixed disk has not been prepared, DOS displays another prompt:

```
Create DOS Partition

Current Fixed Disk Drive: 1


Do you wish to use the entire fixed disk
for DOS (Y/N).....................? [Y]
```

6. Press the Enter key (this means yes). DOS responds:

```
System will now restart
Insert DOS diskette in drive A:
Press any key when ready . . .
```

7. The DOS system diskette is already in drive A, so press any key. DOS is restarted and again displays the date prompt. Set the date and time again as you did in steps 2 and 3.

FORMATTING THE FIXED DISK

Note: Formatting the fixed disk erases any files that may be stored on it, so follow this procedure only if the fixed disk has not yet been formatted or if you don't need any of the files stored on it.

1. Type the Format command:

```
A>format c: /s /v
```

DOS displays a message before starting to format the disk, giving you a chance to cancel the command because formatting erases any files on the disk.

2. Press *y.*

The red light on the fixed disk goes on; DOS displays *Formatting...* and begins checking each location on the fixed disk. This takes several minutes. When DOS finishes, it responds:

```
Formatting... Format complete
System transferred
Volume label (11 characters, ENTER for none)?
```

DOS is waiting for you to type an identifying name, or volume label, for the disk. The volume label is displayed each time you display the directory of the fixed disk; you cannot change this name without reformatting the disk or using the Label command.

3. Type any name of up to 11 characters and press the Enter key. This completes formatting the disk. DOS responds by displaying the system prompt:

```
A>_
```

COPYING THE DOS SYSTEM FILES TO THE FIXED DISK

With the DOS system diskette still in drive A, type:

```
A>copy *.* c:
```

This process takes about two minutes. DOS displays the names of the files as it copies them. When all the files have been copied, DOS again displays the system prompt:

```
A>_
```

Remove the DOS system diskette from drive A and store it in a safe place. If you wish to copy the programs from the DOS Supplemental Programs diskette to the fixed disk, insert the Supplemental Programs diskette in drive A and repeat the preceding command (*A>copy *.* c:*).

TESTING THE FIXED DISK

To make sure the procedures were successful, restart DOS from the fixed disk. Open the door of drive A so that DOS won't try to start from that drive, then restart DOS by pressing Ctrl-Alt-Del (hold down the keys marked Ctrl and Alt, above and below the left Shift key, and press the key marked Del in the lower right-hand corner of the keyboard).

If all went well, DOS prompts you for the date. Enter the date and time as you did before. Now when DOS displays the system prompt, it is C> rather than A>, showing you that the fixed disk is the current drive.

If DOS doesn't restart properly, press Ctrl-Alt-Del again, making sure you are holding both the Ctrl and Alt keys down while you press the Del key. If DOS still doesn't restart properly, repeat the procedures in this appendix.

APPENDIX

B

ADVANCED COMMANDS

This appendix briefly describes some commands that control advanced DOS features. The descriptions are necessarily brief, because most of these commands are intended for programmers and deal with *how* DOS works, rather than *what* DOS does. Although several of the commands give you even more control over the power of DOS, they are not required for most routine use and, therefore, were not included in this book.

These commands are divided into three groups: advanced DOS commands, configuration commands, and DOS programs. For a more detailed description of any command, refer to the manual that came with your copy of DOS.

ADVANCED DOS COMMANDS

The advanced DOS commands, like the other DOS commands described in the body of the book, let you manage the devices, files, and programs that make up your computer system. These advanced commands are used primarily by programmers; routine use of DOS seldom requires them.

Break

Normally, DOS only checks to see if you have pressed Ctrl-Break when it reads from or writes to a device. You can use the Break command to tell DOS to check more frequently.

Command

The Command command loads another copy of the DOS program (COMMAND.COM) that carries out commands. This feature enables programs to carry out DOS commands as if they had been typed at the keyboard.

CTTY

The CTTY command changes the definition of standard input and standard output from the console (keyboard and screen) to another device, such as a serial communications port. This command makes it possible, for example, to operate the computer from a terminal that is at a different location and is connected to the computer by a communications line.

Exe2bin

The Exe2bin command converts a command file with an extension of EXE to a command file with an extension of COM; the conversion can make the program smaller and make it run more quickly.

Link

The Link command combines (links) several programs into one.

Set

The Set command defines one or more values, called the environment, that are associated with the command processor (COMMAND.COM) and that programs can use in order to tailor the system's operation.

Share

The Share command makes it possible for different programs to share the same files. This capability is required if you are using a network program.

Verify

The Verify command tells DOS whether to double-check each time it stores something on a disk, to make sure it stored the correct data. Disk operations are quite reliable, and verifying slows down the disk storage process a bit, so DOS normally doesn't verify.

CONFIGURATION COMMANDS

These commands aren't typed at the keyboard; they are placed in a special file called CONFIG.SYS to define operating characteristics of DOS. Some application programs or accessory devices may require that you create CONFIG.SYS and put some of these or the configuration commands discussed in Chapter 17 in it; the documentation of the application program or accessory device usually includes step-by-step instructions. Programmers also use these commands.

Break

The Break configuration command performs the same function as the DOS Break command described earlier. Although their names and functions are the same, they are different commands.

FCBS

The FCBS command tells DOS how many files opened by File Control Blocks (FCBs) DOS can use at one time. Unless otherwise instructed, DOS can use a maximum of four such files at a time.

Shell

The Shell command names a program (command file) that is to replace COMMAND.COM as the DOS command processor.

THE DEBUG PROGRAM

Just as Edlin is a separate program with its own commands that lets you create and revise files of text, DEBUG is a program with its own commands that lets you examine the contents of memory and manipulate programs stored in memory. You start the DEBUG program with the DEBUG command.

APPENDIX

C

GLOSSARY

Adapter: A term sometimes used to refer to printed-circuit cards that plug into a computer and that control a device, such as a display or a printer.

Application program: A program, such as a word processor or spreadsheet, that performs some specific useful task; an application of the computer to a particular area or need.

ASCII: The information-coding scheme used with most computers to represent letters, numbers, and symbols; an acronym for American Standard Code for Information Interchange.

AUTOEXEC.BAT: A batch file that can be created to perform a desired set of start-up procedures and that is carried out automatically by DOS each time the system is started.

AUX: Short for *Auxiliary.* The communications port DOS uses unless instructed otherwise. Can be either COM1 or COM2.

Back up: To make a copy of a file or a diskette for safekeeping.

Backup diskette: A diskette, stored for safekeeping, that contains copies of files.

BAK: An extension, automatically assigned by Edlin and many word processors, to the next-most-recent (penultimate) version of a text file.

BASIC: A programming language; included with IBM's versions of DOS. BASIC is an acronym for Beginner's All-Purpose Symbolic Instruction Code.

Batch command: The name of a batch file. When a batch command is typed while DOS is at the command level, DOS carries out the commands in the batch file.

Batch file: A text file with an extension of BAT that contains DOS commands. When the name of the file is entered at the command level, DOS carries out the commands in the file.

Baud: The rate at which data is transmitted over a communications link. One character per second equals approximately 10 baud.

Binary: The base-two numbering system whose only digits are 0 and 1. Computers use the binary system because the digits can be represented by the presence (1) or absence (0) of voltage.

Bit: The smallest quantity a computer can measure or detect; corresponds to a binary digit (either 0 or 1). Eight bits make up a byte.

Boot: To load and run a program; derived from "pull yourself up by your own bootstraps."

Byte: The unit of measure for computer memory and disk storage. One byte contains eight bits and can store one character (a letter, number, or punctuation symbol).

Chip: *See* integrated circuit.

Color display: A device that displays color or monochrome images on a screen.

Color/Graphics Monitor Adapter: The printed-circuit card for IBM personal computers that controls all displays other than the IBM Monochrome Display.

COM1, COM2:   Short for *Communications*. The names of the two serial communications ports.

Command: The instructions you use to control DOS.

Command file: A file that contains the program or instructions required to carry out a DOS command. If its extension is COM or EXE, the command file contains machine instructions; if its extension is BAT, the command file is a batch file and contains DOS commands.

Communications: The means by which a computer transmits and receives data to and from devices or other computers; also called telecommunications.

Communications port: *See* port.

CON: Short for *Console*. The name by which DOS refers to the keyboard (input) and the display (output).

Console: *See* CON.

Control key: The key labeled Ctrl; use it, as you do the Shift key, by holding it down while pressing another key. The Control key usually causes something to happen rather than displaying a character on the screen. If displayed, it is shown as ^, as in the end-of-file marker, ^Z (Ctrl-Z).

CPU: Acronym for Central Processing Unit. The term is most frequently used to describe the piece of equipment in large computers that contains the circuitry required to do calculations; sometimes used to describe the portion of a microprocessor integrated circuit that does calculations in smaller computers.

Ctrl: *See* Control key.

Ctrl-Break: Key combination that cancels a command; entered by holding down the Ctrl key and pressing the Break key.

Ctrl-C: Same as Ctrl-Break.

Ctrl-Num Lock: Key combination that stops DOS until you press any other key. Usually used to freeze the display so you can view long displays. Entered by holding down the Ctrl key and pressing the Num Lock key.

Ctrl-P: Same as Ctrl-PrtSc.

Ctrl-PrtSc: Key combination that controls the state of simultaneous printing and displaying. Pressing Ctrl-PrtSc once causes DOS to print everything that is displayed; pressing Ctrl-PrtSc again causes DOS to stop printing everything that is displayed. Entered by holding down the Ctrl key and pressing the PrtSc key.

Ctrl-S: Same as Ctrl-Num Lock.

Ctrl-Z: Key combination that creates the special character DOS uses to mark the end of a file. Entered by holding down the Ctrl key and pressing Z. Can also be entered by pressing the function key labeled F6.

Current directory: The directory in which DOS looks for files unless otherwise instructed.

Current drive: The drive containing the disk on which DOS looks for a directory or file unless otherwise instructed.

D

Data: The numbers and text used by a computer to do its work.

Data bit: A signal used in serial communications to represent the transmission of a character; either seven or eight data bits can be used to represent one character.

Data file: A file that contains the data needed by a program; can be numbers, text, or both.

Device: A piece of computer equipment, such as a display or a printer, that performs a specific task.

Device name: The name by which DOS refers to a device (for example, PRN, LPT1, LPT2, or LPT3 for a printer). Device names are treated like file names by DOS.

Directory: The index that DOS maintains on a disk. The directory contains an entry for each file that gives the file's name, extension, and size, the date and time it was created or last changed, and the location of the beginning of the file. All but the last item are displayed by the Directory command.

Disk: A magnetically coated disk that is used to store files. The term is used when no distinction need be made between a diskette and a fixed disk.

Disk drive: The device that rotates a disk in order to read (retrieve) and write (store) files.

Diskette: A disk for storing files made of thin, flexible plastic, enclosed in a protective jacket.

Diskette drive: A disk drive used for diskettes.

Display: The screen on which the computer shows both what you type at the keyboard and the result of its work.

Drive: See disk drive.

Drive letter: The letter that identifies a disk drive.

Edit: To change the contents of a text file, usually with a word processor or with Edlin.

Editor: A program used to create or change text files; also called a text editor.

Edlin: The DOS text editor.

Enter key: The key you press to tell DOS that you have finished typing a line.

Esc: *See* Escape key.

Escape key: The key labeled Esc; cancels a line you have typed but have not yet entered by pressing the Enter key.

Extension: A suffix of up to three characters that can be added to a file name to identify the contents of the file more precisely.

F

File: A named collection of information stored on a disk; usually contains either data or a program.

File name: A name of up to eight characters that DOS uses to find a file on a disk.

Filespec: The complete specification of a file; can include a drive letter, path name, file name, and extension.

Filter command: A DOS command that reads standard input, processes it in some way (such as sorting into alphabetic order), and writes the result to standard output.

Fixed disk: A disk of large capacity (generally 10 megabytes or more) that cannot be removed from its drive.

Floppy disk: *See* diskette.

Format: To prepare a disk for use.

Function key: One of several keys, usually labeled F1, F2, and so on, that cause DOS (or an application program) to perform a certain function, such as copy characters in a line of text.

H

Hard disk: *See* fixed disk.

Hardware: The equipment that makes up a computer system, as opposed to the programs, or software.

Hexadecimal: The base-16 numbering system whose digits are 0 through F (the letters A through F represent the decimal numbers 10 through 15). Often used in computer programming because it is easily converted to and from binary, the base-2 numbering system the computer itself uses.

Hidden file: A file, usually used only by DOS, that is not listed when you display the directory. Hidden files cannot be erased, copied, or otherwise affected by DOS commands.

Hierarchical filing system: *See* multi-level filing system.

Information: The result of processing data to convert it to a more useful form.

Initialize: *See* format.

Input: The data that a program reads.

Input/output: A generic term that refers to the devices and processes involved in the computer's reading and writing data.

Integrated circuit: An electronic device that combines thousands of transistors on a small sliver, or chip, of silicon. Such devices are the building blocks of computers. Also referred to as a chip.

Interface: The boundary between two systems or entities, such as a disk drive and the computer, or the user and a program.

I/O: Abbreviation for input/output.

I/O redirection: *See* redirect.

K

Keyboard: The device that consists of a collection of labeled keys and is used to give instructions and data to the computer.

L

LPT1:, LPT2:, LPT3:   Short for *Line printer*. The names that DOS uses to refer to the three parallel printers that can be attached to the computer.

M

Microcomputer: A small computer system, usually used by only one person.

Microprocessor: An integrated circuit, or chip, that contains the circuits the computer needs to calculate and to communicate with the other parts of the system.

Modem: A device that permits the transmission of computer data over telephone lines. Contraction of *modulator–demodulator*.

Monitor: A device that displays, or monitors, computer input and output; usually used synonymously with display.

Monochrome: A term used to describe a computer display capable of displaying one color.

Monochrome Display and Printer Adapter: A printed-circuit card that operates the IBM Monochrome Display and a parallel printer.

Multi-level filing system: A computer filing system that lets you define directories within other directories, creating a structure with many levels. Also called a tree-structured or hierarchical filing system.

N

Network: A group of computers, linked by a cable, that share resources such as disk drives and printers.

Operating System: A program that coordinates the operation of all parts of a computer system.

Output: The result of a program's processing its input data.

Parallel communications: A communications technique that uses multiple interconnecting wires to send all eight bits of a byte at once (in parallel).

Parallel port: The communications port to which the printer is usually attached.

Parameter: A qualifier that you include with a command to define more specifically what you want DOS to do.

Parity: An error-detection technique used to check accuracy in data communications.

Path: The list of directory names that defines the location of a directory.

Path name: The portion of a file specification that defines the path to the file.

Pipe: To direct the output of one command to the input of another command.

Port: The electrical connection through which the computer sends and receives data to and from devices or other computers.

Print queue: The list of files to be printed by DOS; you create and modify the print queue with the Print command.

Printed-circuit card: A thin, rectangular card or board, usually made of fiberglass or epoxy and coated with copper. A circuit is etched into the copper, and electronic devices, such as integrated circuits, are soldered to the circuit. Computer systems are made up of these cards.

Printer: A device that produces images of text and graphics on paper.

PRN: Short for *Printer.* The printer DOS uses unless instructed otherwise. Can be LPT1, LPT2, or LPT3.

Program: A set of instructions for a computer.

Prompt: A request by the computer for you to provide some information or perform an action.

Q

Queue: A list. *See* print queue.

R

RAM: Short for *random access memory.* The memory that DOS uses for programs and data; RAM content changes often while you use the computer, and is lost when the computer is turned off.

Redirect: To cause a command to take its input from a file or device other than the keyboard (standard input), or to cause the output of a command to be sent to a file or device other than the display (standard output).

Replaceable parameter: A symbolic reference, consisting of a percent sign followed by a one-digit number (such as %1), that can be included with commands in a batch file to refer to the parameters entered with the batch command.

Return key: A term sometimes used to refer to the Enter key.

ROM: Short for *read-only memory.* A portion of the computer's memory that is permanently recorded, usually containing a program. The content of ROM is not lost when the computer is turned off.

Root directory: The main directory that DOS creates on each disk; the top directory in the multi-level filing system.

S

Serial communications: A communications technique that uses as few as two interconnecting wires to transmit bits serially, one after another.

Serial port: The communications port (COM1 and COM2) to which devices, such as a modem or a serial printer, can be attached.

Software: The programs that are used with a computer system, as opposed to the equipment, or hardware.

Standard input: The device from which a program reads its input unless the input is redirected; in normal DOS operation, standard input is the keyboard.

Standard output: The device to which a program sends its output unless the output is redirected; in normal DOS operation, standard output is the display.

Stop bit: A signal used in serial communications that marks the end of a character.

Subdirectory: A file that contains directory entries; sometimes also used to refer to the group of files whose directory entries are in the same file.

System program: A program whose purpose is to control the operation of all or part of the computer system, such as to manage the printer or to interpret the commands you enter.

System prompt: The characters DOS displays when it is at command level (ready to accept a command); unless you specify otherwise, the system prompt consists of the drive letter of the current drive and a greater-than sign (for example, A>).

T

Telecommunications: *See* communications.

Temporary file: A file that DOS creates in order to redirect command input or output, then deletes when the command is completed.

Text: Ordinary, readable characters, including the uppercase and lowercase letters of the alphabet, the numerals 0 through 9, and punctuation marks.

Text editor: A program that you use to create or change text files. Also simply called an editor.

Text file: A file that you can read (contains ordinary letters, numbers, and punctuation marks).

U

Update: To change a file, creating a new (or updated) version.

V

Virtual disk: A portion of the computer's memory reserved for use as a simulated disk drive. Also called an *electronic* or *RAM* (for random access memory) *disk*.

Volume label: An eleven-character name you can assign a disk at the time you format it.

W

Winchester disk: A term sometimes used to refer to a fixed disk; taken from an internal code name used by IBM for a large, fixed disk.

INDEX

Where more than one reference is listed, the defining, or more important, reference is listed first.

VAN WOLVERTON

A professional writer since 1963, Van Wolverton has had bylines as a newspaper reporter, editorial writer, political columnist, and technical writer. He wrote his first computer program—one that tabulated political polls—for the *Idaho State Journal* in Pocatello, Idaho, in 1965. His interests in computers and writing have been intertwined ever since. As a computer professional, Wolverton has worked at IBM and Intel. His well-honed talents now turned to computer books, Wolverton has written numerous manuals and books for the major national software companies, including Microsoft Corporation. He lives in Scotts Valley, California, with Jeanne, his wife, and their three children, Bill, Kay, and Andy.

The manuscript for this book was prepared and submitted to Microsoft Press in electronic form. Text files were processed and formatted with Microsoft Word.

Cover and text design by Ted Mader and Associates. Drawings by Rick van Genderen.

Text composition by Microsoft Press in Bembo with display in Akzidenz Black and Franklin Gothic Bold, on the CCI-400 composition system and the Mergenthaler Linotron 202 digital phototypesetter.